MUSKIE

MUSKIE

by Theo Lippman, Jr.,
and Donald C. Hansen

W · W · NORTON & COMPANY · INC ·

NEW YORK

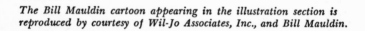

The Bill Mauldin cartoon appearing in the illustration section is
reproduced by courtesy of Wil-Jo Associates, Inc., and Bill Mauldin.

Contents

Illustrations

MUSKIE

MUSKIE

FOR

PRESIDENT

The caravan pulled into Washington, Pennsylvania, shortly before noon—the candidate's car, the cars of the candidate's staff and of other party officials, a photographers'-pool convertible, and a press bus. The candidate was Senator Edmund S. Muskie of Maine, Democratic nominee for the office of vice-president of the United States. It was September 25, 1968; the campaign was nearing its midpoint. Senator Muskie was already well into a typically long day when he arrived in this grim town in southwestern Pennsylvania's bituminous region. He had started the day posing for pictures with labor leaders on the seventeenth floor of the William Penn Hotel in Pittsburgh. Then he had held a press

conference there. Then there had been a television show at
KDKA-TV. Then the thirty-mile drive to Washington. After
his speech here he was scheduled to campaign in little Ali-
quippa, Pennsylvania, and then to move on to Michigan, for
appearances in Taylor, Warren, Hamtramck, and Detroit.
The common theme running through this crowded day was
an appeal to the so-called labor-ethnic vote. Senator Muskie
was a liberal Democrat of Polish extraction. Union members
with Polish and other central European ancestries were heavily and strategically located in Pennsylvania, Michigan, and
the other industrial states surrounding the Great Lakes. They
were flirting with the American Independent candidate,
George C. Wallace, and their defection would be disastrous.
Senator Muskie had been assigned to keep the potential strays
in the Democratic flock. He had doggedly carried out his
assignment for over three weeks now, winning warm support
from his fellow Polish-Americans in union halls around the
country, but little national attention. Before he left Washington, Pennsylvania, however, he would suddenly be well on
his way toward the national recognition and acclaim that had
so far eluded him; and he would begin to be a semihero to
another large and potentially dynamic group of Americans.

Senator Muskie and a few Pennsylvania Democratic leaders
lunched at the George Washington Hotel. From there he went
to the county courthouse. A temporary outdoor platform faced
the street and a row of offices and stores. A few hundred people
waited to hear him. It was a good crowd for a vice-presidential
candidate, larger than many Senator Muskie had appeared
before in the past weeks. Its size was swelled by the presence
of a truculent band of students from nearby Washington and
Jefferson College. College students had plagued Vice-President
Hubert H. Humphrey in his campaigning; he had even had
to have some arrested. Muskie had suggested privately to the
Vice-President that by inviting a heckler up on the stage with
him for a debate, he might stop the interruption and win
back some of the disaffected youngsters, but Humphrey had

rejected this proposal. The students were vociferously anti-war, and since the bloody student-police clashes at the Democratic National Convention, and the defeat there of their antiwar leader, Senator Eugene J. McCarthy—events many of them believed were related—the Democratic party and its candidates had become their special targets. Senator Muskie had escaped, relatively speaking, but only because he was less identified in the public mind with President Lyndon Baines Johnson than was Vice-President Humphrey, and because his campaign had attracted so little attention of any sort. Students had walked out on him at the University of San Francisco exactly one week before, in his only campus visit.

As soon as the senator started to speak in Washington (his prepared text dealt with educational policies), the students drowned him out with chants of "Stop the war! Stop the war!"

"Give 'em hell, Senator," a middle-aged spectator yelled.

Muskie shook his head. He bent his tall frame forward, his mouth turned down at the corners in a schoolteacherish grimace. Under brown, wavy hair, his long face was all planes, tangents, and shadows, slightly lopsided and just craggy enough to nullify the description "handsome." He shook his head again. "No, I'm not going to outshout anybody," he said. He waited for the boos and yells to subside. He began again, speaking of his last visit to the city ten years before. The crowd noise rose and fell, and he started and stopped.

"Say something," a voice shouted.

"If you will give me the chance, I will," he snapped.

A cry more plaintive than the rest came from the babble of the student crowd: "You have a chance, we don't." To the students, this epitomized their plight.

The senator quickly responded. "I will suggest something right now to you young gentlemen. You pick one of your number to come up here right now, and I'll give him ten minutes of uninterrupted attention. There is another side of this bargain . . . and you listen to this part of the bargain: you give me your uninterrupted attention." It was not a particularly inventive solution to the problem, but it was new to recent presidential campaigns. It worked, immediately, and its symbolic meaning attracted attention far beyond that Pennsylvania corner of handsome autumn hills and ugly little industrial towns. A student came up, almost straight out of central casting: His name was Rick Brody; he was twenty-one years old; he had long hair and dirty jeans; and he radiated that special powerlessness and awkward desire to participate which distinguished the American young that year.

"Thank you," he began. "This is a chance we usually don't get, and I think it's fine. You guys [middle-aged members of the audience jeering *him*] say we are dirty and unwashed. We are the true Americans. We love the flag just as much as anyone else. . . . The reason I am out here in the streets is because no one listened to us at Chicago when Senator McCarthy showed through the primaries that seventy per cent of the American Democratic party was dissatisfied with President Lyndon Baines Johnson's stand on Vietnam and domestic issues. . . ." Rick Brody trailed off into near-incoherence after that. Whether anyone listened or not, he said at one point, his generation would not vote in 1968. They were "anti-election." They despaired of the system itself. He finished his speech, thanked Senator Muskie, and stepped back to listen. The situation was a made-to-order setting for a favorite theme of the senator's, the ability of the American political system to react creatively to those who invest in it.

Senator Muskie, towering over Brody, began to speak, with theatrical softness, forcing his excited audience into hushed attention. He described how his father had fled the "czarist tyranny" of Russian Poland when he was seventeen years old to find in America the things "that Rick Brody says you are protesting to find. He tore himself out of his home life, tore himself away from a family he would never see again, to go to a foreign land with only five years' formal education, with a newly learned trade as a tailor, to take up life and to find opportunity for himself and for children who were yet unborn. And the year before he died his son became the first Polish-American ever elected to governor of an American state. Now that may not justify the American system to you, but it sure did to him." A few of the students in the crowd joined the workingmen and their wives in applauding. Senator Muskie went on quietly for several minutes. He recounted the steps leading up to his political triumph as governor-elect, stressing a similarity between Democrats in Establishment-Republican Maine in the 1940's and early 1950's and youth in America in 1968. He said, in effect: If we could do it, you can do it.

Furthermore, he concluded, if the young lent their energies to the right cause, all would benefit. "You young people have got a great opportunity here to contribute to what must be done that the rest of us have not yet been able to do. And all I want to say in closing is this: It is not my purpose to belabor you . . . with any argument, or with any point of view or any personal view. But I want to say to you that there are those of us in this system who have worked for the objectives that I hear you voicing every day. Maybe not as effectively as we might, because of our shortcomings and weaknesses; maybe not in the way that you would and that you will when you are given the opportunity. But don't misjudge the basic good will of this American system toward the objective of making it truly a system responsive to the needs and the will and the voice of the two hundred million Americans who make up this society."

The students applauded him as heartily as the adults. He had said nothing remarkable. His appeal was basically very conservative. But the conflict-resolving drama of it, and the obvious sincerity, and the implied distinctions between the Democratic and Republican tickets, were like rain in the desert to those liberal students and adults who had been revulsed by Chicago and the Democratic party leaders' seeming harshness and insulation from the rank and file. Furthermore, the message was *delivered*. Until this week, Democratic campaign managers had been operating with little money. The party's advertising campaign had barely gotten started. Humphrey and Nixon were mentioned on the news broadcasts every night—and so was the headline-making Spiro T. Agnew —but not Muskie. Republican advertising was swamping the Democrats. That night, Senator Muskie's debate with Brody was featured on all three networks' news reports. It was the first time since the campaign began that he had received such coverage.

The Democrats began to roll at last now, and Muskie's impact was one reason that they did so. (But it was by no means the only, nor even the major, reason. First, enough time had elapsed since Chicago so that some wounds were healing, literally and figuratively. Second, the course of the campaign so far was reinforcing the fears and resentments of liberal Democrats directed toward Nixon and particularly toward his tough-talking running mate. Agnew displayed a casual meanness of spirit by calling a Japanese-American a "fat Jap," and referring to "Polacks." He stirred memories of Senator Joe McCarthy's witch-hunting days by describing Humphrey as "squishy soft on Communism." Third, money was at last coming in to Democratic treasurer Robert Short, mostly in large loans from a few old faithfuls. Fourth, and probably most important of all, the Vice-President, five days after the Muskie appearance in Washington, promised that if elected he would stop the bombing of all of North Vietnam, an act of severance from the then stated policies of President Johnson.) In October, the Democratic ticket made a surprising gain on the Republican, closing a gap measured by the Gallup and Harris polls at approximately 15 per cent. On Election Day the popular votes for the tickets of the two major parties were almost identical.

If Senator Muskie's contribution was not the major one, it was still very important. The contrast with Agnew was so stark. It could be seen even with respect to experience alone, for Muskie was a second-term senator who had been governor of his state twice, while Agnew was halfway through his first term as governor. Their styles and the contents of their messages were also different enough to cause such liberals as Dean Stephen Bailey, of Syracuse University, to announce that "not the least reason" he was voting Democratic was Muskie. While Agnew was speaking twice a day primarily in business clubs and affluent suburban centers, Muskie was making ten appearances a day in ghettos, in union halls, at nationality conventions, on campuses. His stock with students was rising, not only because of his continued willingness to share his platform with them, and the symbolic implications of that willingness, but also because he was saying the things they wanted to hear: He was for draft reform; he favored the vote for eighteen-year-olds; he had urged President Johnson to stop the bombing last January; he was for justice for the poor and the blacks. He had been as unknown nationally as Agnew when the campaign began. In early September, a Harris Poll had shown him only slightly preferred over the Maryland governor, being favored by 33 per cent of those queried, while Agnew was chosen by 30 per cent. By October 21, Harris found the proportions had changed to 41 per cent for Muskie and 24 per cent for Agnew. Humphrey praised him so highly and warned so often of the mortality rate of American presidents, that the joke sprang up that the presidential candidate was the first nominee to promise to die in office. A Bill Mauldin cartoon in the Chicago *Sun-Times* showed Nixon in a track suit carrying Agnew (holding his own mouth shut) over his shoulder, and racing Muskie carrying Humphrey.

This portrayal was the caricaturist's hyperbole, but Muskie *was* an asset. Americans were more vice-president conscious than usual, after the assassinations of the 1960's. Muskie's talents as conciliator in the fragmented Democratic party, his quiet campaign manner, his espousal of old-fashioned verities, his Maine humor—all combined to set him apart in an anxious age from the vociferous Humphrey, the aloof and ad-agency-slick Nixon, the blustering Agnew, the bigoted Wallace. Well before the election campaign was over, the thought had occurred to Muskie and to many other political observers that he would emerge from a Democratic defeat as a contender for a leadership role in his party, and for the 1972 presidential nomination (though in modern times only one defeated vice-presidential candidate, Franklin D. Roosevelt, had made that trip). Back when he had announced in Chicago that he had chosen Muskie, Humphrey had promptly stressed his belief that Muskie's long career proved he could assume the presidency if that need arose. That, of course, is the principal constitutional responsibility of a vice-president.

In the last week of the campaign, at the end of a long day, Muskie was asked if "after all this" he would be content to go back to his old existence. His campaign plane was dipping for a landing in Seattle. Bright lights twinkled up and down the hills and around the coves of that city. Muskie looked out the window, then at his questioner. "Back to being *just* a United States senator?" he asked wryly. He continued on, "It will be hard after this, actually. . . . When a man in public life has had a chance to influence national policy, to think about being at the top, he naturally doesn't like to settle for less. So I am going to think about the prospects."

He ended the campaign with two cross-country dashes. He had played his role as conciliator well. The election results would show that the ethnic vote, or most of it, had come back, after weeks of allegiance to Wallace's third party. He had helped Humphrey bring the party, outside the South, into a semblance of its old compromising, agreeing, happy— or at least good-humored—self. On Election Day he voted in his old home town of Waterville, in central Maine. While Americans voted, he played golf. While the votes were counted, he relaxed, watching slides. The next day at noon, he wired Agnew his congratulations. He met his campaign workers for the last time in the headquarters-motel parking lot. It was a brilliant warm day, with autumn hanging on tenaciously. Muskie was dressed for golf in yellow slacks and a light-blue windbreaker. Several supporters wore "Muskie for President" buttons. Relics of his favorite-son campaign, they had taken on a new meaning. For anyone who missed the point, the loyal wearers of the buttons began to chant, "Muskie in 'seventy-two" and " 'Seventy-two, 'seventy-two."

With rare exceptions, vice-presidential candidates are selected by an electorate of one—the presidential nominee. Even so, candidates for the job often seek it, campaign for it, by indirection at least. Muskie, though aware that Vice-President Humphrey was considering him along with a few others, did not actively campaign to be chosen. "This was a true case of the office seeking the man," Senate Majority Leader Mike Mansfield said later. In part this situation arose because Muskie's character and personality are such that he often avoids political fights involving personal goals, but in larger part it developed because he genuinely believed that the political realities would prevent Humphrey from choosing him. Twice before, in 1960 and 1964, he had been mentioned as a possible vice-presidential candidate. Press speculation on both occasions had been brief. Muskie had believed then that a Democrat from Maine would not help the ticket and therefore would not be on it. In early 1968, still not convinced that this conventional wisdom was wrong, he was given reason to rethink it.

Senator Eugene McCarthy had entered the New Hampshire primary as the only candidate opposed to the President. Against all odds and expectations, he had won the delegates there and almost won the popular vote. The next primary was in Wisconsin, again a two-man race. Polls and other evidence indicated McCarthy would win there, perhaps overwhelmingly. In April, two days before the voting, President Lyndon Johnson announced that he was no longer a candidate for reelection. Between the New Hampshire primary and the President's surprise withdrawal, Senator Robert F. Kennedy had entered the contest. Henceforth, the fight became three-cornered, with Humphrey, McCarthy, and Kennedy opposing one another. The two senators fought each other hand to hand in the primaries after Wisconsin. Kennedy and McCarthy competed for votes in primaries in Indiana, Nebraska, Oregon, California, and South Dakota. Kennedy won in every state but Oregon. In some of these states Humphrey or a stand-in was also on the ballot, but Humphrey didn't campaign and was always swamped. Kennedy's final victory in California might have propelled him on to the nomination. He was assassinated at a victory celebration on primary night.

Humphrey was busy elsewhere during the primary races, seeking nomination in non-primary states. His hope was that the delegates who were selected in party meetings or conventions would stick with him despite the implication of the primaries that he was not the party's best candidate. One non-primary state was Maine, and in May Humphrey and Muskie flew up there to attend the state convention. On the plane Humphrey told Muskie that this time the speculation about his being a vice-presidential candidate was much more realistic than before. "Without mentioning it expressly," Muskie said, "he gave a very strong indication that he was considering me for a place on the ticket, that I was pretty high on his list." When they arrived in Maine, Humphrey bubbled around among the Down East Democrats with high praise for their senator. He conspicuously wore a "Muskie for President" button. Technically, Muskie was a favorite-son candidate, but he did not hold his votes together, and most went to Humphrey.

Thereafter, particularly after the numbing assassination of Robert Kennedy in California in June made Humphrey's nomination likely, the Vice-President told Muskie several times that he was still "high on my list." Whenever there was a new story in the Washington papers speculating on a vice-presidential favorite, Humphrey would reassure Muskie, without making any promises. Muskie continued to have doubts. "Maine is a small state," he explained later. "We didn't have strength in the convention. Also, the party was divided. It seemed to me that Hubert would try to unite it by combining factions." Some of Muskie's critics assert that he uses this sort of thinking as an excuse for his failure to achieve personal goals. He himself has admitted that he found being from a politically unpowerful state "comfortable." He has said that this "insulated" him from national ambitions and national prospects, allowing him to pay more attention to his Senate work, and to enjoy its rewards more. However that may be, the situation as he and others saw it in the summer of 1968 was one in which a little-known senator from a small state with no ties to either the Kennedy or McCarthy camps was not the ideal vice-presidential candidate for a Hubert Humphrey ticket.

His name stayed in contention, however, because the Humphrey campaign staff kept it in contention. By the time Democrats began arriving in the armed camp that their convention city of Chicago had become, the Humphrey nomination was assured. As the convention proceeded, the questions most in suspense were the outcome of the debate on the Vietnam plank, and the choice of a vice-presidential candidate. "Discussion of a Vice-Presidential candidate in the Humphrey camp, with three days to go before a final decision, is centering on Senator Edmund S. Muskie of Maine, Mayor Joseph L. Alioto of San Francisco and former Gov. Terry Sanford of North Carolina," wrote Warren Weaver, Jr., in *The New York Times* on August 27. Elsewhere there was speculation about such possibilities as Sargent Shriver, the Kennedy brother-in-law who was ambassador to France, and Governor Richard J. Hughes of New Jersey. Weaver's story continued, ". . . the law and order issue makes it potentially desirable to have a Vice-Presidential candidate who is both Roman Catholic and a member of an ethnic minority. Senator Muskie, who is of Polish extraction, and Mayor Alioto, an Italian-American, meet these tests and would presumably cut Democratic losses in the so-called "backlash" areas where racial fears are strongest." This was an important consideration. Humphrey later said, however, that the final choice was between Muskie and one of his own strongest supporters, thirty-seven-year-old Senator Fred R. Harris of Oklahoma, that the other names being mentioned in Chicago were not in contention. (But Senator Edward M. Kennedy could probably have had the nomination for the asking.) The next night the convention nominated Humphrey, after a bloody battle between police and antiwar demonstrators in the streets and parks around the headquarters hotel, the Conrad Hilton. Now he had to decide between Muskie and Harris.

Humphrey's suite was on the twenty-fifth floor of the Hilton. The Maine delegation was in the Holiday Inn, five miles away, but Muskie, because he was chairman of the Democratic Senatorial Campaign Committee, was staying at the Hilton, on the seventh floor. The afternoon after Humphrey's convention victory, with the Vietnam plank favored by him and by the administration also approved, all speculation concerned the vice-presidential nomination. Old rumors and some new ones floated through the hotels and the convention center. Humphrey called Muskie to his suite, he also called Fred Harris. Muskie was not insulated by Maine's lack of importance now, and he knew it. His prospects were very good. Eugene McCarthy and Edward Kennedy had announced they were not available for the job. So had Senator George S. McGovern, a Kennedy man with ties to the peace movement. Of all the possibilities still being mentioned, only the nomination of Sargent Shriver met Muskie's old formula of a ticket that combined factions—but few at Chicago took a Shriver candidacy seriously. Harris was still viewed as more of a "Humphrey man" than Muskie.

When Humphrey brought Harris into the room where Muskie was waiting and said to Muskie, "Would you like to meet the man who—is going to nominate you?" the surprise was less than it would have been a few weeks before. Humphrey said later that there were several reasons for his choice of Muskie over Harris. The crucial one had to do with his New England Yankee demeanor. "When it came to making a choice between Harris and Muskie, I went for the quiet man. I know I talk too much, and I wanted someone who makes for a contrast in style. Two Hubert Humphreys might be one too many." Harris' age and relative inexperience also put him at a disadvantage. At 4:34 P.M. Humphrey went downstairs and announced his decision.

The nomination itself was not quite routine. In the call of the states that night, Alabama yielded to Oklahoma. Harris nominated Muskie. All the other states passed until Wisconsin, the next to the last. That state's McCarthy-dominated delegation nominated Julian Bond, a twenty-eight-year-old Negro state legislator from Georgia. He was too young to hold the office, and asked that his name be withdrawn. The McCarthy people were not trying to defeat Muskie; they wanted to get the floor so that they could protest police behavior in Chicago. Their first choice for the symbolic nomination had been not Bond, but Governor Philip H. Hoff of Vermont. He sympathized with what they were trying but said he could not oppose "my friend" Muskie.* In a roaring

* Muskie had various kinds of ties—personal, political, philosophical— to the non-Humphrey factions in the party. According to a Democrat close to Senator McCarthy, Muskie would have been *his* vice-presidential candidate. Some McCarthy supporters even wanted Muskie for president in 1968 when they decided McCarthy couldn't make it. About a week before the convention, one of them approached Muskie about seeking the presidential nomination, but he was cool. The effort continued through Donald E. Nicoll, Muskie's administrative assistant. Nothing ever came of it, and those involved would not discuss it in detail even two years later. Of the various guarded versions offered in 1970, this one seemed the surest: "Pro-McCarthy Democrats concluded that he couldn't be nominated and that Humphrey couldn't be elected. The compromise choice that we felt could be nominated—and then supported after the convention by all factions in the party—was Muskie. It was an outside chance. The President's help would have been necessary, and would have been available, we had reason to believe. Muskie didn't respond because he didn't really believe that we were serious and that it was possible, and because he felt obligated to support Humphrey, and also probably because he is the cautious, thorough kind of person he is—the safe way to play it was to go for the more likely vice-presidential nomination. The moment it was all possible came and went."

turmoil, the roll-call vote began. Delegates and spectators hurled imprecations at Mayor Richard J. Daley of Chicago and his Illinois delegation. Before the balloting was completed, Chairman Carl Albert recognized Daley, who moved that the nomination be by acclamation. Most in the vast hall were unaware of what was going on. Albert put the motion to a vote, said the *yeas* had it, and Muskie was nominated. The recorded vote at the time of Daley's motion was 1,944½ for Muskie, 48½ for Bond and 26½ for others.

In his acceptance speech Muskie stressed the theme of confidence—confidence in the system and in one another—that he would urge upon Americans in dozens of speeches during the coming campaign:

> To make a society such as ours work is not easy. It means learning to live with, to understand and to respect many different kinds of human beings, of different colors, of different races, of different national origins, of different cultural levels, of different tastes and intellectual capacities, of different educational attainments, of different social backgrounds, personalities and dispositions, and to accept them all as equals.
>
> It means learning to trust each other, to work with each other, to think of each other as neighbors. It means diminishing our prerogatives by as much as is necessary to give the others the same prerogatives. It means respect for the rule of law as a dispenser of justice as well as a maintainer of order.

It was a very old-fashioned speech. The next day he and Humphrey flew to Minnesota for a rest together, with their families. Then he flew home to Maine. Then back to his suburban home in Bethesda, Maryland, close to Washington, D.C. That was to be his base for the campaign. On September 8, in San Antonio, he began the thirty-eight-state campaign swing which led, through Washington, Pennsylvania, to national prominence.

"Senator Muskie, A Close-up of the Loser as a Big Winner," said the cover-story title on *Look* magazine not long after the race was all over and the votes all counted. Writer Laura Bergquist described the campaign, told of the guarded hopes Muskie had for the future—expressed as he vacationed in the Virgin Islands—and concluded her article with two questions many people were asking: "Can a non-pushy, non-affluent, self-made son of a Polish immigrant, by personality and virtue alone, still make it in the American political big time? Will those voters regard him as warmly in '72 as they did in '68?" Certainly Muskie was asking himself those questions. He would begin to voice them publicly before long. But on that Virgin Islands vacation, with his own family and the Humphreys, Muskie mostly relaxed. While Hubert Humphrey basked in the sun, to melt away the tensions and the disappointments, the Muskies were "swimming, fishing, golfing. . . . I didn't feel the disappointment as much," he said candidly. When he returned to Washington, the questions became insistent right away. "There were thousands upon thousands of letters from people urging me to consider 1972," he said. "Two people worked all day every day just slitting the envelopes and taking the letters out."

In addition to the pleas that he run for president in 1972, there were commendations of his performance in 1968, offers of help, pleas for him to speak out on issues or to address specific organizations, applications for jobs. There was no money for expanding his staff, much as the torrent of mail made that desirable. The services of those who volunteered part-time and free assistance were quickly accepted. (Those who volunteered ideas and high-level assistance, prestigious men from important law firms, banking offices, university faculties, and the like also found their offers taken up.) Muskie, administrative assistant Don Nicoll, trusted old Maine friends Richard J. Dubord and George J. Mitchell, some senators, Washington lawyer Berl Bernhard, and some others, got together to discuss ways to ensure positive answers to Laura Bergquist's questions. One opportunity was a formal leadership role in the Senate. This finally was not pursued. Another was a nationwide speaking tour. There were more than enough invitations already. Muskie preferred this for several reasons. It would allow him to keep his name before the public. It would allow him to develop friendships in Democratic circles in every section of the country. It would allow him to advance his ideas and work for his programs during a period when the initiative would be with a Republican administration. And it would allow him to earn some money. Many of the invitations offered handsome honoraria. In 1969 he was to earn $74,450 in this way. He was the Senate champion on this circuit.

Seeking the presidency informally is an undertaking as difficult as it is necessary four years before the election. Muskie wrestled with the problem of explaining his position with realism and candor. Near the end of 1968 he said on a network television show that "right now the vice-presidential campaign would appear to bring it [a bid for the 1972 presidential nomination] in reach. But there are problems, and as long as there are problems you don't really generate ambition. But to say I don't even think about it would not be an honest answer." In January, 1969, he told a group of Washington correspondents about his heavy mail, and said, with a shy, sly smile, "It has produced a flicker of ambition."

Also, that month he was on another network interview program. The host said, "I have reached the conclusion that you are very receptive toward 1972."

Muskie replied, "At least I want to explore it. I don't know whether I'll run for president. I really don't know at this point. But I enjoyed the national campaign. . . . But whether I will enjoy it after two or three more years of this kind of activity, I don't know."

"You mean the rubber-chicken circuit?" he was asked.

"Yes, the rubber-chicken circuit and the time-consuming, energy-consuming nature of the thing."

His first reaction to the rubber-chicken circuit was a happy one. He went to Miami to make two speeches and pick up two checks, and came back wide-eyed. He told a group of reporters about his experience. "It's pretty damned hard to get sustained national exposure in Washington, in the Senate," he said. "But when I was in Miami I got more time on radio and television there than I would get from here in a year." He had also been to a conference on education in Connecticut. "All the opinion makers in the state were there." Later on, the wearing pressures of the tour would sap his energies somewhat. The sustained exposure was to fade away. He would ask himself if it was all worth it, and if in any case the prize was within reach. That was in the future. In January he was ebullient. The last week in that month saw the start of what the press characterized as the formal beginning of his informal campaign. As if to suggest that nothing goes as planned in politics, as if to warn him of the rough road ahead, the trip was hectic. He went to Texas for two days of speeches in Dallas and Fort Worth, but had to interrupt his visit in order to fly back to Washington to vote against Walter J. Hickel as secretary of the interior. This came up at a time that had not been anticipated when the trip was scheduled. There was no question of defeating Hickel. Only sixteen senators opposed him. But he had made some remarks about natural resources in his state of Alaska and elsewhere that outraged conservationists, and in recent years Muskie had become a leading spokesman for conservation and for antipollution measures. Hence, the gesture of voting against Hickel was important to him. He managed to get it in and still deliver the Texas speeches, but doing so required some fancy footwork and a lot of extra airplane mileage.

So began a busy winter and spring. In February he spoke in San Francisco and Los Angeles; Oxford and Seven Hills,

Ohio; New York City; Auburn, Alabama; Jacksonville, Florida; Ottawa, Illinois; and Manchester, New Hampshire. He also flew to a meeting in Japan, to show his interest in foreign affairs. He also opened hearings by his subcommittee concerned with pollution. He also made several speeches in Washington. And February is the shortest month. Requests for him to address various groups continued to batter his office. A member of the staff estimated that twenty to thirty invitations that could be considered legitimate and attractive came in each day. Both the senator and his staff would find before the weather turned warm that stoicism was more called for than enthusiasm. The day-to-day workload was heavy. Only a few unpaid volunteers augmented the same staff that previously had felt pushed just doing the routine work of a senator from a small state. This routine work still had to be done, along with all the new business. Muskie fretted over the problems. In mid-February he told a press conference, "It's quite an undertaking for a man without means. It becomes more awesome the more I contemplate it." Was his interest in "exploring 1972"—the euphemism that had developed—decreasing? No, he was "increasingly interested." He still found audiences warm. He still saw his name in the important papers and magazines a lot, saw his face, heard his voice on television. But also in February, he received a rude shock. A Gallup Poll showed Edward Kennedy was the choice of 38 per cent of those asked who should lead the Democratic party. Muskie was the choice of 21 per cent. Humphrey, of 15. Democratic respondents favored Kennedy 2 to 1 over—Humphrey! Muskie was their third choice. About the same time, the *Christian Science Monitor* polled Democratic state chairmen and national committeemen, asking a similar question. Kennedy was a near-unanimous choice.

In March, Muskie made fourteen speeches outside of Washington. In April, he made twenty. He was tired in May, and discouraged, but he made a dozen out-of-town speeches. He made fourteen in June. It was a weary commencement season.

Even after his disillusionment set in, he drove on, he said later, because he had to know for sure whether the favorable reception he had received in the first post-election months was "just afterglow," or something of substance. Or as he explained to his aide Don Nicoll at the time, suppose he did nothing, then in 1972 found his credentials were as good as any Democrat's, but because for three years he had not campaigned and someone else had, he lost the nomination by what would then seem default? That would be hard to take. Ever after he would feel a deep regret. "Up in my part of the country, you don't worry about ifs," he said in another connection once. But New Englanders are not as icy as they sometimes seem to be saying they are. It was a New Englander who said that the saddest words are "it might have been." Muskie had to try.

In April he had marveled at the already booming Kennedy movement. "There really is no precedent for this—having in the ranks of the defeated party an accepted candidate four years in advance," he had said. He was not only surprised at this, he was "irritated," according to William Chapman of the Washington *Post*. His own boom, he was reluctantly concluding, may after all have been just afterglow. In June he said he was ready to stop, more or less. "There was a time when I thought I had a call for the presidency," he said. "But that's over. Of course, if I'm reelected to the Senate next year, I'll take another look at it. And if responsible Democrats thought in 1972 that I should run, I'd consider it. But I can get along without being president." The third and fourth sentences in that statement were the politician's fine print. You don't bow out of anything irrevocably, just as you don't get into anything irrevocably if you can help it. Mike Mansfield was quoted publicly that June as saying, "If Senator Kennedy wants the nomination, as of now I think he's got it." Muskie agreed. He told the Long Island newspaper *Newsday* so, adding only, "unless there is some pretty substantial change in the political climate."

The next month, a car occupied by Senator Kennedy and Mary Jo Kopechne plunged off a wooden bridge into a tidal pond on Chappaquiddick Island, Massachusetts. The car turned upside down. Miss Kopechne drowned. A shocked Senator Kennedy could not explain what had happened, why he had waited long hours before reporting the accident. *Newsweek* magazine said what most commentators were thinking: "For now, [Kennedy's] seemingly inexorable progress toward the 1972 Democratic presidential nomination has come abruptly to a halt—quite possibly for good." A quick Gallup Poll showed Kennedy's image badly tarnished. A later Gallup Poll showed Muskie the people's (and the party's) choice to lead the party now. The *Christian Science Monitor* resurveyed the chairmen and committeemen. Forty were for Muskie, sixteen for Humphrey, only five for Kennedy. "It looks like Senator Edmund Muskie for the Democrats in 1972," wrote columnists Roscoe and Geoffrey Drummond in August, "and he's going for it." And he was.

CHAPTER TWO

"SOMEBODY
HAS TO
DO IT"

Ⅰn a faded, yellowing copy of the Stephens High
School newspaper, *The Broadcast,* dated November 10, 1931,
there is an article by an unknown author about a fellow
student, senior Ed Muskie. The article recounts the youngster's
high-school career and concludes that "there is probably heaps
more to tell of the honorable deeds of this mastermind but the
boy is modest and modest people don't relish being held up as
an example. However, when you see a head and shoulders
towering above those of the common herd in the halls of
Stephens you should know that your eyes are feasting on a
future president of the United States."

Nobody in Rumford today seems able to identify the author

of the piece, whose prophecy is as yet unfulfilled, but a good many of the townspeople are willing to credit him with an uncommon degree of prescience. Most share the opinion of Frank Anastasio, a boyhood friend of Muskie's and now a Rumford barber, who says, "Nothing he does surprises me. We always expected him to reach the top."

The older residents of Rumford, a grimy mill city of ten thousand perched amidst the Appalachian range in western Maine, today largely recall the young Muskie for his high-school accomplishments rather than as a person. He is remembered as valedictorian of his class, as president of the Student Council, as a star of the Stephens High debating team, and in the words of his 1932 graduation yearbook, as a "public man of light and leading." Those who recall him as a schoolboy more often describe him as being "respected" than as being "liked." The stories told today center on his achievements rather than on the boy himself.

Rumford, as a community, is indistinguishable from a number of other Maine papermaking towns. Of it, one may truthfully say, "It stinks." Fumes belching from the giant Oxford Paper Company stacks spew forth an odor that residents say compares favorably with that of rotten cabbage. The wastes from the Oxford mill, along with municipal sewage, have for years been dumped into the Androscoggin River, fouling the waterway until today it is one of the ten most polluted rivers in the nation. Yet Oxford, one of the largest mills in the United States, is Rumford's principal employer; without the mill it is doubtful if the city would exist at all. And residents, knowing that, sniff the odor and say, "That's the smell of money." When Muskie was a boy, an older papermaking process at Oxford produced a sulfur odor that was, to the largely uncomplaining residents, preferable to today's cabbage smell. The rank fumes and the befouling of the water were things the future chairman of the Senate subcommittee on air and water pollution grew up with and accepted.

To Muskie's father, Stephen Muskie, Rumford was home.

Born Stephen Marciszewski, in 1882, he was raised in a small village near Bialystok, a city in northeast Poland close to the Russian border. He had little formal education; when he was twelve his father apprenticed him to a nearby tailor with but one aim in mind: to provide his son with a trade when he fled the country. Seventeen was the age of conscription into the czarist armies, and few Poles were anxious to serve in the army of their oppressor. Stephen Marciszewski's father was determined that his son should leave Poland before he was drafted.

Little is known of young Marciszewski's years in Poland, except that while he was apprenticed he lived in the tailor shop, subsisted on whatever crusts his master provided, and slept on his bench. But he learned his craft, and when he was seventeen left Poland and settled in England, where he lived and worked for three years. In 1903 he emigrated to the United States, settling in Dickson City, Pennsylvania, a small suburb of Scranton. Some of his relatives owned a tavern there and Ed Muskie recalls fondly a family reunion in Union City when he was fourteen. As the oldest boy in the family he was given the honor of drawing the draft beer for the celebration.

When he applied for citizenship in the United States, Marciszewski changed his name to Muskie. A few years later he met, wooed, and married Josephine Czarnecka, of Buffalo, New York. On their honeymoon, they traveled to Maine and visited Rumford, where Stephen's sister lived, and in 1911 they moved there. Irene Muskie was born the next year; Edmund Sixtus Muskie was born on March 28, 1914. Subsequently there was another son—Eugene—and three more daughters—Lucy, Frances, and Betty.

Stephen Muskie's tailor shop did well. Rumford's more affluent citizens had their suits made there and were never disappointed. "He made every suit I wore from the time I began wearing them when I was eleven or twelve," Muskie recalls. "In fact, I still have a suit he made for me. It's double-breasted and I still wear it on occasion. And it's still in good shape."

The elder Muskie, a small, wiry, hardworking man, provided adequately for the family of eight. Lucy, two years younger than Ed, and perhaps still the closest to him, says, "You couldn't call us poor. We always had plenty to eat. We had a car and father always took us riding on Sundays. In the summer he'd hire a camp for a week or two on a lake. There was never more than enough, but there was always enough."

"Father felt very deeply his obligation to provide for his family," Muskie says, "to provide a home and an education if he could. He didn't believe in buying on credit, so he worked hard to build up the cash reserves that were needed. When he bought a car I'm sure he paid cash for it. He was very frugal and yet he provided, I thought, very comfortably." Mrs. Muskie—a strong, independent woman who for years, even after her son became a United States senator, took in washing for a few neighbors—ran the household. There were no favorites. If she brought home a candy bar it was taken to the kitchen table and carefully cut into six small, equal pieces.

As the family grew, the rented Rumford apartment became overcrowded and the elder Muskie purchased, from a relative, a small frame house on Hemingway Street, in the Virginia section of Rumford. Mrs. Muskie still lives there. The house itself was not much of an improvement in terms of space. There was a kitchen, a pantry, a dining room, and a living room on the first floor, with three bedrooms and a bath above. Ed and Eugene shared one bedroom and four girls another.

At five, a shy youngster who had to be pulled along by his older sister Irene, Muskie was sent off to the Pettingill School. There he first felt what he termed during the 1968 vice-presidential campaign "the lash of prejudice." World War I had just ended, the Russian Revolution was still in progress, and there was a definite prejudice in Maine against Eastern

Europeans. The son of the tailor was greeted at school by cries of "dumb Polack." His ancestry and his religion were held up to ridicule. The taunting of the Muskie children at school continued for about five years. He had no friends. Irene and Lucy, who also faced the jeers, came home crying and told their parents. "I felt so awful and ashamed," Lucy said. But the proud tailor told the girls, "Let them call you all the names they want. The names aren't going to hurt you. Be proud to be Polish."

Muskie, sensitive and shy, blinked back the tears and didn't talk to his father about this teasing. "I was at a very impressionable age," he says now. "And coupled with my own shyness it may be that I exaggerated it in my own mind. But there was a definite hostility toward us and we all felt it. It didn't last long, probably by the time I was eight or nine it was over. Perhaps if I'd been a half a dozen years older at the time it might not have meant as much."

But his family was one of the only three Polish families in town, and the experience did have a deep significance for Muskie. He has a vague recollection of crosses burning in Rumford, and even then he knew what they represented. So he retreated, taunted at school, bullied outside, he read and played at home. His mother says that one of her most vivid recollections of the young Muskie has him sitting alone by a window, silently looking out. He pored over books of all kinds—*Tom Swift* and Horatio Alger, books about history, travel, and biography. His father, who had taught himself to read and write the English language, encouraged him. "Father didn't have much formal schooling—he didn't have the chance," Muskie says, "but he had just an intense interest in current events, politics, in the things that were going on. Not in any partisan sense, but in the sense that he wanted to know what was happening. And why." From his father, young Muskie inherited a quizzical combative instinct, a thirst for knowledge, and a temper. Irene doubts that he had any real friends outside the house until he reached high school.

At home Muskie displayed none of the shyness he showed in public. "He was never shy around the house," says Irene. "Mostly it was his terrible temper." The children played casino, whist, and rummy, and "Ed just couldn't bear to lose a game. If he lost he'd throw the cards, yell, and stamp off. He just hated to lose." Once, when Irene had been teasing him for losing, Muskie became so enraged that he chased her into the pantry, and Irene screamed in fear that he was going to hit her. He has never completely conquered either his shyness or his temper; he remains essentially a private person for all his public successes, and has a temper that can approach the volcanic. As governor, he once hurled a heavy book at an aide during a heated discussion, missing only narrowly. During his 1964 reelection campaign, shortly after presidential aide Walter Jenkins was arrested on a disorderly-conduct charge in the Washington YMCA, Muskie's opponent challenged him during a televised debate to agree to another debate, on the issue of morality in government. Muskie was literally quivering with rage as the program ended. "Did you see that? Did you see what he did?" Muskie bellowed at gentle Edward T. Folliard, the Pulitzer Prize winning Washington *Post* reporter, who was traveling with him at the time. During the vice-presidential campaign he would fume at advance men and aides who established schedules he was incapable of meeting. "Who are these faceless bastards that are responsible for this schedule?" he wanted to know during one torturous daylong motorcade through Pennsylvania. The phrase caught on, and today some of Muskie's advance men still refer to themselves as "FB's."

As Muskie grew older he would help his father in the shop after school, doing odd jobs around the place. His father would sit on his bench working and talk with the customers. "He loved to talk and to argue," Muskie recalls. "He used to get into vigorous arguments with people. It didn't matter who the customer was, it might be the shopkeeper or the business-man next door, or it might be one of his more wealthy clients.

I can remember him engaging them, challenging them on issues and questions. And he usually knew his facts and what he was talking about." Later, when Muskie was in college, he and his father would argue heatedly in the evening over current issues. "I can remember some of their arguments, with both of them yelling and going to bed thinking that they'd never speak to each other again," says Lucy. "But the next morning you'd never have known there had been an argument. That's the way they were." Says Muskie with a smile, "Father had his views and he was a hard man to shake."

Not all the customers appreciated the elder Muskie's probing questions. One, a wealthy Republican, after arguing with Muskie for some time asked him his political affiliation. "I'm a Democrat," shot back Muskie. The customer, one of Muskie's best, turned on his heel and left the shop. He never came back. Yet years later, in 1956, when Muskie died, the former customer was the first to call and express his sympathy to the family.

The Muskie family was close-knit. Father ran the shop and mother the household. The elder Muskie was a disciplinarian in the sense that he required the children to behave, but he did not lay down a strict regimen of life for them, and rarely attempted to interfere with their plans for their own lives. "We grew up knowing that there were certain things that had to be done around the house and we did them," Muskie says.

At home the children would often prepare shows or "entertainments" in the pantry and then call their parents to watch the recitals. Young Muskie, who had a fine voice, would as often as not sing his favorite, "The Whiffenpoof Song," the Yale drinking song popularized by Rudy Vallee, another Maine boy.

The strong sense of family has continued, although his sisters confess that Muskie's innermost thoughts remain as much of a mystery to the family as they do to the nation. "We never really knew and we don't know now what he's thinking about when he's with us," says Irene. "He just doesn't talk about himself with us. When he's with us he'll sit and read the paper or go upstairs and take a nap; you feel as though you don't mean much to him. And then he'll do something, make some gesture, and you'll know that he's concerned about us."

Perhaps nothing more illustrates Muskie's sense of family than an episode that began on election night in 1968. His entire family was invited to come down from Rumford to Waterville to join him for a private dinner at his motel head-quarters and to watch the election returns together on tele-vision. The family watched the returns until about 1 A.M. and then Muskie went to bed. His mother and four sisters all had rooms at the motel, but the elder Mrs. Muskie, then seventy-six, decided at about 3 A.M. that she wanted to go home to sleep in her own bed. The daughters tried to convince her to stay the night but she was adamant, so they drove her home. The next morning Muskie awoke to find himself a defeated candidate and his family gone. He was deeply hurt. Shortly thereafter he left for his post-election vacation in the Virgin Islands with Humphrey. When he returned to Washington he called his sister Lucy, and his first words were, "You walked out on me." "He thought that we had left him because he was a loser, and it wounded him," Lucy says. "He felt it was our place to be there with him."

As the children entered high school they began to move their separate ways. Muskie, still withdrawn and a loner, turned increasingly to religion, so much so that many thought he would become a priest. Frank Anastasio, who first began learning his barbering trade when he was about twelve years old, using Muskie as a guinea pig, was certain of it. "During Lent he and I would go to mass every day. I guess I went along because he did." Muskie still retains strong religious convictions. Richard J. McMahon, his campaign manager and factotum during the 1954 campaign, remembers that Muskie always made a point of getting to church on Sunday no matter how tight his schedule. "One morning in Presque

Isle he was cold broke and I had a dollar and a half. We went
to church and he borrowed the dollar from me to put in the
collection plate, leaving me to put in the fifty cents. It was
my money but I had to put in the fifty cents." Catholicism
and its principles remain deeply rooted in Muskie and continue to shade his outlook on social problems. During the
1968 campaign he dodged the issue of birth control entirely
and when pressed would say hotly that "I don't intend to issue
an encyclical." Speaking at heavily Protestant-oriented Choate
in 1970, Muskie said during an interview that while "I think
we must change our stand on abortion" he was unclear about
how to go about it. However, he was "deeply concerned" at
the prospect of legislation being expanded "to the point that
anyone can get an abortion if she can get a doctor to approve.
This carries the entire idea further than I am prepared to
go." To talk of birth control, Muskie said, echoing Catholic
dogma, is to talk "about the beginning of life. Life in a free
society is at the very essence of freedom. If life is not sacred,
freedom is meaningless."

In high school Muskie's grades remained excellent but his
friends were few. Then, during his sophomore year, in an
effort to overcome his shyness, he ran for the Student Council
and won. Shortly after this first venture into elective politics,
a young English teacher at Stephens, Miss Celia I. Clary,
stepped into Muskie's life. "I had always thought that debating would be a way to overcome my shyness," Muskie recalls,
"but I couldn't bring myself to take the initiative on my own
to go out for the team. Miss Clary, the debating coach, encouraged me to do it. She got me interested in debating during
my junior year. She pushed me into it."

Miss Clary, who left teaching in 1932, the year that Muskie
graduated, is now Mrs. Barry Fossett, and with her husband,
runs a small department store in Oakland, Maine. "I wouldn't
say that I was responsible for getting him interested in debating," she says of Muskie. "He was interested in all manner
of school activities, and being the scholarly type that he was,

he would just naturally drift to debating. And he was a good debater; he was good at anything he undertook."

To Mrs. Fossett, young Ed Muskie "always had dignity. He would always carry himself well. He was the type of boy who was very respected by all of his classmates. . . . If he says I was the one that got him interested in debating then I thank him for that. I remember him as being a very wonderful young person."

Debating, and the encouragement of Miss Clary, provided Muskie with the assurance he needed. Already six foot four, Muskie was lured because of his height onto the basketball and track teams. But athletics were not his first love and he was never more than a substitute center on the mediocre Stephens High teams. During a March regional basketball tournament in Lewiston in his junior year, Muskie could not be located. He was finally discovered in the locker room reading a book when he should have been on the bench.

During his junior and senior years, Muskie blossomed. He became president of the Student Council. He was a member of the Latin and dramatic clubs and during his senior year was named general manager of the school fair. He delivered the valedictory address for his class.

Although Muskie had come out of his shell by the time he was graduated from high school, he has always remained somewhat naïve, particularly about sex. In one of his stock speeches on urban disorders during the 1968 campaign he used a quote from Jefferson—who foresaw the problems of urbanization—in which Jefferson warned that when people became jammed together in cities "they would begin to eat one another." The phrase, because of its sexual connotations, drew some titters on college campuses but Muskie continued to use it. Finally, some aides suggested that he drop it entirely. Muskie wanted to know why, and seemed genuinely bewildered when it was explained to him.

When he applied to Bates, a small liberal-arts college in Lewiston, he was rewarded with both acceptance and a $250

annual scholarship which would pay his tuition. But total
annual college costs, including clothing and spending money,
ran to $750, and Muskie's father dug deep, those Depression
years, to make up the difference.

Ed himself also contributed. A Rumford classmate, Charlie
Taylor, who had been accepted at Bates too, had worked the
summer before at Narragansett-by-the-Sea, a resort hotel at
Kennebunk. With Charlie's help Muskie was hired as a dish-
washer at $10 a week plus room and board for the ten-week
season. Since he worked for two summers in the kitchen, it is
understandable that when, on the day following his election
as governor in 1954, some Boston photographers descended
on the small Muskie home in Waterville and asked him to
pose for a picture washing the dishes with his wife, he refused.
"Why, that wouldn't be right," Mrs. Muskie said. "Ed hasn't
helped with the dishes since were were on our honeymoon."

At Bates, Muskie shared a dormitory room with Charlie
Taylor and earned his board by working as a waiter in the
Bates Commons. In his third summer at the Narragansett, he
was taken out of the kitchen and made a bellhop. The pay
was $5 a week plus uniform, bed, and board, but the tips
more than made up the difference. Muskie found he was
making $35 a week in the summer season during the depths
of the Depression. But money remained scarce and he seldom
came home from college on weekends because of the expense.

Toward the end of his career at Bates the financial situation
eased somewhat, in part due to the Roosevelt New Deal.
Muskie was named a dormitory proctor, and was paid with
funds provided by a federal assistance program to college students. The additional income went toward his dormitory
payments, his scholarship paid the tuition, and his job in the
Commons (he was now the headwaiter) provided his meals.
Despite the need to work his way through college, Muskie
neglected neither his studies nor student activities. When
he was graduated from Bates in 1936 he was a member of
Phi Beta Kappa and president of his class.

Muskie next entered Cornell Law School. There the situation was more difficult, both scholastically and financially, and he didn't want to work while in school because of the pressure of studies. "I had a $400 scholarship for tuition, but the total costs were then about $1,100 a year. By that time there was a lot of slack to pick up because my summer job as a bellhop didn't provide enough. My father carried me through the first year at Cornell, but now my father and I had come to the end of our rope. There wasn't any way that we could see of doing the rest of the job."

About two weeks before his second-year classes were scheduled to begin at Cornell, Muskie, who was frantic because of the lack of money, learned of William Bingham II, of Bethel, Maine, an eccentric millionaire and brother of Representative Frances Bolton of Ohio. Bingham was one of New England's leading philanthropists, and one of his hobbies was assisting Maine college students who had already begun their education but were in financial difficulty. Quickly, Muskie wrote him a letter, briefly and simply explaining his problem. Within a week he received a reply from Dr. George B. Farnsworth, one of the managers of Bingham's affairs, asking that Muskie visit him at Bingham's vacation home at Christmas Cove ("I always thought it was aptly named," Muskie says). Muskie saw Farnsworth the next day, and after a lengthy discussion, the doctor wrote the student a check for $900, given as a ten-year, interest-free loan. "If you need any more next year come and see me again," he told Muskie.

Muskie did again talk to Dr. Farnsworth before his last year at Cornell, and received a second check, this time for $1,000, on the same terms. Shortly after Pearl Harbor when Muskie had enlisted in the Navy, he received a letter from Dr. Farnsworth, who wrote that he understood Muskie had entered the service and that he and Bingham didn't want him leaving for duty with the financial burden of the loan hanging over his head. Enclosed with the letter was the note for

$900, canceled. "Next year," Dr. Farnsworth wrote, "if you are still in the service I'll send you the second canceled note." The next year the $1,000-note was returned.

After graduation in the spring of 1939 Muskie returned home to Rumford, and while waiting to take the Maine bar examinations, served as a substitute teacher in Rumford and nearby Mexico. He passed the bar and was admitted to practice on March 19, 1940. Rupert Aldrich, the Oxford County clerk of courts, whom Muskie had met while visiting the court, told him that Carl Blackington, a Waterville attorney, had died and his widow had the practice up for sale. It looked like a good opportunity, Aldrich told Muskie, since much of Blackington's practice had been as a collection agent. "That was important to me because it meant that some money would be coming in while I was waiting to get established," Muskie says. "It isn't a particularly attractive way to practice law but it does pay the bills."

Muskie and Aldrich drove to Waterville to meet Mrs. Blackington and look over the practice. "It looked like a good proposition. There was a library which was very good and there were all the supplies. I remember that there were several hundred dollars' worth of stamped envelopes on hand, and the collection accounts looked as though they'd be productive. And there were some small estates that looked worthwhile. The only problem was that Mrs. Blackington had a price of $4,000 on the practice and I certainly didn't have that kind of money."

Again, Muskie's father came to the rescue. He convinced some friends that they should lend Muskie $1,000 to use as a down payment on the practice, and Mrs. Blackington agreed to accept the balance over a three-year period. "But before we signed the final papers with Mrs. Blackington I asked her what she would take for a cash sale. It was probably the only financial brilliance I have ever shown," Muskie says. Mrs. Blackington said she'd accept $3,000 in cash and agreed to leave that option open for six months. Within six months Muskie was able to make a $2,000 bank loan and buy the practice for $3,000.

With the practice had come Mrs. Blanche Nadeau, who had been Blackington's secretary. The young lawyer had quickly discovered that she was close to indispensable to the office. When she stipulated as a condition of her staying on with him that Muskie not run for office or undertake any other outside work that would interfere with his law practice, Muskie quickly agreed. "After all, a good secretary was hard to find and she was a good secretary."

Waterville, a clean bright city of nineteen thousand, seemed to like Muskie, and Muskie liked Waterville. The city, the home of Colby College and the Hathaway shirt (the only shirt Muskie now wears), was friendly and growing. It was also probably the only city in America with a Chinese restaurant named The Jefferson which was run by a Jewish family and featured strawberry shortcake. Muskie was just settling down to building a law practice when the United States entered World War II. Muskie, then twenty-eight, enlisted in the Navy and made arrangements to keep his office open during the war. Rupert Aldrich agreed to look in from time to time and Mrs. Nadeau, who planned to retire, was replaced by Mrs. Marjorie Hutchinson. Today, Mrs. Hutchinson remains both as a close friend and as the secretary at his Waterville law office, which serves as his district office in Maine.

In the Navy Muskie wrote to his sister Lucy that because he knew nothing of engines, he'd been assigned to a naval engineering school. He served uneventfully as a junior officer on a destroyer escort, the U.S.S. *Brackett,* in both the Atlantic and Pacific during the war and was discharged in late 1945 as a lieutenant. In his absence the law practice had failed to pay its own way, but Muskie did not regret that he had maintained it. "I felt it was important," he has said, "to keep my name active in Waterville."

Returning from the service to law practice in Waterville,

Muskie was elected head of the local AMVETS post, while
Richard McMahon, then the manager of a local finance office,
was elected head of the Marine Corps League. The war dead
were being returned home and the several veterans' organizations in town formed a council to provide pallbearers at
military funerals. "That was when I first got to know him,"
McMahon says. "I remember one day we were both picking
up our mail at the post office and I asked him—he was
running for the Maine Legislature in 1946—why he was a
Democrat. In those days being a Democrat in Maine was a lot
like bumping your head against a stone wall."

"Well, if I lived down South I'd probably be a Republican,"
Muskie replied with a smile. "Somebody has to do it."

The decision was natural enough. Muskie's experiences—
as the son of a Polish immigrant, a Roman Catholic, a
student struggling for an education during the Depression
years—all shaped his political instincts; but none more than
the Roosevelt New Deal, which had provided both funds for
his education and the controversy which whetted his interest
in public life. Few first-generation Americans in Maine became Republicans; the chances for acceptance were rare, the
opportunities for advancement slight. The party leaders were
almost exclusively Anglo-Saxon, with names like Hildreth,
Sewall, Hale, Brewster, and Smith.

The only Democrat to succeed in Maine in decades had
been Louis Brann, a florid-faced Lewiston politician who had
been elected governor in the Depression year of 1932 and reelected in 1934. In the unrest of the 1930's three Maine Democrats also had won congressional seats, but none had left an
imprint on the electorate and none had been reelected.

Brann had been the exception. Victorious in 1932 by a
margin of less than three thousand votes, he had been reelected with ease two years later. A gregarious chief executive,
he was a handshaking, backslapping politician that reserved
Down Easters accepted for a time but never really understood.
Once, Maine Democrats recall, while handshaking his way

through a Democratic rally he clasped the hand of the son of of a man he knew casually. "Hello Jim," said Brann, pumping away, "how's your father?"

"He died last week," said Jim sadly.

But Brann had already grabbed another hand to massage. As Brann worked his way around the hall, he eventually made his way back to the disconsolate Jim. He grabbed the hand again, shook it warmly, and asked, "Well, Jim, how's your father?"

"He's still dead, Governor," Jim replied.

Years later, Maine Democrats would fondly recall that story, coupling it with one concerning Muskie during his reelection campaign in 1956. By then, handshaking had become almost a reflex. One evening, returning home from the hustings, he was greeted at the door by his wife. Muskie automatically stuck out his hand and asked, "How are all the folks up your way today?"

But Brann had been an oddity, a freak spawned by the Depression. In 1936 he had run for the United States Senate and lost. Two years later he had been defeated in his attempt to rewin the governorship. The two Brann successes were discounted for what they were, temporary aberrations of the Maine electorate.

In 1946, F. Harold Dubord, then the Maine national committeeman of a bankrupt Democratic party and a well-known Waterville attorney, was looking for legislative candidates and came to Muskie's office to talk to the young war veteran about running for a seat in the Maine House. Dubord explained that a young, bright veteran might be able to win. Muskie listened with enthusiasm. "I was interested," he said, "because of my father's general interest in public affairs. And the whole New Deal period had coincided with my own personal life and problems. But it had never occurred to me to get into politics until Harold Dubord came to my office and asked me."

There was another reason. Business was far from booming at the walk-up office of Edmund S. Muskie, attorney-at-law.

"I wasn't busy. I was waiting for clients to show up and it seemed to me that it would be very useful and very interesting to spend one term in the Legislature. I didn't have anything more than that in mind." The money was not much of an inducement. A legislator received $850 for the two-year term, from which he was expected to pay for his room and meals. Fortunately, the state capital, Augusta, was only seventeen miles away, so renting a room would not be necessary. If Muskie won, Dubord pointed out, he could drive back and forth.

But there was no assurance that Muskie could win. The Democrats were in as sad shape in Waterville as elsewhere in the state. They had lost the mayor's office the year before and the city's two House seats had been held by Republicans for the past four years. Muskie, who campaigned hard, was as surprised as anyone else when he won. His running mate for Waterville's second House seat, Roland Poulin, was also elected.

Muskie's legislative record was not overwhelming. He came to Augusta as one of twenty-four Democrats elected to the 151-member House of Representatives. He was assigned, as a freshman House member and a Democrat, to two forgettable, unimportant committees, Federal Relations and Military Affairs. He voted with the Democratic minority most of the time and near the end of the session joined with most Democrats and many Republicans to defeat a bill which would have established a personal income tax and a sales tax to finance increased state services, arguing that the bill had been hastily prepared. He supported a measure to provide a veterans' bonus with funds to be raised from horse-racing revenues. It failed.

But Muskie learned how to play the legislative game. He kept his mouth shut most of the time—a virtue his fellow Maine legislators respected—and he was easygoing and friendly. When he opposed the Republican majority he did so without either heat or hostility. Republican House leaders, sensing that Muskie was no partisan gadfly, responded by naming him to the Judiciary Committee, a plum appointment, when he was reelected in 1948. His Democratic colleagues chose him as their House minority leader at that time and again at the start of the 1951 session. He was then, as now, cautious, careful; he burned few bridges behind him. A legislator who served with him during those years remembers him best as "a very quiet young man, always an extremely intelligent man, the kind of fellow who always thought things out very carefully before he opened his mouth and expressed an opinion."

In 1947, while serving his first term in the Maine House, Muskie suffered his first—and until he and Humphrey were beaten in 1968, his only—political defeat. He ran for mayor of Waterville; his opponent, Republican Russell M. Squire, a popular politician who had at one time been mentioned as a GOP gubernatorial possibility and was now the president of a local bank, defeated Muskie by about four hundred votes. Muskie was defeated in large measure because some of the heavily Democratic wards in an area known as "the Plains" of Waterville failed to produce on Election Day. "There was a rumor the day before the election that Ed was Jewish and that hurt him," McMahon said. "Ed lost that election in the Democratic wards." It was to be several years before Muskie was accepted in the French community in Waterville and around the state and began to attract that heavily Democratic bloc vote.

About the time Muskie first ran for the Legislature he met Jane Gray, a beautiful, photogenic nineteen-year-old Waterville girl whose father, a paper-mill employee, had died when she was twelve, leaving a widow and five children. The mother took in Colby College students as boarders, and Jane's older brother, Howard, became the head of the family. He is now the business manager of the Waterville *Sentinel,* one of the

Guy Gannett newspapers in Maine, then a strong, vigorously partisan Republican newspaper chain which in 1954 would urge the relection of GOP Governor Burton M. Cross over Ed Muskie.

After graduating from high school, Jane had taken a job as a bookkeeper, salesgirl, and occasional dress model in a local fashion shop operated by two sisters. The sisters decided that she would make a fine catch for the young lawyer with wavy brown hair who had moved into town. The problem was Muskie. He simply wasn't interested in girls. Jane began to frequent the same restaurant as Ed on her lunch hour. But he always seemed preoccupied, often reading as he ate, and took no notice. Finally, in desperation, she purposely stumbled into Muskie as he rose to leave. "Excuse me," she said.

"Certainly," said Muskie and walked on.

Jane had about given up hopes on Muskie when she and a friend attended an open-house meeting of the AMVETS chapter. Muskie spoke and Jane was entranced. As they were leaving, someone came to tell the two girls that Muskie would like to meet them, and the introductions were made. The following day he invited Jane to lunch, and they dated for the next eighteen months. "I don't think you could say that Ed really courted Jane," McMahon says. "I think they just went together and then they got married.

According to Jane, Muskie proposed after he'd been serving in the Legislature for about a year. "I've been carrying the ring around for quite a few months but I didn't want to give it to you until it was paid for," he said. Jane immediately accepted. When they were married, in the spring of 1948, she agreed to two conversions. A Republican and a Baptist, she consented to become a Democrat and a Roman Catholic. It's been a happy marriage and Muskie became a devoted father as the family grew. Perhaps because he had married relatively late in life he doted on his children and missed them deeply when they were apart. During his 1964 reelection campaign the children were in school in Maryland as he stumped the

state, and Muskie was lonely without them. At one evening
cocktail party held in his behalf at the home of Roger V.
Snow, Muskie disappeared about 8 P.M. Searching the house
and grounds for the guest of honor, Snow discovered Muskie
sitting in the nursery reading bedtime stories to three of the
young Snow children. "I hope you don't mind," Muskie said
quietly as Snow entered. "I miss my children and I was enjoying yours."

The newlyweds bought, for $8,000, a small yellow clapboard
Cape Cod cottage in Waterville, a four-room expandable.
Muskie had also purchased, while still a bachelor, a rough
camp on nearby China Lake, for $4,000. The Muskies spent
the summer after their marriage there. Until a few years ago,
when Muskie paid $26,500 for a handsome summer cottage
in Kennebunk Beach, a cottage nestled between a golf course
and the ocean (and within walking distance of the Narragansett, where he had bellhopped), these were the only Maine
homes Muskie owned. The Cape Cod was sold for between
$13,000 and $14,000 after he became governor, when the
family had outgrown it. The China Lake cottage was sold
later for about $9,000.

McMahon, who was then working for a woolen mill, presented the Muskies with two blankets as a wedding present.
When he was himself married five weeks later he received an
electric clock from them. "I've still got it at home and it's a
good one because it still keeps perfect time. I've always been
a little suspicious of that clock. He probably got two of them
as wedding presents when he got married."

Although McMahon says it with a smile, Muskie is known
as a man close with a dollar. Only recently, since money has
become somewhat more plentiful, has he begun to pick up an
occasional luncheon tab when eating with friends. "The last
two or three times I've eaten with him he's surprised me by
paying the bill," says George J. Mitchell, a former Muskie
aide in Washington, a speech writer during the 1968 campaign and now Maine's Democratic national committeeman.

Muskie's frugality used to rankle Maurice Williams, his administrative assistant when Muskie was governor.

"As a governor, he used to get all kinds of little gifts," Williams, now Maine's commissioner of finance and administration, recalls, "and it seemed to me he was always getting golf balls in the mail. In those days I used to play golf but he didn't. And Jesus, he'd get those golf balls by the dozen and I'd sit there in the office and look at them and drool and then I'd watch him take those goddamned golf balls over to the Blaine House and stick them in the attic. I never got one. But if he wasn't free about giving things away, he was very sentimental. At Christmas he always had a party for his staff at the Blaine House and it meant a great deal to him."

Muskie didn't serve long after his election to a third term in the Maine House in 1950. The House convened in January, 1951, and on February 8 he resigned to become state director of the Office of Price Stabilization, a federal post. When Muskie told the House of his decision to leave, a fellow member, Representative Lloyd T. Dunham, a Republican, said, "As a new member two years ago, I listened to Ed time after time and I enjoyed his logic, his straight thinking, and I thought to myself, it is too bad that he is a member of the minority party. If he belonged to my way of thinking, I think Ed would go an awful long way."

Muskie resigned to take a job that didn't promise to make many friends for a budding politician. Nationally, prices had soared in 1950 and inflation had become a major concern, forcing the Truman Administration to announce a general price-wage freeze early the next year. The move was unpopular and in many areas the administration of the stabilization program was controversial—drawing charges, sometimes leading to congressional investigations, of profiteering and influence peddling. When he became state OPS director, Muskie said, "We are trying to accomplish an almost impossible task. We are trying to stop almost overnight a flood of rising prices. It cannot be done that easily. Prices are going to continue to rise; for how much longer we don't know." Then Muskie added, "It is going to be my effort to make the OPS in Maine a public agency, not a police agency. We will, naturally, crack down on violators in the interests of the welfare of our people but we are set up to help you in tackling a vicious problem and we hope you will look upon us as people to whom you can come for advice and assistance."

There may have been controversy surrounding the OPS nationally, but in Maine, Muskie adopted an evenhanded approach that won him new friends around the state. Where controls were highly unpopular, as in potato-growing areas and along the coast, Muskie made a number of personal trips to discuss problems with businessmen and labor leaders. And despite the controversy, inflation was held in check in 1951. Wholesale prices began a slow but steady drop, and although the consumer price index continued to rise, the rate of increase was markedly slowed. Nevertheless, Muskie was dissatisfied, and he resigned from the OPS in the summer of 1952, to return to his law practice, saying that a combination of "public apathy and active business opposition has resulted in a weakening of the controls law" in Congress.

Expansionary pressures were evident in the Muskie household as well. A son, Stephen, born in 1949, had been joined in 1950 by a sister, Ellen. (She was to be followed in 1956 by another girl, Melinda.) The four-room Cape Cod was beginning to bulge. Muskie, a tinkerer and do-it-yourselfer, decided early in 1953 to finish off two additional rooms upstairs. One evening as he was working, a stair rail gave way and he fell a full flight, breaking his back. He was unconscious for two days, and only after two weeks was it certain that he would live; he remained in the hopital for two months. In the spring, wearing a large back brace and using crutches, Muskie was released from the hospital, and moved to the China Lake camp to recover. Each day he would crawl down to the lake for a swim, using it as therapy. Now national committeeman (he had been elected a year earlier by the Maine delegation at the

Chicago Democratic convention), he also spent the summer thinking about the Democratic party and the state ticket for the coming year. For himself, he settled on seeking the Second District congressional seat, opposing incumbent Republican Charles Nelson. By late fall he had discarded the crutches and was able to return to work. In his spare time he headed a fund-raising committee for the Waterville Sisters' Hospital, which was threatened with closing, and raised more than $100,000 to keep the facility open.

Muskie's own finances remained in poor shape. At the time of his accident he had no money in the bank, and it was not until he became governor in 1955 that he worked his way into the black. Insurance covered the hospital and nursing bills, but the doctor bills remained, as did payments on his house and car. The election victory of September, 1954, was to prove a financial lifesaver. Between September and the national elections in November, Muskie, the upset Democratic winner in a solid Republican state, was a hot property at Democratic affairs in other states. Honoraria and fees for his appearances throughout the country brought in about $5,000. The money was used to pay Muskie's office rent, his secretary, and his living costs, and provided a "draw" of $100 a week for his own expenses between his election and his inauguration. At that time Maine law provided no funds to be used by the Governor-elect in preparing a staff or a budget, so the fees and honoraria kept Muskie afloat. "I was in the red at the time, all right," Muskie says, "but I don't think my debts were overwhelming. But if I'd lost that election," he says, shaking his head, "I would have been in sad shape."

CHAPTER THREE

THE

$18,000

UPSET

In Maine, late June is not a political season. The frantic, if traditionally well-mannered, primaries are over and the public interest has turned to more immediate, more important matters. In northern Aroostook the farmers have emerged from the long, bitterly cold winter to sow the annual crop which is the economic lifeblood of the largest potato-producing county in the nation. Farther south, lobstermen have begun to tend in earnest the more than half a million traps which dot the state's rugged and forbidding 3,478-mile shoreline. In resort communities from Bar Harbor to Kennebunkport caretakers carefully remove the shutters and turn on the electricity in thousands of summer cottages, while shop owners and restaurateurs from Moosehead to Sebago Lake check their stocks, obtain uniforms for the pretty co-ed waitresses, and spruce up for the coming season. Road commissioners work their crews feverishly to repair the potholes and frost holes in roads and streets before the summer residents and tourists arrive in droves and make highway reconstruction not only difficult but economically disastrous. For along the Maine coast summer means tourists and tourists mean money. And money, largely earned between Memorial Day and Labor Day, means survival through yet another winter.

In the larger cities of the state, the commercial and industrial centers such as Portland, Lewiston, and Bangor, which are only peripherally dependent upon the tourish trade, the paper, textile, and shoe factories begin to hum with renewed vigor as the sun daily moves higher across the sky from East Quoddy Head, the easternmost point in the United States, to Fryeburg, on the New Hampshire border. The crusty Mainer may be forgiven if he abandons politics in the summer; he's working to survive.

But though the average Maine man is too busy in late June to be interested in matters political, in the early summer of 1954 they were of principal concern to Ed Muskie, the Democratic nominee for governor, and to his campaign manager, Richard McMahon, the Waterville tax collector and former finance-office manager. The two had come to Portland on a fund-raising expedition and were eating at the Pagoda Restaurant owned by Henry Wong, one of a minority of ardent Democrats in a strongly Republican city. There were other reasons for going to Henry Wong's. He was a friend of Ed Muskie's. The food was good. And it was the only place in Portland where the two were always assured of a free meal.

This was the first time McMahon had traveled with the candidate in the young campaign. A week earlier Muskie had driven his temperamental secondhand 1949 Lincoln alone on a six-hundred-mile, four-day swing through Aroostook and

Washington counties. The weather had been damp—foggy and rainy—throughout the trip. The reception of the candidate had been poor. Local Democrats had been largely unenthusiastic or uninterested. Muskie had returned home late Saturday night—tired, lonely, and discouraged. Richard J. Dubord, a close friend, had taken one look at him and immediately telephoned McMahon. The candidate couldn't be expected to travel the state alone, Dubord said, and McMahon agreed to accompany him. The following Monday they had left for Portland on the fund-raising effort.

Not until they had arrived in Portland did McMahon discover that Muskie had packed to stay overnight: He had put his toothbrush and razor in the pocket of his suit. "God, it was a shock," says McMahon. "Even in those days I wasn't used to traveling that light." At the Pagoda they were met by Jack Agger, a local attorney and businessman, who offered to share his Longfellow Square bachelor apartment with them.

"When we get up to Jack's place that night it turns out there's only one bedroom and a couch in the living room," McMahon says. "Jack says he's going to sleep on the couch, so we go into the bedroom and there's only this one three-quarter-size bed."

Muskie, the party's national committeeman and candidate for governor, claimed the outside of the bed, relegating McMahon to the portion abutting the wall. In the morning, McMahon, who is five foot seven and weighs over two hundred pounds, told Muskie, "Never again. The next time we travel together we're going to have to make better arrangements than this." Later he commented, "I made up my mind it was the last time I was going to have to crawl over that lanky, bony son of a gun every time I had to go to the bathroom. And he hadn't even told me to bring my toothbrush."

The story is not atypical. For to appreciate the Maine election of 1954 one must understand that the Democratic party, which existed in name only, was as broke as were its candidates. At very best the campaign of 1954 was designed as a dry run for 1956, when the small band of young Democrats who were attempting to rebuild a political party hoped to make a legitimate drive for major offices. Of all the major Democratic candidates in 1954 only Muskie and James "Big Jim" Oliver, a political maverick who had served as a Republican congressman during the 1930's and then deserted the GOP, could lay claim to any substantial legislative experience.

In 1954 Democratic strength was centered largely in the party organizations in the mill cities of Biddeford, Lewiston, and to a lesser extent, Waterville. These were largely fiefdoms, controlled by local parochial party leaders, who in many instances saw personal advantage in a permanent minority status. Patronage, both from Washington and from the state capital in Augusta, was funneled through these local leaders.

Of 480,658 registered Maine voters, only 99,386 were listed as Democrats. Independent voters, those enrolled in neither party, totaled 118,928. The Republican party claimed 262,344 members. In only one of Maine's sixteen counties, Androscoggin, did Democrats outnumber Republicans; elsewhere the GOP was in firm control. In Washington County, hard by where Franklin Delano Roosevelt had summered at Campobello and where he had proposed harnessing the giant Passamaquoddy tides to provide low-cost electric power to a chronic economically depressed area, Republican voters outnumbered Democrats 4 to 1. Farther south along the coast the picture was even bleaker; in some counties Republicans held an 8-to-1 advantage.

The Republican enrollment figures were reflected and magnified in terms of the only figures a politician finds meaningful—those denoting political victory. In the elections of 1952 Republicans had won all but 24 of 151 seats in the state House of Representatives and held all but 2 of the 33 state Senate seats. Not only did the GOP control both United States Senate seats, three congressional seats, and the governorship, but its influence extended to courthouses and sheriffs' offices throughout the state. For a full century the Republican party had been the dominant political force in Maine, winning elections with so few exceptions that by the 1940's it had made a mockery of the slogan "As Maine goes, so goes the nation." In the twentieth century, save for defections to the Progressive party and for reactions to the impact of the Great Depression, Maine had gone Republican. Period.

Yet the general belief that Maine has always been a one-party state is incorrect. For Maine had come to statehood in 1820 as a Democratic state in the Jeffersonian tradition. Between 1820 and the state Democratic party's collapse in 1856, after the party became identified with proslavery in an abolitionist state, Democrats won all but a handful of the then annual gubernatorial elections. Only once in the first thirty-four years of statehood did Democrats lose control of either branch of the Maine Legislature.

That had all been long ago. A century of Republican control, during which such national figures as James G. Blaine and House Speaker Thomas B. Reed had made "Maine" synonymous with "Republican," had dimmed the knowledge that the state could support a Democratic party.

The prolonged Republican successes, however, had left their marks upon the party. One-party control had led to intra-party squabbling; human resources were misallocated by an organizational structure that all but ignored younger party members. As far back as 1948 there were indications that rank-and-file Maine Republicans were looking for an excuse to kick over the traces. That year they had, amazingly, rejected their party chieftains in a bitter primary to nominate a former Skowhegan telephone operator named Margaret Chase Smith as their candidate for the United States Senate. A relatively unknown congresswoman, she had defeated two former governors, Horace A. Hildreth and Sumner Sewall. Again, in 1952, when Burton M. Cross, the president of the state Senate, had won the gubernatorial primary in a hard, three-way fight, one of the losers, a Stockton Springs farmer named Neil S. Bishop, had run as an independent candidate in the fall general election and polled a surprisingly high 35,000 votes.

In the winter of 1953–1954 a few Maine Democrats saw the signs of Republican discontent, but they were inclined to underestimate them. Even earlier, back in 1952, Dick McMahon and Dick Dubord had both urged Muskie, the new national committeeman from Maine, to run for governor. Muskie had rested his chin in cupped hands, considered the situation, and decided, "This isn't the year; let's wait until 'fifty-four and look it over." The Democrats had gone on to nominate "Big Jim" Oliver, and he had been, predictably, swamped by Burt Cross in the Eisenhower landslide.

In 1954 the prospects looked no more inviting than they had in 1952. The only difference seemed to be that now Democratic party control at the state level was swinging into the hands of a small band of reformers, including Muskie, Dubord (whose father had unsuccessfully run for governor in 1936), and a thirty-four-year-old Lewiston attorney named Frank Morey Coffin. No one was to be more instrumental in refurbishing the Democratic party than Coffin. He was the grandson of Frank Morey, a six-term Lewiston mayor, who in 1911 was elected speaker of the Maine House. Frank Coffin's father was a respected attorney; his mother for several years was a Democratic state committeewoman from Androscoggin County. Coffin, a brilliant Bates College and Harvard Law School graduate, was slight and pale, with jet-black hair, a widow's peak, and narrow eyes that gave him an almost satanic appearance.

Muskie, at forty the oldest of the group, had recognized both Coffin's brilliance and his potential. He had read some of Coffin's speeches urging a new Democratic party, and while convalescing from his broken back at his China Lake camp, during the early fall of 1953, had invited Coffin to explore the possibilities with him. The China Lake meeting had ended with Muskie urging Coffin to play a more active role in party politics. Coffin, in fact, was anxious to assume more responsibility, but in Lewiston his aloof attitude, and the fact that his name was not French, had hampered his progress.

There is no doubt that Muskie, the national committeeman, wanted Coffin as state chairman. The problem was to get him elected to the Democratic state committee. Once Coffin was there, it would be possible to put the party apparatus into his hands. "We knew it wouldn't be easy to get him elected from Androscoggin because there were several popular Franco-Americans who wanted the job," McMahon, by then a state committeeman from Kennebec County, said, "but we wanted him badly. So some of us let it be known to a few people in Lewiston that the worst thing they could do would be to elect Frank Coffin to the state committee. So naturally they went right ahead and elected him." Louis Jalbert, a veteran legislator and one of the ablest schemers in the maze that is Lewiston politics, rejects McMahon's theory. "We elected Frank Coffin that year because he was the best man for the job," he says.

Even before his election to the state committee and to the post of state chairman, Coffin had put his imprint on the 1954 campaign as chairman of the Platform Committee. The platform, a masterpiece of political showmanship, was developed as a "grass-roots" statement of Maine beliefs and aspirations. It was drafted not by party leaders behind closed doors, but by schoolteachers, mill workers, and farmers. Questionnaires were circulated throughout the state, exploring citizen sentiment on a broad range of state issues. The public reaction was enthusiastic: Mainers, long accustomed to being either scolded or ignored by the Republican party, took the formulation of the platform seriously. By February, 1954, Coffin had held an open "issues conference" that attracted about 250, including many who had never before participated in politics.

Maine men jealously guard the concept of participatory democracy. In small towns across the state the March town meeting brings together the rich and the poor, the lobsterman and the lawyer, in an annual exercise in practical civics that is unsurpassed anywhere else in the nation. Now, more modestly, a political party was inviting the same sort of involvement. For the first time fishermen were asked what ought to be done to preserve the lobster, educators were asked what was wrong with their schools—and they responded.

By the time of the 1954 Democratic state convention in Lewiston, where an old lion of the party, W. Averell Harriman, drew an enthusiastic reception as keynote speaker, the Democrats had a platform to submit for approval, but no candidates. Muskie was certainly not the party's first choice for governor, nor did he particularly want to run. "I guess at that time I was probably more interested in Congress, if I was to run for anything at all," Muskie said.

Immediately after the March convention a number of older Democrats were approached as possible gubernatorial candidates. Among them were Dr. Clinton A. Clauson of Waterville, who was to become governor four years later, and F. Harold Dubord, who had run unsuccessfully in the 1930's. There were no volunteers.

With less than three weeks to the mid-April filing deadline, Muskie, Lewiston attorney Alton A. Lessard, Professor Paul Fullam of Colby College, and Dick McMahon met in Room 211 of the Augusta House in a frantic attempt to produce a ticket. Then throughout the afternoon Muskie was on the telephone, trying to locate candidates. Perry Furbish, an old-line Democrat from Palmyra, said he'd run for governor if no one else could be found. "But, you ought to run, Ed," he told Muskie. "The Republicans are split. This is the year we can go somewhere."

Slowly, as the afternoon passed and Muskie telephoned throughout the state in search of a gubernatorial candidate, the possibility of his own candidacy emerged. "The more he called people," McMahon says, "the more he talked to people, the more they began to throw back at him: 'Well, what's the matter with you?' So finally he decided to run. And he really was a reluctant candidate. But he figured that he ought to do it now, get it over with, because somebody had to do it, and after all, he was the national committeeman."

Almost until the end, Muskie assumed that if he ran at all, it would be as a candidate for Congress from the Second District. Certainly, running in the Second District would be less wearing in terms of both time and money than a statewide campaign. In any case, there was only one realistic prediction for a Democratic candidate—defeat. Some participants in the 1954 campaign believe, in fact, that the entire ticket that year was really designed to lay the groundwork for Frank Coffin's assault on the governorship two years later, when, most believed, the party would be on firmer footing. So widespread was this belief, that two years later Coffin was compelled publicly to deny that there was truth to the rumors that he would be the candidate for governor and that Muskie would step down after a single term in order to run for Congress. Coffin, who was elected to Congress himself in 1956 and 1958, did return to Maine to seek the governorship in 1960, only to be buried in the anti-Kennedy landslide that engulfed Maine that year.

Finally, with the state filing deadline for the primaries only a week away, the ticket was secured: Ed Muskie would run for governor; Ken Colbath, Tom Delahanty, and the irrepressible Jim Oliver would seek the three congressional seats. Paul Fullam, after being told by his doctor that he had a heart condition and might live three years or thirty, at first decided not to run for the Senate. He went to Muskie's home to deliver the bad news personally. Muskie glumly received it, and the two talked at length about the possibility of finding a replacement. The next morning, at about seven thirty, Muskie's phone rang. It was Fullam. "I've decided to run after all," he told Muskie. "You looked like a big, sad bear when I told you last night, and I couldn't sleep thinking about it." Fullam was to run and lose. Three years later he would be dead. Within a week, the nominating petitions had been circulated, returned, and filed with the Secretary of

State. The ease with which the signatures were secured gave McMahon the "first indication that we might have some sort of an organization after all. And from then on the campaign was under way and we were traveling by the seat of our pants."

In seeking reelection to the United States Senate in 1970, Edmund S. Muskie would spend more than $150,000. In 1954 the Democrats could muster only $18,000 to finance campaigns for the Senate, the governorship, and three congressional seats. And to the money shortage was joined another factor. Although no one spoke of it, the truth was that a Roman Catholic had never been elected governor. Maine is preponderantly Protestant, and prejudice against the 270,000 Catholics runs deep, if silent. "Pope Night" in November, which featured torchlight parades and was climaxed by the burning of the Pope in effigy, had continued in parts of New England almost into the twentieth century. The spread of the Ku Klux Klan followed; in the 1920's the Klan had an estimated 150,000 members in Maine, more than in any other New England state. In Portland, the state's largest city, the Klan flourished and in 1923 plunked down $76,500 for a Forest Avenue estate which was turned into a permanent meeting place, featuring an auditorium and a sixty-foot-high electric cross. In some Maine communities the Klan was given official recognition by the town fathers. Crosses were burned across the state, some bombings and fires were blamed on Klan activity, and Jews, Catholics, and the tiny Negro population were intimidated. To be sure, some Republicans of the 1920's denounced the Klan and its burning crosses, but the Republican party in Maine is basically Protestant in composition, while Catholics —primarily Franco-Americans in the mill cities and in the St. John Valley, along the Canadian border—have formed the nucleus of the Democratic organization in Maine in the twentieth century.

Today, Mainers may claim that the prejudice is an illusion, that Muskie is proof that a Roman Catholic can make his way politically in their state. Yet he remains the only Roman Catholic ever to be elected to major office in Maine. The prejudice exists. In the hierarchy of Maine business—in the banks, the investment houses, the giant paper companies, and the private utilities—the governing offices are almost exclusively Protestant. As late as 1958 a young college graduate seeking a job in Boothbay Harbor was interviewed at length and then was bluntly asked, "Are you a Catholic?" Assured that he was not, the owner told the applicant, "Well, of course, I've got nothing against them, but a lot of people in town do." Two years later a wave of anti-Catholicism was a definite if unmeasurable factor in the Maine defeat of John F. Kennedy.

Moreover, the vote obtained by Muskie, running unopposed, in the June primary, was unimpressive. He had polled 17,221, compared to 97,052 votes for Governor Cross, also unopposed, in the Republican primary. And no governor in Maine history had ever been refused a second term by the electorate.

Cross, in fact, had every reason to be elated at the primary results, and he was. He called a press conference to point out gleefully to newsmen that he had received a greater percentage of the total Republican vote than Muskie had received of the Democratic. What's more, he had run ahead of the GOP incumbents in the First and Second Districts and neck and neck with the GOP congressman in the Third District. And he had run as well as the popular Senator Smith. Overall, said Cross, "I think this was a whale of a vote of confidence."

So it seemed. Cross, who had been privately worried for some time about his popularity in the party, felt vindicated by the GOP primary results. He had run better than anyone had expected and could look forward to appearing on the ballot in the fall neatly sandwiched between Senator Smith and three incumbent congressmen who seemed certain of victory in Maine's first-in-the-nation September election. Cross could even afford to give a backhand compliment to the opposition. He had, he said, a "great deal of respect" for Muskie, but confessed that he hardly felt that he was the strongest candidate the Democrats could have mustered.

But the primaries had been deceiving. Cross was unpopular, and political reporters, as they nosed through the state, could not help detecting the odors. The trouble, much of it of Cross' own making, had been long fermenting. Early in the year he had angered Washington County residents by making a cavalier visit to one of the poorest areas of the state (with an unemployment rate of about 15 per cent and a per capita income of less than $1,400 a year) and reporting that "no depression" existed.

"In fact," Cross had told the Washington County Chamber of Commerce, "there is no place in Maine where I'll admit that there's a depression." Then he had added gratuitously that he commended those in the county who were "resentful of people pitying you on the outside." Finally, the Governor had offered one last bit of free advice to the people of Washington County. They might, he had suggested, "lift themselves up by their bootstraps." That single statement, more than any other, was to plague Cross throughout the campaign. For it somehow crystallized in the public mind the image of the Republican party as the party controlled by the giant paper companies (which either directly or indirectly owned half the land in the largest New England state) and by the private utilities (which furnished electric power at rates among the highest in the nation). It was the kind of unfeeling, aristocratic comment that could only have been uttered by a politician leading a firmly one-party state. Somebody grumbled that it grew a trifle wearisome to hear Republican governors comment "on how noble it is to dig clams, grow blueberries, teach school, and wait on table."

Burt Cross, a successful florist turned politician, had risen in the GOP according to the prescribed practice, coming up through the legislative chairs to the presidency of the state Senate in 1952, after which he had won a bitter primary fight and a first term as governor. But he had never been able to avoid the unfortunate phrase or the untimely act. "He was the most stubborn man I've ever known in my life," says one GOP state official. "And he never learned the knack of political compromise."

Cross, who until 1954 had never lost an election, and who subsequently would never run in another, had sought the Senate presidency in 1951 after two House terms and two Senate terms, opposing Senator Robert N. Haskell. When Cross had won, his supporters were rewarded with choice committee chairmanships, as expected; Haskell's supporters were dumped altogether from their preferred committees. Cross declined, as the victor, to hold out the olive branch of reconciliation to the vanquished.

As governor, Cross continued to exhibit a lack of compromise, a lack of tact. "In twenty years of public life Burt Cross never learned to let a man down easy," says a Republican colleague. "A governor, when it comes to appointments or jobs, has to have the knack of saying No gracefully. Ed Muskie could turn a man down for a job and the fellow would come out of his office saying that he was a wonderful guy. Burt Cross never learned to do that."

Yet if he is judged by his accomplishment, Cross emerges as an able chief executive. He tackled the Highway Commission and abolition of the politically popular but wasteful pork-barrel program which permitted legislators to take small road-building projects home to their constituents each year. In the face of considerable legislative opposition, Cross pulled the Highway Commission out of the quicksand of politics and placed it on a solid professional footing, appointing the state's first full-time Highway Chairman, a career state administrator. He reorganized the scandal-ridden State Liquor Commission, and established a state hospital program providing care for the indigent. He carved an impressive, progressive record, which was overshadowed only by his ineptness in public relations.

In the campaign of 1954 it was Burt Cross, now fifty-one, who would survey the havoc of Hurricane Carol and comment that "it wasn't as great as I had anticipated," never realizing that the observation, however honest, would not be accepted by the farmers, orchardists, fishermen, and homeowners who had been severely injured financially by the storm. And he would remain amazed that he was criticized for refusing, during the campaign year, to approve a grant of ten thousand dollars to the city of Portland for port and harbor development. It was a matter "of principle" to Cross that the money could not be granted until he had received specific legislative authorization and that closed the question so far as he was concerned. In Aroostook County he could not understand the objections when he urged closing the Presque Isle tuberculosis sanatorium and combining it with another more than a hundred miles away; after all, wasn't it perfectly clear that the facility was uneconomical and unnecessary? Nor did he seem to realize that a campaign year was no time to suggest that many miles of state-maintained highways be turned back to the towns for upkeep with local dollars. As governor and as candidate in 1954 he symbolized all that was wrong with an insensitive political party; as a loser to Muskie he came to personify the reason for the decline of the Maine Republican party. In the third-floor rotunda of the State House it is customary for the portraits of the past four governors to be placed in specified positions of prominence. The portrait of Burton M. Cross was never hung there; instead it was placed around a corner. Cross deserves better, for, in fact, he represented only the inevitable end product of a stagnant political party that had lost touch with the public.

Despite the drawbacks and limitations of Burton Cross, the Democrats continued to view the campaign of 1954 as only a prelude to 1956. Although Muskie maintains that "I thought there was a chance we could win—I saw the reception we were getting around the state and the packed rallies in Grange halls where there had never been a Democratic rally before," no one else in the campaign shared that optimism. The campaign was laughable even by rustic Maine standards. There is no documented evidence that Muskie stayed even once in a hotel or motel during the campaign; while on the road he would sleep at the homes of obliging local Democrats. Whenever possible he tried to spend the night in Waterville, where Jane could iron shirts and wash out underwear. He was constantly broke even though he had deferred payment of all his personal bills, except for the house mortgage and electricity, until the campaign was over. One discouraging night Muskie and McMahon pulled into a roadside diner in Newport and counted their money. Between the two there was just enough change to buy a package of cigarettes, a doughnut, and two cups of coffee. They split the doughnut.

As the improbable campaign wore on, Muskie's car wore out. The end came one night as the two drove through the fog of the Haynesville woods, a desolate thirty-mile stretch which separates central and northern Maine. The road was so barren and dangerous that a folk singer once recorded a song about it, which did rather well; the song was called "A Tombstone Every Mile." The tires on Muskie's car were so bare and the steering so erratic that a terrified McMahon crawled over the front seat and lay down on the floor in the rear as the candidate careened through the night. Throughout the remainder of the campaign, they used McMahon's year-old Ford.

Muskie would travel the state, speaking wherever an audience would listen, while back in Lewiston, Frank Coffin and Donald E. Nicoll, a former radio newsman and the party's first executive secretary, ground out press releases and attempted to scrape up money. Intellectually, Muskie and Coffin blended perfectly. Muskie would telephone Coffin that he was making a speech somewhere that night on economic development, and spell out his major points, and Coffin would produce a lengthy press release that captured not only the general theme but often the exact language of Muskie's speech.

There was a closeness of thought between the two that approached the uncanny.

It was perhaps not until early July that Muskie began to exhibit signs of being more than a perfunctory candidate. Hitherto he had been largely greeted with the reserve Mainers characteristically exhibit to any stranger who has yet to prove his reliability. True, there had been some previous indications that some Republican voters were not openly hostile. On the day following the uncomfortable night in Jack Agger's bed, McMahon had been surprised that on Portland's Exchange Street, the center of the city's legal district, "they didn't ignore Ed. They were willing to look him in the eye and talk to him. Some of the Republicans even went so far as to actually wish him luck. But they and we thought it was hopeless. Nobody thought we could win, not for a minute."

McMahon believes he can pinpoint the moment when Muskie's campaign began to sparkle with promise. It was, he says, a Saturday speech in early July in Rangeley, a small resort town—the kind that attracts hunters and fishermen— in the Longfellow Mountains of Maine, about forty miles north of Rumford. They had gone to Rumford to visit with Muskie's father who was then now seventy-two, semiretired, and ailing. The father and son had talked long and quietly and then Muskie and McMahon had driven north toward Rangeley.

As they drove, Muskie began to muse about the surroundings and to point out spots where his father had taken him fishing when he was a boy, where they had camped, the tailor and the shy, gangling youngster. "He was very fond of his father and I didn't realize how much until that day," says McMahon. "That was the only time I saw him get emotional that way. He'd gone back to the days when he was eleven or twelve with his father, and how those were the days and how much he missed them." The two had pulled to the side of the road when they reached the Height of Land, a spot that reveals a breathtaking panorama of Mooselookmeguntic, the state's third-largest and most beautiful lake. They sat there quietly for several minutes and then drove on.

That night in Rangeley, Muskie was to speak to a fish and game club, McMahon recalls, about the "put and take" method of fish stocking. Fish are put into a lake by the state in the spring and taken out by fishermen during the summer. The subject was a dry one, even for sportsmen, but Muskie, still moved by the drive from Rumford began to talk about his youth and fishing with his father. "He just got carried away by the memories and he carried everyone there away with him," McMahon says. "Pete Damborg [a political writer for the Guy Gannett newspaper chain] had come up to get a look at Muskie in action and he was impressed. We're sitting in the back of the room and you could hear a pin drop, the guy was so sincere. They came there expecting to hear him tell them about why he ought to be governor and instead he's telling them about fishing with his father. It was wonderful."

The mood was still present two days later in Castine, where Muskie addressed the first elderly audience of the campaign. Castine is a pretty coastal town nestled in Hancock County, midway up the Maine coast, and Hancock County, like much of Maine, has for years been experiencing an emigration of its youth. Heavily dependent upon the sea for its subsistence, Hancock County has watched as youngsters have finished school, failed to find work, and moved south to Massachusetts and Connecticut for factory employment. Muskie, who was to peg much of his campaign on the need for increased economic opportunity, talked to the group of Maine's elderly about the exportation of Maine's youth. He spoke of the need for creating jobs that would make it possible for the young to drop their welding torches in Bridgeport, Hartford, and Worcester and return to the good life in Maine. "Oh, I actually began to get tears in my eyes," McMahon says. "I had to leave, I couldn't stand it. The guy was hot and he had the women going for him. They loved him. They were all Republicans but they loved him that night." They loved him in September as well. Castine in 1954 could count only 62 enrolled Democrats, compared to 239 Republicans: Muskie carried the town by a vote of 125 to 108.

There were two factors, in addition to Muskie's personal allure and Cross' ineptitude, that must be weighed in considering the reasons for Muskie's success in 1954. The first was a Stockton Springs farmer named Neil S. Bishop; the second, a new entertainment medium in Maine—television. The impact of these is difficult to measure, yet it is possible that Muskie would have lost the election if both had not been available to him.

Bishop in 1954 was a moustached and moose-jawed fifty-year-old Republican with four terms in the state Senate behind him and a public record that included proposals calling for, among other things, the elimination of milk pricing controls in Maine and the sterilization of sexual perverts and imbeciles. He was a morose political maverick. Two years earlier he had battled Cross and an Augusta hardware dealer, Roy Hussey, for the GOP nomination for governor. Defeated in the primary, he had run as an independent in the fall and had kept the 35,000 votes he had won in the spring. Laconic, unpredictable, and politically unorthodox, he became the first prominent Maine Republican publicly to endorse Muskie's candidacy. Working actively, he formed a "Republicans for Muskie" club in Waldo County and urged that those who had supported him vote for Muskie. "I am absolutely certain that most of my supporters went along with me to vote for Muskie," Bishop says. "I led, and I believe they followed." Democrats today are less certain of Bishop's influence. Says one who was close to the campaign, "Neil Bishop was a help all right, but perhaps no more so than several dozen fairly prominent Republicans who were, either as Neil was, overtly for Muskie, or covertly for him. I just can't assess whether we would have won without Bishop. But it was a significant move for a real respected, established Republican to kick the traces, and that undoubtedly encouraged others and helped create an atmosphere that made being seen with Muskie respectable."

Muskie was to win by 22,000 votes in 1954; certainly some of the Republican defectors had followed Bishop's plea. Two years later Bishop had broken with Muskie (the young governor had been appreciative but unwilling to give Bishop a voice or a hand in the new administration), By 1958 Bishop was firmly back in the GOP, running for Congress as the Republican candidate, against Frank M. Coffin. When he lost, he went into a self-imposed political exile for a dozen years, then emerged in 1970 as the GOP candidate—ironically—for Muskie's Senate seat.

The impact of television on the 1954 election, like that of Bishop's involvement, was deep but difficult to measure. Until 1954 Maine political campaigns revolved around shaking hands at factories during the day and speaking at rallies in Grange halls and auditoriums in the evening. Billboard, newspaper, and radio advertising were all used regularly. It was possible for many voters never to see the candidates, particularly the Democrats. The advent of television in Maine changed all that. By 1954 four stations were in operation in the state— one each in Lewiston and Bangor, and two in Portland. According to one estimate, in 1954 there were slightly more than 100,000 receivers in use in Maine, with a potential audience of close to 400,000. Actually, it's likely that there were considerably fewer sets in the state at the time. But in any event, television offered two advantages to the Democrats—time was cheap (a fifteen-minute slot could be bought for two hundred dollars) and the medium was so novel that families spent the evening watching whatever was aired.

"We were lucky in 1954," says McMahon. "We had a captured audience with television. It was new, and because there was only one channel in all but the Portland area, if we bought the time you couldn't help but see us. And it was so new that people would watch whatever was shown, even politicians. We reached Republicans that year we couldn't have reached any other way."

What many Maine viewers saw that year was the first Democrat ever to appear in their living rooms. Some rural Republicans may even have been surprised to find that the Democratic candidate for governor didn't wear horns. It may be significant that the revival of the Democratic party in Maine coincided with the appearance of television in the state. While television was available to Republicans—and they used it heavily—it had less impact for them; they were known—indeed, in some instances, shopworn. The Democrats offered the new show, the new faces, on television. Rural Mainers found that Democratic candidates were worried about the same problems as they, that they spoke with the same accents, and that they appeared to be as knowledgeable as the Republicans. Moreover, watching television many discovered for the first time that some respected Maine men were Democrats. The venerable Portland attorney Leonard Pierce appeared on television to endorse Muskie and with him came the beloved president of Bowdoin College, Kenneth Sills, to profess his belief in the Maine Democratic party. If "Casey" Sills could be a Democrat, Mainers reasoned, the party must have some merits. And so they watched when the thoughtful, earnest Democratic candidate for governor came into their living rooms and talked about the need for moving the state forward, the necessity for two-party government, and of his desire for change. "Maine desperately needs two-party competition at the polls and in the development of sound programs for the benefit of our people," Muskie said in his initial announcement, stressing his belief that progress could only be made in a two-party system. It was a belief that would echo throughout the campaign.

As the campaign wore on, Coffin and Nicoll became increasingly convinced of the value of television, and shifted the allotments in their meager budget until in the end they spent slightly more than four thousand dollars in airing their major candidates. "There is more and more interest in our candidates," the boyish Nicoll said in explaining the expanded use of television by Democrats as the campaign moved into late August and early September. "People are eager to hear them, and the demand to see them is increasing, especially in the urban areas. The days of the political rally," he said, "are numbered."

The September elections in Maine were considered by Republicans to have a psychological effect on the rest of the nation. They were particularly important to the GOP in 1954 because of its desire to keep the newly won Republican Congress for Eisenhower. On one of the closing days of the campaign Vice-President Nixon made a half-hour television appeal in behalf of the Maine GOP ticket. That same evening young Senator John F. Kennedy of Massachusetts came to Portland for a television appearance with Fullam.

As the campaign drew to a close, Governor Cross was just as confident as he had been at the start. On the Friday before the Monday election, the Governor confidently predicted a victory margin of 45,000 votes. He had flatly refused Muskie's challenge to a television debate. "I'll be happy to talk with Ed at any time—after the campaign," he had said haughtily.

The next day Hurricane Edna tore into Maine, killing eight, causing damage estimated at seven million dollars, and diverting interest from the finale of the campaign. The hurricane did nothing to increase Muskie's optimism, although some Democrats said hopefully that if enough bridges were washed out it might succeed in keeping some rural Republicans away from the polls on Monday. As he sat in the Pilot's Grille in Bangor on Sunday night after giving his final speech, with the flame from a candle on the table playing over his face, he reviewed the campaign. "At least," he concluded, "they can't say we haven't worked at it. We've given it everything we've got." Could they win? McMahon asked. "Maybe," said Muskie thoughtfully. "If people do what they've said they're going to, we've got a chance." But he didn't sound as though he meant it.

"You know," Muskie said recently, "there was only one time when I thought I didn't have a chance. That was the day of the election, when everybody started to vote and there wasn't anything else I could say or do. And I thought, 'Well, this has been a pleasant interlude; now I can stop this foolishness about wanting to be governor and get down to earning a living.' "

Muskie and Jane awaited the decision of the Maine electorate in a small two-room suite at the Elmwood Hotel, in Waterville. They had voted earlier in the day under cloudy, still windswept skies that would slowly clear toward evening in the aftermath of Hurricane Edna. Jane had been physically ill during the day from the excitement and had finally taken the children, five-year-old Steve and three-year-old Ellen to her mother's, rejoining him later.

Across the state that day Maine men and women had slogged through mud to the polls—248,000 voters, more than half of those eligible. Edna wasn't keeping the voters home after all, Democrats fretted; the turnout was clearly going to be large by Maine standards. During the day Governor Cross announced that the Federal Government had approved his request for rehabilitation assistance for storm damage. It would be the last official public pronouncement he would make before his defeat. Confident, he then returned to the Governor's mansion, the Blaine House, to await the returns.

The voting in Maine was by paper ballot, and it was after 9 P.M. before the first returns started to trickle in from smaller towns across the state. The tiny town of Wade, in Aroostook County, with an enrollment of 90 Republicans and but 2 Democrats, had chosen Muskie 17 to 16 over Cross. This one-vote edge was promptly nullified by Blaine, in the heartland of the heavily Protestant northern Bible Belt, which opted for Cross by a vote of 82 to 40. Then along the coast, where Republicanism is most deeply entrenched and where crusty Down Easters still place Democrats and tourists on the same plane—regarding both as a trifle odd and definitely unreliable—the islanders voted. The fishermen of Matinicus went for Cross by 32 to 1; on Isle-au-Haut Cross was chosen

14 to 3. Farther south, in Cumberland County, wealthy residential Cape Elizabeth went for Cross by 2-to-1 ratio but with only 82 Democrats among the 2,253 registered voters in the community, Muskie had polled a surprising 419 votes. As returns from the larger towns began to come in, it became apparent that in Republican town after Republican town Muskie was cutting into the Cross vote. Clearly, "Muskie Republicans" were splitting their ticket to vote for the Democrat. A waitress at the Elmwood asked Muskie for his autograph. "You know, tomorrow I think you're going to be governor," she said. Muskie, in shirt sleeves, munched on a sandwich and continued to watch the returns. By 11 P.M., as the cities began to report, it was clear that he was winning. McMahon, sensing victory, looked over the suite and found only a single bottle of bourbon. Rumford, Muskie's home town reported; it had gone for the local boy 3 to 1. Then heavily Democratic Lewiston reported—Muskie had carried the city 5 to 1, polling 10,000 votes to Cross' 2,000. Muskie was winning by more than 10,000 votes; he was capturing 55 per cent of the total. Finally, the report came from Biddeford, late as usual ("they always wait until the end to report," one Republican groused, "to see how many votes the Democrats need"). It was icing on the cake: Muskie had carried Biddeford 6 to 1 and had established a lead over Cross of more than 20,000 votes. The Governor conceded, and Maine had elected its first Democratic governor in twenty years.

Frank Coffin arrived late from Lewiston carrying the news: Muskie was the only Democrat to win. Senator Smith had taken 58 per cent of the vote to defeat Fullam. In the congressional races, Oliver, Delahanty, and Colbath had all been trounced. "It's hard to believe, isn't it?" Coffin shouted at Muskie.

"It's amazing. Incredible," said the Governor-elect. Then he and Jane began to cry.

CHAPTER FOUR

GOVERNOR
MUSKIE

Whom manner of creature had Maine citizens elected as their governor? He had walked among them, a rawboned, friendly, open candidate, talking about the need for change, advocating a strong two-party system and increased industrial development, but he had told them little either of his plans for the state or of himself. The citizens of Maine had voted for change, they had rejected an unpopular governor; now they looked closer to assess the results of the September madness.

What they discovered was an unmistakably powerful intellect coupled with a naïveté that bordered on the ludicrous. Muskie was capable of absorbing and understanding the complexities of state government with an almost remarkable ease. Yet he was surprisingly unsophisticated. The day Muskie moved into the Blaine House, a formal, twenty-seven-room mansion which had once been the home of James G. Blaine and since 1919 had been the residence of Maine's chief executive, he and McMahon smuggled three bottles of liquor into the house. While tradition dictated that liquor not be served at formal functions in the public rooms of the Blaine House, governors had long routinely served liquor in their private quarters. But Muskie and McMahon innocently assumed that liquor was taboo throughout the mansion.

"The inauguration was the next day," McMahon says. "He'd just moved in and we wanted a drink. But we were frightened to death about having one in the Blaine House. Here was the first Democratic governor elected in twenty years and we didn't want people to think we were drunkards. We could just imagine having a drink and then having the help all quit the next day in horror."

Unable to find any ice cubes in the upstairs refrigerator, Muskie had finally screwed up his courage and asked one of the maids to bring some up. She arrived shortly with four ice cubes in a small saucer, and a spoon. "I guess they thought we were going to eat them," McMahon says. "Anyway, the whole thing put us off so that we finally hid the liquor up in the attic." It was some time before Muskie felt sufficiently at home to unwind with a drink at the end of the day.

The extent of Muskie's drinking has been a subject of rumors in each election year since 1954. In some tales his consumption has been prodigious. Yet there is no one close to him who will admit to ever having seen him drunk. Nor is any evidence that he has been. He enjoys a drink, and when he finishes one he noisily chews the ice cubes. During the 1968 vice-presidential campaign he restricted himself to two Manhattans daily and there is no indication that he found that limit a difficulty. George Mitchell, who served as a Washington aide for three years in the early 1960's has said flatly,

"I've never seen the senator anywhere remotely near intoxicated. He's careful about his drinking. If he had, I would have known about it because I saw him late in the evenings and early in the mornings." McMahon, who accompanied Muskie on fishing trips, confirms Mitchell's assessment: "I've been with him when there was just a gang of us together at a camp, when Jane wasn't around and when everybody was drinking. He never drank too much. And what he does drink, he holds well." Maurice Williams, Muskie's administrative assistant during his years as governor, recalls that once "he was making a speech to a group of businessmen in York County at a country club and there was a reception first. I'm sure some of the men there were purposely trying to get him drunk. They kept pushing drinks at him. I was watching him because I was worried. But they couldn't do it. He had a few and then he went ahead and made his speech."

Not until after Muskie became governor did newsmen discover that his bow ties, a trademark of his campaign, were clip-ons. The Governor, a Phi Beta Kappa, confessed ruefully that he had never been able to master tying a real bow. Michigan Governor G. Mennen "Soapy" Williams, another devotee of the bow tie, sent him one after the election but he was unable to wear it. A year later Muskie did finally appear in public with a bow tie he had tied himself, this a gift from Republican House Speaker Willis A. Trafton, Jr. Muskie responded by swamping Trafton in the 1956 gubernatorial election. When he became a senator in 1959, the bow ties were replaced by four-in-hands.

The Maine voters appreciated the homeyness of the new young governor. They chuckled when five-year-old Steve proclaimed loudly the day after the election that "my dad's the boss of the whole state." They guffawed when they learned that on a boat trip with the seven staid Republican executive councilors he stripped naked on a deserted section of Vinalhaven Island and cajoled them into following him for a swim in the frigid Maine waters. They laughed when Jane told of the time Ed was invited to dinner at the exclusive Clover Club, in Boston. She had accompanied him, unaware that the Clover Club had never permitted a female inside its doors, and she had been asked, politely, to leave. And the voters winced at reports of some of the most atrocious puns ever uttered by a Maine governor. "He may have been a great governor," said one Maine newsman who covered the State House. "But all I can remember are those awful puns. They were terrible."

Maury Williams, who was probably subjected to more of the puns than anyone else, has mercifully forgotten them all, save one. "The Governor had been invited to present the ribbons at a dog show and he'd decided to send me to represent him," he says. "I'd never represented him, so I asked him what I was supposed to say and do. He told me just to make a little speech before I awarded the prizes. And then he said, 'Look, I've done this before and I know some of these dogs can be a little nervous and excited. When you're presenting the ribbons, if a dog should get excited and bite you in the rear, you know what to do, don't you?' " Williams had shaken his head. "Why," Muskie had said, with a smile, "you just turn the other cheek."

Mainers had to wait until after the inauguration for the human touches of the new governor to emerge. For if the campaign had been an ordeal, the interregnum was a nightmare for Muskie and the Democrats. "We hadn't expected to win, so we hadn't given it any thought," McMahon says. "After the election was when the work really started. Thank heavens we had that platform." A loose-knit group of advisers —among them Frank Coffin, Dick Dubord, Tom Delahanty, Dick McMahon, and Don Nicoll, the executive secretary of the Maine Democratic party—began meeting weekly with Muskie to develop a program. Acting on a suggestion from Coffin, Muskie asked Maury Williams, who was an employee of the state budget office, and a Republican, to become his administrative assistant. Lloyd Nute, a wire-service reporter, was hired as press secretary. Often the group would meet at Nute's Augusta home to plan budget and program proposals. One participant says, "November and December of 1954 was as an intensive a period as I can recall. Maury was just essential because he was only one who had any real budget experience. I look back on it now and wonder how it was that we were able to come up with responsible suggestions that would fit into a budgetary framework when none of us had ever done it before. When it came to taxes and specifics we were babes in the woods."

Williams, who was to prepare the bulk of the first budget himself, watched the new group develop and was impressed. "None of the others had a great deal of experience in state government, but they accepted assignments and they developed a knowledge. Muskie kept that group together all during the first term and it served him very well." Gradually, as Muskie became more accustomed to the governorship, the role of the group in formulating policy faded, and eventually it was disbanded. Coffin, after two congressional terms and an unsuccessful bid for the governorship in 1960, was named deputy director of the Agency for International Development (AID); in 1963 President Kennedy had already decided to name him ambassador to Panama when he was assassinated in Dallas. President Johnson substituted his own appointment, and Coffin was later named to the First Circuit of the United States Court of Appeals. McMahon, a Boston business-school graduate, was named by Muskie to the state's Public Utilities Commission, where he established a reputation as a fighter for lower power rates. He is now Maine director of the Federal Housing Administration. Delahanty, who had replaced Muskie as minority floor leader in 1951, was in 1958 named to the Maine Superior Court in one of Muskie's last appointments as governor. Dubord in 1955 took over the law office of his father, F. Harold Dubord, whom Muskie at that time appointed to the Superior Court. Dick Dubord was a short, stocky attorney who played clarinet in a Dixieland band in his spare time.

He had a gift of laughter and mimicry (in 1956 he drove a sound truck down the middle of heavily Franco-American Lewiston urging voters, in a broad British accent, to support Muskie). Over the years he was to be Muskie's closest friend. He served as Maine's Democratic national committeeman for twelve years, unsuccessfully sought the Democratic nomination for governor in 1962, and for two years was Maine's attorney general. When he died unexpectedly at forty-eight of a brain hemorrhage in early 1970 Muskie was sincere when he termed him "a good and dear friend, a warm and delightful companion." Williams was to become the Maine director of the federal Small Business Administration before returning to state service in 1967, under a Democratic governor, as commissioner of finance and administration. He had left Muskie during the late stages of the governor's second term after asking for assurances that he would be taken to Washington if Muskie won a Senate seat. "At the time he asked I hadn't finally made up my mind to run for the Senate," Muskie says, "so I was in no position to give him any assurances." Williams, with Muskie's permission, gave up his job as administrative assistant to become deputy commissioner of the state's industrial-development agency. Nicoll, slim, short, and with an almost icy reserve, seemed to be the odd man in the group. Yet he, of whom much more will be said later, has become the central figure in Muskie's career.

Williams first got to know his new employer closely during the preinaugural planning sessions, although they had worked together on budgeting problems while Muskie was a legislator. "As we met," Williams says, "it began to dawn on me that many times the people in the room would make recommendations for a program that Muskie would object to. Then they'd thrash it out until it was resolved one way or the other. And if the group insisted, Muskie would yield." To Williams, this approach was "the secret of his success at the time. It indicated to me that he didn't think of himself as a one-man show." Another participant puts another face on it: "In a generalized discussion of broad program goals his participation would naturally be quite different than in the highly targeted kind of decision he would have to make as Governor. In the early [preinaugural] kind of discussion, say a general debate on what organizational form the new industrial-development agency should take, Muskie wouldn't try to lead the discussion or necessarily to impose his will on the group. He might have strong views on particular items, but the probability was that he was learning as much as the rest of us." No one considered this method of developing policy to be government by committee. Williams, for instance, saw it as "two heads being better than one."

Another aspect of Muskie's personality that began to emerge was his slowness to reach a decision—some call it procrastination—his willingness to explore all facets of a problem, his tendency to recite alternatives without committing himself publicly to any one of them. This trait is both a strength and a weakness. A strong sense of accommodation is a virtue in a Maine governor, and it was particularly useful for a Democratic governor in 1954; in a United States senator too it may be desirable. That same quality, however, may be a distinct handicap in a presidential aspirant. Certainly Muskie's cool, slow approach, his availability to compromise, has accounted for a large part of his success both as a governor and as a senator. "In terms of his timing I think there were occasions when each of us would become aggravated by his not coming out for a certain proposal or making some statement," says one close friend. "And yet in retrospect I must say that it's very hard to fault him on his sense of timing. When he finally did move you found that the problem was either fairly resolved by the passage of time or else when he did act it was with such authority and deliberateness that he was far more impressive than if he had jumped the gun." Williams found that Muskie "always looked for public opinion. He would suggest a candidate for a job and then he'd sit back and wait for public opinion before he'd officially post him. And time and time again I saw it pay off for him. By moving slowly he got facts he wouldn't have had if he'd moved rapidly. But public opinion was never a gauge to his own decision. If public opinion was against a man and Muskie was convinced that he was the best man for the job, then he'd conclude that public opinion was wrong and go ahead and nominate him." McMahon perhaps sums it up best: "His sense of timing was always good. He could make you mad because he tended to take his time—procrastination he's good at—and yet he was nearly always right."

Muskie maintains, "I wasn't aware that I took a lot of time making up my mind" while governor, although he concedes that compromise was a necessity. "We had a problem then in presenting issues in a way that would make them salable to a Republican Legislature and nominations that would be acceptable to a Republican Executive Council. I had to be effective if my party was to survive. If I'd been stubborn and said that there was only one way to do things—my way—I'd have gotten nowhere with the Republicans. And so I tried to present options. If all I'd been interested in was confrontation and in proving that I could shout louder than Republicans, well, not much would have been accomplished. I believe in effectiveness."

The first Muskie program, a distillation of the best thinking of the November and December committee meetings, was presented in his 1955 inaugural address. It was, by Maine standards of the time, a bold statement of policy, but it was couched in the conciliatory language of a governor who recognized that he was facing a Republican-dominated Legislature that saw him primarily as a young upstart. "It wasn't their inclination to roll over and play dead," Muskie says. Muskie called for the creation of a new industrial-development agency, increased state support for education, an upgrading of state hospital facilities, and a modernization of the machinery of state government itself. When he came to the question of how to finance his program, Muskie characteristically turned to a discussion of alternatives. One was to raise the sales tax, which had been established four years earlier, at the same time increasing exemptions—on water, electricity, and clothing—to make the basically regressive tax more equitable. The second was to adopt a personal income tax. "These," said Muskie, "appear to be the alternatives available to provide the funds necessary. . . . It should be added that I do not have a closed mind with reference to new tax sources." There was nothing to indicate where Muskie actually stood; he had spelled out the possibilities and it was up to the Legislature to decide. In the end it chose neither, instead adopting a patchwork program of minor taxes and increasing the gasoline tax over Muskie's veto. "I tried to present options," Muskie says, looking back to the 1955 session. "And you must know that the preference option might not necessarily have been the one that I wanted. But you have to learn to work with people."

Muskie's conciliatory spirit paid modest dividends. A new Department of Development of Industry and Commerce was created, increases in the state subsidy for local public-school education were approved, and hospital modernization and expansion was begun. The only major failure was in the effort to streamline state government; Republicans emphatically rejected his suggestions for increasing gubernatorial authority. Today, modernization proposals offered by Muskie during his first two terms are still being introduced, debated, and killed. Muskie's first inaugural address had also placed some emphasis on water pollution, calling for completion of the task of classifying all Maine waters within two years and for increased "public" representation on the state's Water Improvement Commission by persons having no direct connection with industry. At the same time, recognizing that major Maine industry had significant influence on the voting habits of Republican legislators, he once more showed his willingness to accommodate. "Solution of the [pollution] problem," Muskie said, "has serious economic implications for existing industries which must not be disregarded." And again: "The necessity for action is easier to spell out than is the solution. Patience, ingenuity, and cooperation on the part of all those interested will be required before the problem is brought under control if we are to avoid undue burdens for existing industries and our municipalities." And finally: "It is essential that our policy in this field be firm and progressive while avoiding damage to our industrial structure." The Legislature responded with inaction; major water classification and a timetable for ending pollution were still two years away.

But if Muskie was accommodating during his first term, he was far from being a pushover. When, in the closing days of the 1955 legislative session, it appeared that Republicans would scuttle the new industrial-development agency, Muskie, sensing the public mood, threatened to go directly to the people on television, to make his case. The Republicans, led by Senate President Robert N. Haskell, who is perhaps the finest, most knowledgeable student of Maine government to serve in the state Legislature in this century, capitulated. Haskell, who had seen Muskie's cooperative spirit as a sign of weakness, decided he was wrong. From that point on, they worked together. Strategy for the coming week was spelled out at Monday-evening leadership sessions held by the governor at the Blaine House. Muskie could command the minority of Democrats in the Legislature, while Haskell, a ruddy-faced, cigar-smoking public-utility executive could almost single-handedly bring the legislative Republicans behind him on any given issue. Muskie and Haskell would agree on what should be done; between the two it was done.

Muskie's reelection was largely a foregone conclusion. Republicans nominated House Speaker Willis A. Trafton, Jr., an Auburn banker. A tall, angular, amateur politician who wore bow ties, he emerged from the campaign as a sort of pale shadow of Muskie. The Maine mood on Election Day was typified, in Trafton's home town, by Mrs. Gertude Bouttenot, a young housewife. She woke up early that morning with labor pains. Her husband backed out the car and was taking her to the hospital when she remembered that it was Election Day. The Bouttenots detoured to a polling place, where they were told that the polls would open in another fifteen minutes, at 6 A.M. Tentatively, she timed the labor pains. "I guess I can wait a few minutes, she said. At 6 A.M., while her husband paced nervously outside, Mrs. Bouttenot, a lifelong Republican, cast her ballot for Eisenhower and then split her ticket to vote for Governor Muskie. Then they sped off for the hospital. Mrs. Bouttenot, now a telephone-company employee and still a Republican, says simply that "Muskie had a lot of appeal for us in those early days."

Muskie drove with Jane to Waterville to vote early in the day, and then returned to the Blaine House to watch the returns. This time there were no surprises. The only moment of concern came early in the evening when Steve, then seven, was alone watching a comedy on television and heard a report during a station break that his father had lost one of the first small towns to report and was trailing on the basis of that fragmentary return. Jane found him a few moments later sobbing, "Daddy's losing." He consented to go to bed only after he had been reassured that his father was ahead. Muskie did win easily, defeating Trafton by 56,000 votes and gathering a larger total than had ever been given a Maine governor.

There were also strong indications that the Democratic party, apart from Muskie's own personal successes, was reviving. Frank Coffin, then thirty-seven and indisputably the Maine party's resident intellect, had decided to seek the Second District congressional seat. Neil Bishop, the foremost of the "Muskie Republicans" of 1954, had early approached the new governor and his advisers, asking if he would be acceptable as the Democratic Second District candidate. "We had Frank coming along at that time and we felt we had to build our own party with our own candidates," Muskie says. "I think Neil recognized our responsibility, so he decided that his place was in the Republican party." In 1956 Bishop unsuccessfully sought the Second District GOP nomination, losing to James L. Reid, a Hallowell attorney. Coffin won the Democratic primary by defeating a Franco-American opponent who made blatant appeals for the French vote by terming Coffin "a Little Lord Fauntleroy with soft hands and slick hair who has jumped the bandwagon which we, the little fellows with dirty hands, have built through effort and heartaches in the lean years when the weak of heart dared not run for office." Coffin licked him, soft hands and slick hair notwithstanding.

In the general election Coffin faced an uphill fight. The old Second District, which was abolished after the 1960 census, contained 81,000 Republican voters, only 38,000 Democrats, and 42,000 independents. Nor had Coffin any of Muskie's personal dynamism. If Muskie was said to be Lincolnesque, Coffin resembled a sinister Douglas. If Muskie was open and warm, Coffin was cold, aloof, and remote. Four years later, while campaigning unsuccessfully for governor, Coffin visited the Derby Athletic Club, then a center of political Lewiston life, where the most strenuous athletic endeavor was elbow bending or an occasional bout with a pinball machine. Coffin swept through the front door, raised an arm in greeting, and swept out again. Derby Club regulars, who like their politics to be laced with liquor and their candidates to belly up with the boys, were amazed. "God," said the bartender with disbelief as Coffin disappeared, "doing something like that is worse than not coming in here at all."

Given Coffin's personality, the Republican domination of the district, and the strength of Eisenhower in Maine, the GOP should have attempted to separate Coffin from the coattails of the popular Muskie. Instead, Maine Republicans, who have shown an incredible ability to turn almost any asset into a liability, succeeded in binding the two inextricably together. The vehicle was an article in the Boston *Herald* a week before the election which told of heavy CIO influence, financial and otherwise, in the Muskie and Coffin campaigns. The story was accompanied by a photograph showing Muskie seated next to Denis A. Blais, the Lewiston-area director of the Textile Workers Union of America (CIO). Maine GOP leaders expressed varying degrees of public shock, amazement, and dismay at this journalistic revelation. The Republican state chairman promptly wired Muskie, asking him to explain the extent of union activity in the campaign and concluding with the query "Is the second party which Misters Muskie and Coffin seek to rebuild in Maine the Democrat party or the CIO party, or a combination of both?" Muskie, who has the ability to be as righteously indignant as any man in public life when he puts his mind to it, took to television to reply. The *Herald* photo was a phony, he said. It had been cropped. The original had been made when Muskie was attempting to mediate a labor dispute, and had included, in addition to Blais, a management representative. Moreover, the *Herald* had managed to imply that the picture was current, although it had been taken eighteen months ago. Since the picture was false, the article was false, and the Governor refused to waste any more time commenting on a false issue. Coffin carried the matter a step further in a final televised confrontation with Reid three days before the election. Coffin readily admitted receiving $2,000 from organized labor in campaign aid but noted that Margaret Chase Smith had, two years before, accepted $3,000 from labor groups. Had Senator Smith done wrong in accepting the money? Coffin asked. Reid mumbled that he didn't care to comment. The issue had been turned to Coffin's advantage; the fact that organized labor was and is a heavy contributor to Maine Democrats was obfuscated; Second District voters could scarcely reject Coffin without repudiating Muskie. Coffin was elected by seven thousand votes. He and Muskie were the only major Democrats to win in Maine that year.

Muskie's second term as governor was more impressive than his first; having won a clear mandate in September and proven that the 1954 election was no fluke, the governor approached the Republican-controlled Legislature with more confidence. His second inaugural address was smooth, almost conversational, without the heavy tone of deference he had assumed two years earlier. The proposals he made during this second term sparkled with the progressive spirit that had been muted in 1955. To continue a program of industrial development he proposed using the state's credit to attract risk capital for the construction of new industrial buildings through creation of the Maine Industrial Building Authority; he urged adoption of a reorganized school-subsidy program which incorporated a plan to encourage school consolidation; he won approval of a $24,000,000 highway bond issue— larger than any previously authorized in Maine—as well as a $13,000,000 improvement program for hospitals, the university, and teachers colleges. To pay for increased services he requested and received a 1-per-cent increase in the sales tax. The Legislature also implemented his proposals that the governor serve a four-year term and that Maine hold its elections in November along with the rest of the nation. Now, too, he was more positive about the need for attacking water pollution: "Surely it is beyond argument that an abundant supply of clean water is essential to our industrial growth, to meet our domestic needs, to encourage the natural reproduction of fish in our streams, and to our coastal economy. This imposes responsibilities upon industry and upon our communities. Each must make progress to the maximum extent possible." He lost proposals to abolish the Executive Council, to establish annual legislative sessions, to increase maximum grants to public-assistance recipients, and to reorganize the Maine Milk Commission. But overall the record was strong. Muskie won passage of about 65 per cent of all bills he had supported, and more significantly, nearly 90 per cent of his most important proposals were accepted. Two years earlier he had been successful with only about half of his program.

His dealings with the all-Republican Executive Council improved steadily. The Council, a carry-over from the colonial days when the citizenry had suffered at the hand of Crown-appointed governors, is elected by the majority party in the Legislature. In Maine it can confirm or reject gubernatorial appointments, and until recently acted as the patronage agent for all state insurance. The authority to confirm appointments is the Council's greatest source of power, for it narrowly limits the influence of the governor, particularly if he is of the opposite party. Maine Republicans have consistently opposed efforts to scrape away this barnacle on the ship of state. If Muskie wanted to place a Democrat in a state post, the seven Republican councilors could simply fail to confirm his choice; usually they could do so with impunity, since they were not popularly elected and hence were comfortably insulated from voter wrath. Muskie used three instruments to overcome resistance in the Council: his basic let's-be-reasonable personality, the creation of broad public support on behalf of the candidate of his choice, and finally, the *quid pro quo* "package deal," in which he agreed to nominate some Republicans if the Council would agree to confirm an equal number of Democrats. It wasn't always easy. When Muskie nominated Republican Obed Millett to the Maine Milk Commission, the Council balked on the ground that Millett was a "Muskie Republican" and thus tainted was unfit for service.

One of the appointments most difficult for Muskie to get confirmed was to be his last as governor. Late in 1958, when he had already been elected to the United States Senate, he proposed Tom Delahanty, one of the unsuccessful congressional candidates in the 1954 campaign, for the Maine Superior Court. When Muskie discussed Delahanty's appointment privately with the Council, it was rejected. "Then I tried to put together a package that the Council would approve," Muskie says, "but we wern't getting anywhere." Finally, with his term drawing rapidly to a close, Muskie went to the Council with an ultimatum. Although his term as governor didn't expire until January 8, 1959, he had been considering resigning on January 2 to avoid losing seniority to other newly elected senators. "I told the Council that I felt I ought to resign early but that I felt so strongly about the right to appoint Tom Delahanty to the court that I would just stay on to the end of my term if necessary to fight for him," Muskie says. The Council didn't care whether Muskie stayed on to the end of his term or not, but another Republican, Bob Haskell, the Senate president, did. If Muskie resigned, Haskell would take over his office until Governor-elect Clinton A. Clauson was inaugurated. Haskell would be governor of Maine, if only for less than a week. "I didn't discuss this with Bob," Muskie recalls with only the trace of a smile, "but I heard interesting rumors that my staying on until the end of my term made him unhappy. When I told the Council of my intention to stay on, I speculated to myself that it might have some influence." Apparently it did. The Council, which had been adamant in its refusal to consider Delahanty, suddenly confirmed him. Muskie resigned on January 2 and Haskell, who still enjoys the title Governor, became Maine's chief executive for five and a half days.

The decision in 1958 to seek the United States Senate seat held by Republican Frederick G. Payne was not difficult for Muskie to make. Aside from abandoning politics entirely, entering the Senate seemed the only course open to him. A third term as governor was out of the question. A year earlier, at Muskie's urging, the Legislature had approved the lengthening of the governor's term to four years, and in supporting the four-year term Muskie had given "implied assurances that I did not seek selfish advantage."

Furthermore, Payne was an inviting target. In 1952, while governor, he had been implicated in a charge by Herman Sahagian, a Maine wine bottler, who claimed to have paid $12,000 in bribes to ensure that his products were stocked in state-owned liquor stores. Payne was exonerated, but two men, one of them a former Liquor Commission chairman appointed by Payne, were indicted on a charge of conspiracy to bribe a public official. The Liquor Commission official was acquitted, but the other man was found guilty. Payne went on to Washington under a cloud of public doubt. In 1958 Payne's problems multiplied when it was learned that he had accepted a vicuña coat from Boston industrialist Bernard Goldfine, who then under congressional investigation in connection with charges that high government officials—including Presidential Assistant Sherman Adams—had pressured federal regulatory agencies on behalf of Goldfine-owned companies. The subcommittee turned up evidence that Goldfine had paid $1,196.55 in hotel bills for Payne and two other New England senators. Payne protested that he and Goldfine had been "close personal friends" for a quarter of a century. In the 1958 GOP primary Payne's old political foe, wine dealer Sahagian, emerged from the past to oppose him for renomination, reviving the 1952 liquor scandal in the public mind and fanning the Goldfine issue by saying that when he needed a coat "I bought it myself." Though Payne easily defeated Sahagian in the primary, his troubles were not over, for straitlaced Maine Yankees demand the appearance of honesty as well as honesty itself in their public servants.

Despite Payne's obvious handicaps the campaign was no lark for Muskie. He was faced by an incumbent whose voting record was difficult to assail. Early in 1958, for example, Payne and Democratic Senator Paul Douglas had teamed to sponsor the Area Redevelopment Bill to provide loans to both economically depressed industrial areas and low-income rural areas. And Muskie had problems in his own party. Dr. Clinton A. Clauson had defeated state Grange Master Maynard Dolloff for the Democratic gubernatorial nomination, and the Waterville chiropractor's campaign was scarcely a thing of beauty. In the first place, he'd spent $15,000 in winning the nomination and felt that it was up to the party to provide general election funds. Second, Clauson and Jim Oliver, who was again running for Congress in the First District, in southern Maine, seemed unfamiliar with operating as part of a total coordinated campaign. Oliver had a penchant for flights of rhetoric that could lead to embarrassment of the party at any time. Clauson's campaign seemed to be founded almost exclusively on the premise that he would follow Ed Muskie around and immediately shake whatever hand Muskie shook. "If Muskie went into a men's room to take a leak during the campaign, you just knew that Clauson was standing at the next urinal," said one witness. "Doc just shadowed him. He took the phrase 'riding on Muskie's coattails' literally."

According to McMahon, Muskie called him at his office in the Public Utilities Commission midway through the campaign and said in desperation, "Look, you've got to get off your ass. We've got to start tying this thing together or he [Clauson] is going to take me down with him too." "You're kidding," McMahon replied. "He can't be that bad."

Investigation proved there were problems. "I went down to where Doc was going to give a speech, out in front of the Old Orchard House," McMahon says, "just to listen to him. And somebody gave Doc a press release of the speech he was going to give. I'm leaning there on a parking meter and the good doctor is introduced and he starts reading the press release to the crowd, saying, 'Dr. Clinton A. Clauson said at the Old Orchard House tonight that, . . .

"And there's this guy standing next to me and he turns to me and he says, 'Is he serious? Did he say what I thought he said?'

"And I said, 'Yep, I heard him too.' "

The upshot was that McMahon began coordinating the campaigns of the major Democratic candidates in all their aspects, including the purchase of materials and the distribution of funds from union organizations. "Representatives of all the candidates would meet every Wednesday in Waterville and we'd sit down to be sure that everybody was on the same wavelength," he said.

Muskie was also under some pressures within the party because it was widely believed that he had supported Dolloff over Clauson in the primary. "The press speculated that Dolloff was the Muskie candidate and they never believed me when I said I was neutral," Muskie maintains. "But I never mentioned any preference, even to my closest staff. I didn't try to maneuver behind the scenes. At the outset of the 1958 campaign I brought Dolloff and Clauson to lunch at the Blaine House and I said, 'I want you to understand that I'm taking no part in this primary. I want to say it right now at the beginning and in the presence of each of you. Each of you has my commitment to that fact. And that's the way it is.'" Don Nicoll, who in 1958 was Coffin's administrative assistant agrees. "Frank was quite open in his support of Dolloff, and yet Muskie caught much more hell for his supposed support than Frank did for his open support," Nicoll says. But if Muskie was neutral in the campaign, most of his closest associates, including Coffin, McMahon, and Dubord, were working for Dolloff's nomination. The same thing was to happen four years later when Dubord was defeated by Dolloff for the nomination. In 1962 all of Muskie's close supporters were actively behind Dubord, again leading to speculation that Muskie had backed the loser. "I often think I should have come out and supported a candidate," Muskie recently said wearily. "After all you get accused of it anyway."

Once the several races had been coordinated, Muskie's own campaign began to heat up. In late August, former Maine Senator R. Owen Brewster surfaced on television to endorse Payne and to discuss the number of wars that had occurred during Democratic administrations. He also revived the 1956 charge about the amount of money that unions were pouring into the Maine Democratic campaigns. Muskie assumed what the Associated Press referred to as "an obviously anguished manner" and replied that Brewster had sunk "to a mere hatchet man. This spectacle . . . makes me cringe." A few days later Muskie accused Payne of "the lowest type of politics" after Payne had said that "in those few cases where he [Muskie] has taken a definite stand on my voting record he has shown himself to be strictly in the wing of his party which advocates handouts, unnecessary spending, and increased government controls over private industry." That kind of statement scarcely seems to merit labeling as "the lowest type of politics," but then it doesn't take much to offend Muskie. For Muskie is at his campaign best when he feels he has been unjustly attacked. His anger, whether uncontrolled or summoned, rises to the surface; his eyes blaze, his forefinger waggles, his great head shakes, and his jowls quiver, as he decries an opponent's unwarranted attack. As a campaign technique it has been remarkably effective in Maine.

In any event the angry exchanges in 1958 served to enliven a campaign that had produced few substantive issues. Muskie, in fact, in mid-August candidly said in a television interview that "there isn't a single overriding issue at the moment." There were, however, two factors of overriding importance in the campaign. One was the silent issue of Sherman Adams and Bernard Goldfine (to which Muskie did not address himself during the campaign); the second was the personal appeal of Muskie himself. He had become the state's most popular governor in memory and the Maine Democratic party's leading attraction. There was nothing Payne could say or do to change the public's mood. He seemed actually relieved after the election that the ordeal was over. "Maybe the voters have done me a favor," he said. "This way I'll probably live longer." Two weeks after Payne's defeat, Adams resigned his presidential post.

Muskie's election was predictable; not even the large victory margin—61,000— came as a surprise. The Muskie popularity was sufficient to pull Clauson into office with him, as the first Maine governor elected to a four-year term. Frank Coffin easily won a second term in Congress and persistent Jim Oliver finally won in the First District. Republicans were able to win only one major race, retaining their hold on the congressional seat for the Third District, in northern Maine. The Republican Administration's cold response to the problem of unemployment in general and to the needs of chronically depressed areas in particular was widely considered an important reason for the strong gains Democrats made in the 1958 congressional elections. Early in September, President Eisenhower had vetoed the Area Redevelopment Bill, saying that it provided for too little local responsibility. Two days later, Muskie defeated Payne. In the Maine Legislature, Democratic candidates made significant progress, winning twelve Senate and fifty-eight House seats.

As the Muskies entertained election-night guests, actress Bette Davis and her husband Gary Merrill, at the Blaine House and breakfasted the next morning with Governor-elect and Mrs. Clauson, reporters checked their files and discovered that Muskie had become the first Democrat ever to be popularly elected in Maine as a United States senator.

There was one other bit of news. Jane Muskie announced on election night that she and Ed were expecting their fourth child in December.

CHAPTER FIVE

THE

DEMOCRATIC SENATOR

FROM MAINE

The Muskies experienced two shocks when they went to Washington to make plans for their move down there. The first was the high cost of real estate. The house they bought, a new split-level in the Springfield section of Bethesda, Maryland, cost $35,750, over four times as much as their Waterville home. For a flickering instant, Muskie said later, he wondered if being a senator was going to be worth it. They liked the neighborhood from the start, however. It was not far from Washington by local standards. There was a parochial school within walking distance. There were plenty of children for the young Muskies to play with (sixty-five on one street, by unofficial census). The neighbors were a good mix of business and government people. "Very congenial," said Muskie, and Jane agreed, but nevertheless adjustment was necessary. They came down after their fourth child, Martha, was born on December 17. When they arrived, their furniture hadn't been delivered and the furnace was broken. A more lasting problem for Jane was the fact that for the first time in four years she had to manage without a household staff. "It was difficult," she says. "Maine treated its first family very, very well." She made the adjustment because with New England practicality she had kept reminding herself while in the Blaine House that their stay was temporary. The second year in Washington, with a fifth child on the way and official social obligations increasing, they moved around the corner to a larger house (costing $49,000) with maids' quarters. Edmund junior was born on July 4, 1961.

The second shock of their arrival in Washington was solely Muskie's, and it was painful. Like all newly elected Democratic senators, he paid an early courtesy call on the man who would be his political leader, Senate Majority Leader Lyndon Johnson. This was before the new Senate went into session. Johnson talked for half an hour about the difficulties of adjustment, particularly when the new senator had been a governor. "He said the greatest difficulty probably was the roll-call vote, where you had to put yourself on record," Muskie says. "He said many times you won't know how you're going to vote until the clerk calling the roll gets to the *M*'s. I thought it was a very good fatherly talk."

Then Johnson began pressuring Muskie about how he would vote when the Senate took up its first order of business, the rules relating to unlimited debate, or filibuster. The existing rules required a two-thirds vote to halt a filibuster, but *unanimous* consent was needed to halt a filibuster on a proposal to change the rules themselves. The filibuster had been used chiefly to prevent majority sentiment in favor of civil-rights legislation from having its way. The Senate in 1959 was to be the most liberal in years, thanks to the previous November's recession-triggered Democratic landslide. Liberals decided to challenge the traditional view that Senate rules carried over from Congress to Congress since the Senate was a "continuing body," with only one third of its members elected anew for each Congress. The liberals claimed that new rules could be adopted every two years by majority vote. Johnson favored a mild compromise: to allow cloture (the imposed ending of debate) when it was favored by two thirds of the senators present, rather than by two thirds of the total membership, and to follow this procedure even in rules debates.

Muskie favored a compromise between this plan and the proposal of the liberals to impose cloture when it received the vote of a simple majority. He favored a three-fifths vote to end debates. But he wasn't sure. "When Johnson finished, inasmuch as I wasn't ready to support him, I felt it tactful to use the clue he had given me. At that point he said, 'Well, Ed, you haven't had much to say.'

"And I said, 'Well, Lyndon, the clerk hasn't gotten to the *M*'s yet.' I wasn't trying to rile him. I just wanted him to know that I wasn't ready to buy his proposal, and that I hadn't yet committed myself to any other. He regarded it as an impertinence, I guess."

Afterward, according to another report, "Bobby Baker passed the word around the cloakroom that Johnson had written Muskie off as 'chickenshit.'" Baker was majority secretary. Then, shortly after Johnson had won his compromise on the rules in the Senate voting, with the help of a majority of the fifteen freshmen Democrats, the Johnson-dominated Steering Committee penalized Muskie by denying him membership on the committees which were his first, second, and third choices—Foreign Relations, Interstate and Foreign Commerce, and Judiciary. No freshman got on the Foreign Relations Committee, but four were assigned to Interstate and Foreign Commerce and two to Judiciary. Muskie got a seat on Banking and Currency, which was fourth on his list, and on two committees which were not his choices at all—Public Works and Government Operations. Muskie took the rebuff personally. Johnson took the challenge the same way. The two men did not speak socially for almost a year. "If I had asked for Banking and Currency I might have gotten Commerce," Muskie said years later. His wryness did not conceal an edge of bitterness in his voice, vague and interesting, like a tiny scar. For his part, Johnson must have been aware of Baker's gossiping, and he must have been harboring a memory of the confrontation when in 1968 he told people that *his* choice for the vice-presidential nomination was Senator Daniel K. Inouye of Hawaii, a respected legislator but highly unlikely as a vice-presidential nominee that year.

Even in his chagrin and frustration, Muskie found the Senate a heady place. The debate on the rules impressed him. He wrote in his newsletter home, "The debate was fascinating . . . when it was all over, I was left with a tremendous respect for the ability, the dedication, and the effectiveness of my colleagues in the Senate—those with whom I disagreed as well as those with whom I agreed." This despite the fact that as Johnson had forecast, the difficulties of the transition from governor to legislator were already becoming noticeable. Muskie told the Women's National Democratic Club that winter, "One thing I've learned very quickly is that one never gets one's way all the time here . . . [but] the governor is at the center of things. He selects the time and place of presentation." He said that he felt Washington social life to be "a bewildering experience," and that he found himself constantly "buffeted about by the whims of political leaders and the pressures of commentators and lobbyists." In the same speech, Muskie joked about the Democratic ladies' even wanting to hear from a lowly freshman senator such as himself. He exhibited this streak of humility several times in the early years in the Senate. Some regarded it as a small-state inferiority complex. In Maine some took it as an indication that he would not seek reelection. Indeed by 1962 there were enough rumors to that effect to lead Muskie to deny them publicly. By then he was moving toward influence in the Senate, and shedding his frustrations.

An able senator works himself into Senate power in various ways. Party loyalty sometimes helps. Hard work and long hours of attention to detail almost always help. Muskie displayed the inclination and the temperament for both. He took his ugly-duckling committee assignments and buckled down to tedium. Later his expertise on these committees would be celebrated, but in the late 1950's and early 1960's only his peers appreciated his work. In Banking and Currency he labored at urban problems, especially on the Housing subcommittee. He also worked in this field in the Government Operations Committee, being particularly concerned with relations among cities, states, and the Federal Government. On the Public Works Committee he pioneered in anti-pollution legislation. Recognition was not long in coming. While still in his freshman term he was named chairman of the Intergovernmental Relations subcommittee and of the Special Air and Water Pollution subcommittee. These appointments were rewards for his developing legislative skills. He also was named first a member, and then chairman, of the Democratic Calendar, or Legislative Review, Committee. This appointment was more of a political reward, for a loyal Democrat who was also an insistent spokesman for the younger liberal Democrats. Because of this chairmanship he automatically became a member of the Senate Democratic Policy Committee, a powerful group.

Muskie left no doubt of his party loyalty, though, like a few other liberals, he occasionally opposed Lyndon Johnson's arbitrary ways. In 1959, the freshman from Maine voted with the majority of his fellow Democrats 71 per cent of the time. That was about the party average. He supported President Eisenhower only 41 per cent of the time, approximately the average for all Democratic senators. The next year he voted with his party's majority 62 per cent of the time, and supported Eisenhower 44 per cent of the time. He voted to con-

firm the appointment of Mrs. Clare Boothe Luce as ambassador to Brazil, as did most liberals, and of Potter Stewart as
associate justice of the Supreme Court, as did all liberals, but
against confirmation of Lewis Strauss as secretary of commerce,
again siding with the majority of liberal Democrats. Eisenhower vetoed four pieces of legislation in 1959 and two in
1960, and each time Muskie voted to override the veto. On
the most controversial legislation of this period, the 1959
Labor-Management Reporting and Disclosure Act, he supported the position adopted by organized labor and by his
party's national leadership on each of the seventeen amendments for which a roll-call vote was taken.

Meanwhile, he was winning friends by influencing voters
belonging to Polish and other ethnic groups in behalf of
Democratic candidates in other states, as he had been doing
ever since his election as governor. He was popular in such
constituencies. Muskie was careful about the approach, however. "I always made the point that I wasn't elected because
I was a Pole, and the fact that I was a Pole wasn't held against
me by non-Poles," he says. In 1958 he had turned down a
request from a member of the staff of New York Governor
Averell Harriman to campaign for him in a way he thought
would be exploiting his ethnic background. In 1960, he turned
down an aide to John F. Kennedy who wanted similar assistance in the Wisconsin presidential primary.

By 1960, Muskie's demonstrated party loyalty, his little-
known but still appreciated legislative activities, and the memory of his vote getting in Maine combined to make his name
one of those mentioned by commentators who were looking ahead to the Democratic national ticket for that year's
presidential election. Muskie was a very early backer of
Senator Kennedy. His announcement of that support in January caused raised eyebrows; two New Englanders—and certainly two Catholics—could never be on the 1960 ticket.
"Some Democrats are thinking . . . [he] acted hastily," a
story in the Washington *Post* said, envisioning either a John-

son-Muskie or a Symington-Muskie ticket. Like Lyndon Johnson, Senator Stuart Symington of Missouri was a leading presidential hopeful. The story continued, "Buildup for Muskie
lists him as a rising star that turned the Republican tide in
Maine; a liberal; a Catholic; one of the party's most telegenic
figures; and he has a wife who is charming."

This sort of speculation pleased Muskie, but he did not
take it seriously. When he and other Maine Democrats were
trying to decide in late 1959 how best to make Maine influential in the party's national affairs the next year, the vice-
presidential prospects were never considered. For one thing,
he and Johnson, while speaking again, were still cool. For
another, he liked Kennedy and thought his chances of nomination were good. Other Catholic Democratic officeholders that
year were reluctant to see a Catholic run for president, feeling
that he would lose and the campaign would be divisive.
Muskie disagreed; he liked to point out that he had defied
the same tradition in Maine in order to run for governor.

Partisanship took on a different meaning in 1961, with a
Democrat in the White House, one the liberals in the Senate
identified with. Lyndon Johnson, newly elected vice president,
was gone. The new majority leader was Mike Mansfield of
Montana, a solid liberal; his assistant, or whip, was Hubert
Humphrey, a veteran liberal leader. This was the year liberals
expected to begin to exert real influence in the Senate, in
harness with a like-thinking president. The Class of 1958
was flexing its muscles. At this time, for example, Muskie received his appointment to the Calendar Committee. In 1961,
too, he had an opportunity to display to advantage his ability
to work out compromises. The liberals in his party favored
filling vacancies on the Policy and Steering committees by vote
of the full Democratic caucus. In the past the majority leader
had appointed new members to those important posts, and
conservative and middle-road Democrats wanted to go on as
before. Muskie suggested in the caucus that the majority

leader nominate senators for seats on those committees with
the caucus then voting to approve or disapprove. The Democrats accepted this proposal.

Other members of the Class of 1958 were rising in importance, too. Close friendships were forming as they rose together. For Muskie, there were growing attachments to the
men whom he saw most often as a result of accident, of
alphabet or home address or Senate seating. Senators Philip
A. Hart of Michigan, Eugene McCarthy of Minnesota, Frank
E. Moss of Utah, Gail W. McGee of Wyoming, and Muskie all
sat together in the last ten seats assigned to the Democrats on
the Senate floor. They were neighbors or near neighbors in
Maryland. They were all liberal Democrats, vigorous men in
their early or middle forties. They liked to talk shop, and they
had had plenty of opportunities to do so in their first two years.
As majority leader, Johnson had often kept the Senate in
session at night. These young senators, and others, had often
met in the Secretary of the Senate's offices for bull sessions
during those long evenings. When Mansfield did away with
night meetings of the Senate in 1961, the bull sessions were
a casualty. Occasionally, Muskie, Hart, and McCarthy would
get together for supper and talk on summer evenings when
their families were out of town. Those sessions gradually faded
out over the years, to Muskie's sorrow. In 1970, he discussed
their passing. "I think it is one of the real regrets of the past
few years. You get to know the senators in that way. The
time available for this kind of comradeship and discussion is
much more limited than I thought it would be. In that sense,
the Senate isn't really a deliberative body, in the sense that
we find opportunities to actually get into policy questions in
an informal way, that makes it possible for us to pick each
other's brains and probe each other's instincts and feelings
about these issues. That is a great loss. The cloakrooms aren't
that sort of place. The committee hearings aren't. Markup
[bill drafting] sessions aren't. There is just very little opportunity to sit down in a bull session to talk about the state of

the nation and the state of the world, to examine each other's ideas on the national goals and the objectives we ought to be following internationally."

In John Kennedy's first year as president, Muskie's support of his new liberal party leaders in the White House and Senate was well above the average. He voted with a majority of his party on 88 per cent of the roll calls that year. He supported Kennedy 75 per cent of the time, while the average Democratic senator did so 65 per cent of the time. In the following years he continued this high level of support. A study of roll calls in 1963 showed he supported the President 88 per cent of the time, compared to an average of 63 per cent for all Democratic senators. His loyalty went beyond voting. He was quick to respond to Republican attacks on the new administration, and was its principal defender when its first scandal broke.

Muskie was a member of the Permanent Investigating subcommittee of the Government Operations Committee. That subcommittee studied the Billie Sol Estes case in 1962, at Republican insistence. Republicans believed they were on the track of a scandal at least as juicy as the Sherman Adams case. Estes was a thirty-seven-year-old wheeler and dealer from Pecos, Texas, active in finance, fertilizer, grains, and cotton. He had made a fortune. When agents of the Federal Bureau of Investigation arrested him in 1962, charging him with fraud, Republicans immediately insisted that Estes' successes were in great part due to his influence in the Department of Agriculture. He had many friends there, and was a member of the department's Cotton Advisory Committee. Both Secretary of Agriculture Orville L. Freeman and Estes' fellow Texan, Vice-President Johnson, were in the Republicans' sights. Senate Minority Leader Everett M. Dirksen, of Illinois, called the case a "glaring symbol" of the "sickness" of the Democratic party and the Department of Agriculture. The subcommittee's investigation and hearings were not conclusive. The partisan nature of the attacks and the defense did not lend themselves to a search for truth. Muskie was the sharpest cross-examiner of witnesses. Years later he would express dissatisfaction with the reputation as partisan he had achieved. He conceded that there were partisan "overtones" to much that touched the investigation, but denied that he had done anything to thwart justice. "Billie Sol Estes was guilty of something, and he went to jail, but it wasn't a guilt that was shared, in my judgment, by Secretary Freeman." Muskie was instrumental, with Senator Sam J. Ervin, Jr., of North Carolina, in getting the subcommittee to write a report on the investigation that cleared Freeman and the Administration. In addition, Muskie and Ervin issued supplemental opinions saying that the department itself could not be accused even of favoritism.

Muskie was as stunned as the rest of America when President Kennedy was assassinated. He rallied to his old adversary Lyndon Johnson in those dark days. Johnson's bereft appeal to the nation for help touched him. The reactions of both men were simply human, not related to politicis. Muskie's natural political inclinations would in any event have led him to support the liberal programs the new President proposed. His sense of party loyalty was never deeper than in the first Johnson years. In 1964 he supported the President in 78 per cent of the roll-call votes in the Senate; the Democratic average was only 61 per cent. In 1965 Muskie supported the President 71 per cent of the time, while the Democratic average was 64 per cent. In 1966 Muskie's support score was 68 per cent, compared to a party average of 57 per cent. In 1967, when things began to fall apart for Johnson and the Democrats, Muskie was his leading backer, voting for his programs 76 per cent of the time. In 1968 the average Democratic support score in the Senate fell below 50 per cent; Muskie's was 60 per cent. (In 1969, Nixon's first year, Muskie supported the President 51 per cent of the time, just a little more than the Democratic average in the Senate, 47 per cent. He opposed Nixon's nomination of Walter J. Hickel as secretary of the interior, of Otto F. Otepka as a member of the Subversive Activities Control Board, and of Clement F. Haynsworth, Jr., as associate justice of the Supreme Court. In 1970 he opposed the appointment of G. Harrold Carswell to the Supreme Court. In 1969, Muskie's liberalism, as revealed by his voting record at least, was at a near record high. The organization Americans for Democratic Action measures senators' "liberal quotients." Muskie's was 94 in 1969; it was higher only in 1961, when it reached 100.)

Muskie displayed his partisanship in other ways during the Johnson years. He voted against an investigation of Bobby Baker by his own Permanent Investigations subcommittee, as did most liberal Democrats. Baker was a Johnson-trained Senate employee who had become rich and notorious in his spare time. The clash between Republicans and Democrats over how and when to investigate Baker came with Johnson facing his national political campaign for the presidency. Democrats in the Senate smothered Republican pleas for a full airing.

In 1968, Muskie returned to the Senate for only one vote during his vice-presidential campaign; he voted for Abe Fortas, the president's choice for chief justice.

In 1964, Muskie—and Hubert Humphrey—voted with other liberal Democrats against suspending the equal-time broadcasting law. Suspension was needed if there were to be debates between the two major presidential candidates, as there had been in 1960. Johnson wanted no debates, so Senate Democrats scuttled them. The Muskie and Humphrey votes were the difference between victory and defeat. In 1968, their actions came back to haunt them when they challenged Richard Nixon and Spiro T. Agnew to debates.

Muskie believes his partisan temperature is a normal 98.6. He says his philosophy of party is best expressed in his early speeches in Maine. To him, party is an instrument of good government, nothing more; it can never be an end in itself. Instances of his partisanship abound in Washington, however, and Robert Albright of the Washington *Post* once wrote of him, "No Democrat was ever more active in his role of chairman of the Democratic Senatorial Campaign Committee." Muskie served in that capacity during the campaigns of 1966 and 1968. His appointment to this position was a reward for his energy and ideas as well as his loyalty. It was also another sign of his rising stature.

A better indication of his growing prestige was the frequency with which his name was circulated whenever an important new Democratic assignment was to be made. The 1960 talk about Muskie as a vice-presidential candidate was not serious, as much because neither of his projected ticket mates, Lyndon Johnson and Stuart Symington, ever had a chance to be nominated for president as because he was still too little known. In 1964, speculation that he might be Lyndon Johnson's running mate had some substance. That speculation began in January, when Johnson showed up unexpectedly at a fund-raising affair for Muskie at the Army-Navy Club. The new president stood up in an upholstered chair and told the crowd that Muskie was "more fearless and active" than the great majority of the "more than two thousand" members of Congress he had known in his time. Rasa Gustaitis of the Washington *Post* asked Muskie if he would like to be Johnson's running mate. He replied that he was a candidate for reelection to the Senate only. In reporting this answer, she added, "but as the tall Texan shook hands with the man from Maine, there were those who thought the two looked right well together."

The leading candidate for the vice-presidential nod was Attorney General Robert Kennedy. United Nations Ambassador Adlai E. Stevenson was given a good chance. So was Peace Corps Director Sargent Shriver. In July, as the Democratic convention drew near, President Johnson ruled out all three favorites by announcing that Cabinet members and those who met with the Cabinet would not be considered. Then speculation centered on the President's old arena, the Senate. Senators Muskie, McCarthy, Humphrey, and Mansfield were named on most of the journalists' and politicians lists. Muskie did not discount his chances until about three weeks before the actual nomination, when a request came to him from presidential aide Walter Jenkins to second the nomination of the President. Something in the way Jenkins phrased this request caused Muskie to interpret it as a signal that he would not be the running mate. Johnson played out to the end the national interest in his choice. The field narrowed down to Humphrey and McCarthy. Then it was Humphrey, Johnson announced on the day of the vice-presidential nomination. That night the Muskies and the McCarthys had dinner together in Atlantic City. Until then, the prospect of national office had remained alive for both. Muskie, though convinced he had correctly interpreted the Jenkins call, could not be absolutely sure until the choice was made official. When a call had come from the White House to their Atlantic City motel, a few days before, Jane's hand had trembled on the telephone. It had indeed been the President calling, but about something else.

Muskie ran for reelection instead. He swamped a conservative Republican, Clifford G. McIntire, getting 67 per cent of the vote. He had hardly rested up from his campaign when he was again in a position to expand his Senate horizons. His endeavors as a loyal and hardworking Democrat, and his hard, productive activity in his committees and subcommittees, had earned him a reputation after one six-year term as a steady, dependable Senate mover. At least, he was a Senate-mover *type;* the problem was to get into a position where he could do things. Senator Hart and some others understood him to be interested in replacing Hubert Humphrey as whip. To many Democratic liberals he seemed a logical choice. And it was a logical spot from which to begin a rise in the Senate hierarchy. Nevertheless, Muskie's own recollection is that he was not a serious candidate, and so informed his supporters. He thought his fellow New Englander John O. Pastore of Rhode

Island had a more evident claim. As a senator, Pastore was senior to Muskie by nine years. He had been the keynoter at the convention. He was more partisan than Muskie in his rhetoric, and enjoyed a good floor fight. And he was openly interested in being the liberal candidate. Another liberal seeking the post was Mike Monroney of Oklahoma. Russell B. Long of Louisiana was the conservative candidate. Muskie recalls that he offered Pastore his support from the start. Then, in mid-November, someone announced to the press that Muskie himself wanted the position. Muskie said he was available, but was not an "overt candidate." Two weeks later Senator Hart announced that he was supporting Muskie.

By year's end it was obvious that the only way to beat Long was for all liberals to unite, but they did not attempt to do so. (Actually, it was probably too late. Long, wise in the ways of the Senate, had made a determined and personal campaign for votes from the moment Humphrey had been named as the vice-presidential candidate.) Muskie announced his support for Pastore's candidacy. In January, Long was elected whip. In later years, some versions of this story made it appear that had Muskie forced Pastore out of the race, he could have defeated Long, but this is not likely.

Liberal apprehensions about Long quickly proved justified. His erratic behavior as a party leader was so disturbing to other senators that in January, 1966, Mansfield named Muskie and three other Democrats to the new posts of "assistant whip." According to syndicated Washington columnists Rowland Evans and Robert Novak, "what Mansfield had in mind became clear in whispered cloakroom comments by Frank Valeo, Mansfield's floor leader and alter ego. The majority leader, Valeo carefully explained, wants a reliable stand-in— not Long, the elected whip—available to take his place running the Senate whenever Mansfield himself cannot be present." Being chosen an assistant whip meant power, but it was not the same as election into the real ruling circle. When Senator George A. Smathers of Florida announced later that year that he would resign his post as party secretary, the number-three job, it was inevitable that Muskie's name come up, and that he consider the prospects. A conservative candidate, Senator Robert C. Byrd of West Virginia, entered the contest, with assured southern support; Muskie, his friend Philip Hart, and Senator Joseph S. Clark of Pennsylvania were the liberal senators interested. The outcome of the contest between Russell Long and John Pastore was on most liberals' minds, and Muskie, Hart, and Clark accordingly met in Clark's office to work out a single candidacy. Of the three, Clark was the weakest candidate. Muskie had already called a few senators. He felt he had a chance, if he became an all-out candidate. He also felt that Clark was not serious in his bid. The Pennsylvanian had made a career of opposing the Establishment—the leadership—in the Senate. Indeed, he had published two books attacking the Senate. But Muskie and Hart yielded to Clark's insistence that he was senior to them and deserved the job. Muskie said later, after Byrd had defeated Clark with ease, "I guess that Phil and I were both too softhearted. Probably we yielded too quickly." When critics (and some supporters) said that this episode proved that Muskie eschewed responsibility and fights, or that he had no ambition, he replied that he did want responsibility, but "was just too deferential to Joe Clark."

In 1968, Muskie's ten years in the Senate paid off with the vice-presidential nomination. After the Democrats had lost, a third opportunity arose for him to be elected to a position of leadership in the Senate. He and Hubert Humphrey were in the Virgin Islands, recuperating from their arduous campaign. He saw a story in the papers quoting Senator Long as saying that he had the votes to beat Muskie, if Muskie challenged him. Long was reacting to efforts that Senator Hart had initiated, tentatively, to secure the whip's job for Muskie. Hart's reasoning was that with a Republican in the White House, a Senate leadership more responsive to the "national Democratic" philosophy was needed. Only Mansfield of the leadership trio of floor leader, whip, and secretary truly met that standard. When Muskie returned from vacation, he met with Hart and Senator Walter F. Mondale of Minnesota, a leader of the younger liberal Democrats in the Senate. "If you fellows think it is important to challenge Long in terms of party," he told them, "I would suggest you probe a few other Democratic senators to find out if they think it is an important fight to make now. I don't want any poll." He said he didn't want to put anyone on the spot. No poll was taken; at least, many Democratic senators said after the event that they were never asked to support Muskie. Muskie said later, "We couldn't find anybody who thought it was important. This finding coincided with my personal preferences, and so I didn't run. His personal preference was to accept some of the many offers to speak that were pouring in from all over the country, to find out if the talk about his being the 1972 presidential nominee had any substance. One thing on his mind was the memory of Lyndon Johnson's presidential campaign in the preconvention months of 1960. Johnson had been limited by his senatorial obligations in Washington, while John Kennedy was able to campaign about the nation.

Unfortunately for Muskie in some respects, the 1968–1969 leadership contest did not end with his decision. That December, Senator Edward Kennedy, vacationing at Sun Valley, read a story in the Los Angeles *Times* about the reluctance of Muskie to make the fight. He called Muskie in the east and asked if he was going to challenge Long. When he said No, Kennedy asked Muskie if he would support him in the same fight, and Muskie said he would. On December 30 Kennedy publicly announced his candidacy. On January 3 he was elected whip by a vote of 31 to 26. Kennedy aides said later that they encountered "no softness." Once they started asking senators to support them, they said, they quickly accumulated enough votes. Of course, when they needed assistance, the unique Kennedy network of friends across the country provided it. Senator Long pointed to that network in his first statement after the vote: "It was a nationwide race. I had him outgunned in the Senate, but he had me outgunned in the country." By and large, the press comment on the Kennedy victory concluded that it made him a front-runner in the race for the 1972 presidential nomination, at the expense of Muskie and the other hopefuls (all of whom, except Senator McCarthy, had voted for Kennedy in the caucus). Much of the comment also recalled Muskie's earlier involvement in Senate leadership contests, and observed that there was a pattern of unwillingness to fight.

A Muskie aide conceded the pattern, but described it as one indicating an unwillingness to fight for unimportant things. Senator Hart, who was Muskie's manager in the whip contest, agreed with that assessment. "Our count indicated Senator Muskie likely would lose that fight. When he reached the same tentative conclusion, his judgment was not to make it. He knew that in the eyes of the nation the fight would have seemed personal. A defeat would have seemed personal. So he chose not to make the race." Hart continued, "I think it is unfair to say of Ed Muskie that he is afraid of a fight. He is the fellow who went into the Polish neighborhood halls in September and October of 1968 and spoke the hard truth about racial tensions." That had been a ticklish assignment. At that time, those sections were high in backlash potential, and there was an ugly mood in the land. On several occasions Muskie has also shown in the Senate that he is not afraid of a personal conflict. He has been quick to assert his jurisdiction, or that of his subcommittee when other senators or subcommittees seem to him to be overreaching. As we shall see, Senators Abraham A. Ribicoff of Connecticut, Henry M. Jackson of Washington, and Fred Harris of Oklahoma, found this out on separate occasions.

Still, his "main character," as Majority Leader Mansfield puts it, is "non-pushy. He is not a man who shoves himself." Mansfield, who is believed to favor Muskie as his successor, has interpreted this character trait in a positive light. "This is in his favor as a legislator," the taciturn Montanan has said. Looking back on the leadership changes of 1965, 1967, and 1969, Senator Mansfield said in 1970 that Muskie's lack of ambition was as much a factor as his reticence in his failure to be chosen. Jane Muskie agreed, and so did many of Muskie's friends, but Muskie himself did not wholly agree. He said he was not specifically ambitious in 1965 and 1967, but had begun to think of himself "before 1968" as a possible Senate Democratic leader someday. Being eleven years younger than Mansfield, he could expect to still be active when Mansfield retired. "This seemed like it might be a satisfying and stimulating culmination to my Senate career," he said of the leader's job. "I was in line for it."

Many in Washington shared this view. In June, 1967, Washington *Post* reporter Robert Albright said Muskie was "widely regarded as the coming man in the Democratic leadership." In December, 1967, the columnists Rowland Evans and Robert Novak, in a report on the rise to power of Senator Robert Byrd, said, "If an election for Senate Democratic leader were held today, Byrd would probably lose to his chief challenger, the highly respected and liberal-backed Senator Edmund Muskie of Maine."

Of the 1969 contest for the whip's job, Muskie later said that not a lack of ambition, but "an oversupply of ambition for something higher" caused him to drop out. Here is how he put it: "In terms of my long-range position in the Senate and prospects of getting into the leadership at some point, I suppose I might come to regard that as the wrong decision. But in terms of freedom to do what I've wanted to do since that time, I think it was the right decision. It may be that I'll never run for the presidency. I may reject national ambition. At that point I may look back and say, 'Well, God, I wish I'd run for whip.'" He went on to say that he realized at the time he agreed to support Senator Kennedy that he might later regret his decision. "It didn't trouble me. You have to make choices. I felt an overwhelming compulsion to explore this other possibility [the presidency]." He had caught that itch in the fall of 1968. It would be better to look back some day and think that one had missed the opportunity to be majority leader of the Senate, than to look back and think that one had missed the opportunity to be president of the United States.

In 1970 it was apparent that whatever happened to Muskie in the coming decade, or to Ted Kennedy, or to other members of the Democratic party, in terms of assignments in or out of the Senate, the senator from Maine was going to play an important and influential role in public affairs. As his second term in the Senate came to an end, he was definitely and comfortably a member of what his old friend Senator Clark had called the Establishment, though it was now more liberal than when Clark described it. The 1958 elections and the 1960 exit of Lyndon Johnson changed the Senate enormously. Muskie belonged to the post-Johnson version of what Senate historian William White called the Inner Club. He was on everybody's list of most powerful senators. He had that ultimate symbol, a luxurious hideaway office in the basement of the Capitol. When Stewart Alsop described "people and power in political Washington" in a book in 1968, he came up with a "Club" which included members of both the House and the Senate: "In general the Club consists of the official hierarchy of both parties in both houses; the chairmen of the important standing committees; plus most of the ranking minority members of the standing committees. There are also one or two, notably in the Senate—like Senator Edmund Muskie of Maine or Senator John Stennis of Mississippi or Senator John Pastore of Rhode Island—who have no exalted standing in the hierarchy or key committee chairmanships, but who are members of the Congressional ruling class for reasons of personality, intelligence, energy, or absorption in the affairs of Congress." Alsop and a friend who reported on the Senate regularly compiled a list of "able" and "very able" senators. Muskie was one of the twenty-two who were considered "very able." The year before, Clayton Fritchey wrote in *Harper's* magazine that the senators could be classified as members of an "inner club," "potentials," "non-members," and "anti-members." Muskie was one of twenty-seven "club" members, and one of only three who were not southerners, westerners, or the chairmen of standing committees. But according to Majority Leader Mike Mansfield, "There is no club," and such political scientists as Nelson Polsby agree. Still, some senators are more influential, and some are more highly regarded, than others. In the late 1960's Richard Riedel, retiring after forty-seven years as a Senate attaché, compiled a list of fifteen senators be believed future historians would regard as the "great men" of his day. Muskie was one.

Muskie's first two terms were fulfilling to him as a politician and as a legislator. They were also happy years. In 1970, with another senatorial election ahead, and no one knew what after that, Jane Muskie thought back on her twelve years in Washington and Bethesda. "This has been a good time for us," she said. "We've had good friends. We've watched the children grow up. [Ellen, and then Steve, were married in 1970. Ellen presented her parents with a grandson that year.] Whatever happens now, I think we'll always look back on this period as perhaps our happiest."

CHAPTER SIX

TRIUMPH

FOR A

"BAREFOOT BOY"

In 1966 President Lyndon Johnson had reason to be glad that in his pique seven years before he had seen to it that Senator Edmund Muskie was assigned to the committee which was his fourth choice, the Banking and Currency Committee. Though Muskie would have preferred the glamour of the Foreign Relations, Commerce, or Judiciary committees, once on Banking and Currency he buckled down to hard work, and he soon began to like his assignment to the Housing subcommittee. This subcommittee, almost a separate committee in itself, wrote most of the legislation dealing with urban problems. For Muskie the work was in a sense an academic exercise, since Maine was a predominantly rural state. The early and middle 1960's were an exciting time to be involved with urban affairs, however. The urban crisis had become the number-one domestic problem, and the men who dealt with urban decay were beginning to find themselves in the national limelight.

That decay was real and alarming. Years of political powerlessness had combined with other forces of modern America to lead the cities, at least many of the largest ones, to the point of fiscal and physical collapse. In accelerating waves of migration, white and black families with few skills and little education had settled in the bigger cities across the nation during and after World War II. Federal highway-building programs and an enormously successful clutch of federal incentives to suburban home building and home buying drained the cities of their middle class. Businesses and industrial employers followed. When Muskie joined the subcommittee in 1959 these problems had not yet excited enough people in Congress and the nation to make a crusade to save the cities possible. But the evidence of the 1960 census and the transition from the relaxed Eisenhower years to the relatively more innovative Kennedy-Johnson years changed all that. So also did the shift from an administration with an essentially suburban, rural, and small-town base to one which drew support from the troubled big cities. Not much was done in the early 1960's. Congress remained apathetic or hostile. John Kennedy attempted to create a Cabinet-level department to help the cities but Congress rebuffed him.

The 1964 landslide elections brought in the Eighty-ninth Congress, the most liberal in a generation. President Johnson sought to use that liberal strength to create a bold new assistance program for the cities. After he first won approval for the Cabinet-level cities agency, the Department of Housing and Urban Development, he proposed his new approach to the ills of big cities, a plan which he called the Demonstration Cities Program. The program, based on recommendations made in late 1965 by a special urban task force as well as on ideas put forward earlier by Johnson and his aides, it was a drawing together for concerted action of all existing programs that might be useful in urban areas. In January, 1966, Johnson formally asked Congress for 2.3 billion dollars to be used in a five-year attack on blight and the causes of blight—fiscal and human—in the worst neighborhoods of sixty or seventy cities.

Even in the Eighty-ninth Congress, the bill was not a sure winner. As House and Senate subcommittees conducted hearings that winter and spring, its supporters began to suspect that it might not pass. And if it couldn't pass in that Congress, there would be a long wait before it was made a law, if it ever was. The measure was too much a big-city bill to appeal to many representatives; and some senators too, especially those up for reelection that year, had personal-political misgivings about committing themselves in its favor. Also, since the bill was obviously going to mean special assistance to Negroes, who comprised so large a percentage of the urban poor, southerners were not going to support it. "The bill is in trouble," reported *The New York Times* in May. It was in so much trouble that even Senators Paul H. Douglas and John J. Sparkman, the Housing subcommittee's two most respected and senior Democratic housing and urban experts, refused to serve as floor managers. On the House side of the Capitol, the Housing subcommittee was so convinced that no such bill could become law that a meaningless substitute was prepared. The prospect was that not only would there be no aid to the cities but that the President would be humiliated by failing to win support in a heavily Democratic Congress for a priority item. At a White House strategy meeting, Administration leaders decided to press ahead first in the Senate, and they decided to get Muskie to lead the fight.

But Muskie did not favor the bill. He liked the concept, he told emissaries of the President, but had doubts about some of the details. He strongly questioned the prospects of the bill's getting through Congress in its original form. Administration officials were welding together an unprecedented lobbying coalition of such special-interest organizations as union, business, and local-government groups—the urban alliance—but still Muskie's political apprehensions worried them. Administration pressure and maneuvering won House Banking and Currency Committee support for the bill, basically in its original form, in late June. (The full House was not going to vote unless the Senate did, however.) When President Johnson learned of the committee vote, he sent aides Joseph A. Califano, Jr., and Lawrence O'Brien to negotiate with Muskie again. They could not convince him, they reported back to the President. Muskie went to Maine for a brief rest as June came to an end. Before he left, he agreed to let his assistant, Don Nicoll, attempt to work out compromise language with White House and Budget Bureau aides. They agreed on changes in the bill that would make the pressure for integration less obvious, to win over southern support, and on language making assistance to small cities possible, to win over members of Congress without big cities in their districts or states. The aides' work was completed over the July Fourth weekend. On July 6, at President Johnson's order, Califano, O'Brien, Nicoll, and Phil Hannah of the Budget Bureau flew to Maine to present the compromise to Muskie. They talked it out with him in his Kennebunk Beach home, overlooking the ocean and the golf course. The long session included a meal break, and a Jane Muskie lobster stew that became famous when Robert Semple reported later in *The New York Times* that "all four participants remember [the stew] as fantastic." Muskie now agreed to manage the bill.

Muskie got the bill through the subcommittee and the full Banking and Currency Committee with dispatch. Semple reported one further adroit maneuver in the subcommittee by the Maine senator that may well have been crucial.

> The swing man was a conservative Democrat, Thomas J. McIntyre of New Hampshire, who clearly opposed the full $2.3 billion authorization [the *Times* story said]. At

this point there occurred, unknown to most of the senators in the room, another of those incidents that altered the course of the bill. For use in an emergency Mr. Muskie had drawn up an amendment cutting the bill from $2.3 billion spread over five years to $900 million over two, a safety valve to which the Administration had assented—reluctantly—on grounds that $900 million was all they had planned to spend in the first two years anyway. Mr. Nicoll, who had accompanied Mr. Muskie to the meeting, leaned forward and asked his boss: "Do you suppose McIntyre would like to offer this amendment?" Mr. Muskie nodded. Mr. Nicoll turned to Senator McIntyre and whispered: "Would you like to offer this, Senator? It cuts it back to two years and $900 million. But the Administration says it's within the ballpark." Senator McIntyre studied the piece of paper for a moment, thought of how well this would go over with his constituents, then boomed out, "Mr. Chairman, I have an amendment I'd like to offer." The motion was seconded and passed by a voice vote. Administration strategists later agreed that if Senator Muskie had decided to fight for the full authorization he might have wound up with nothing.

This instinct for the right time to compromise, this willingness to accept half a loaf, the desire to avoid a fight, and the dependence on Don Nicoll's judgment that this episode demonstrates are all traits whose recognition is central to any understanding of the legislative, governmental, and personal philosophy of the senator from Maine.

The prospects of the bill's becoming law were still iffy. Sidney Spector, a housing specialist at Housing and Urban Development who had been pressed into service as the legislative liaison man for the project, could not count a sure majority in the Senate. There were more than the anti-urbanists and archconservatives to contend with. The snowballing expense of the war in Vietnam threatened the costly new program also. The minority report on the bill, signed by committee members John Tower of Texas, Wallace F. Bennett of Utah, Bourke B. Hickenlooper of Iowa, and Strom Thurmond of

South Carolina, shrewdly appealed to a broader group than these men represented by reminding their colleagues of the ready excuse the war gave for voting No: "Aside from the obligations we face in Vietnam and second front fighting against inflation in our nation, the judgment in planning this demonstration cities program is questionable." The cost of the program was the bill's most vulnerable aspect. Muskie and the Administration had overcome subcommittee opposition with the sleight-of-hand change from a five-year to a two-year program, but that wouldn't work again. No more cuts were possible, no more juggling. Muskie decided instead to meet the minority objections head on.

The Senate began debate on the bill on August 18. Senator Muskie was its manager; Senator Tower led the opposition. Tower, and other opponents, decided on the time-honored tactic of changing the bill from an action measure to a planning one. The key vote would come on Tower's amendment to authorize only planning funds, with any decision on program spending deferred at least until the following year—when there would be a predictably less liberal Congress. Senator Muskie began the contest with a compelling speech about the destiny and plight of the city and the hopes of those who had worked out the bill:

> Throughout history cities have been mainsprings of social and economic growth. Men have gathered in them for common protection, for trade, for industry, for the exchange of ideas, for social intercourse, and for the comforts and attractions urban life could offer.
>
> Men have been drawn to cities as if by magnets. Cities have used the power and imagination of their people to create states, nations and even civilizations. However much we may be attracted to rural scenes and quiet places, we still return to the cities and towns for our business, for government, and for the fruits of learning and the arts.
>
> In a real sense cities are creators of life—and at the same time they can be destroyers of lives. The pages of

history are full of the tales of those who sought the promise of the city and found only despair. From the book of Job, to Charles Dickens, to James Baldwin, we have read the ills of the cities.

Our cities contain within themselves the flowers of man's genius and the nettles of his failures.

We are all familiar with the photographs of our Capitol, with slums blocking the foreground. We know of the explosive forces rumbling, and sometimes bursting, out of the crowded slums not far from the glitter of Broadway, the soaring new buildings of Chicago or the palm-lined streets of Los Angeles.

At one point in his discussion of the complicated bill, Muskie was interrupted by Senator Albert Gore of Tennessee, who asked a common question: What was the difference between this approach and the old urban-renewal approach? Muskie explained that "the emphasis in this legislation is to supplement programs dealing with the physical reconstruction by other programs designed to reconstruct the lives of people who live in those cities." He went into detail briefly, for perhaps a minute or two. When he finished, Gore said, "Mr. President, I think the senator by his extemporaneous answer has given more life and meaning to the program than any explanation I have yet heard. I want to observe that, not only in this instance, but also in many others, I have been impressed with the fact that the distinguished junior senator from Maine speaks with a clarity, elocution, articulateness and grammatical perfection that few senators possess." Even by the standards of the Senate, where gentlemanly compliments are swapped with hardly a thought, those were sweet words. They were only the first of many that would come Muskie's way in the next two days, his finest hours in the Senate.*

* "I only regret that I must debate what I consider the lack of merit in this measure with so formidable and estimable and eloquent a gentleman as my distinguished friend," said Senator Tower a few minutes after Muskie finished his opening remarks. He also commended Muskie for "some very significant improvements in this measure in committee."

On August 19, just before Tower's amendment came to a vote, Muskie challenged its basic premise:

> The minority views of this committee, which were signed, among others, by the distinguished Senator from Texas, the distinguished Senator from South Carolina, and the distinguished Senator from Iowa, said that we should not spend $900 million for this program because our economy is in high gear and we would feed the fires of inflation. A week ago today on the floor of the Senate there was another $900 million program brought up to add to the transportation and housing bills that that committee had reported. The amount involved was $900 million; coincidentally, the same amount which is involved in the pending bill. Senators on the other side of the aisle, including the 3 Senators whose names I have mentioned voted 24 to to add that $900 million. That did not add to the fires of inflation. That was not inflationary. . . .
>
> There was a lot of talk last Friday about a proper order of priorities. There has been a lot of talk today about priorities. There have been many programs that we have talked about in connection with priorities other than college housing and demonstration cities. The priorities have been highlighted by these situations. In connection with this argument, which was made persistently yesterday and today, as far as my list of priorities is concerned, the explosive problem of these diseased cities is No. 1 on the list of domestic problems in this country.
>
> I come from a small State. Only a dribble from this program can seep into my State. We do not have disease. But that disease, wherever it exists is a disease which should be of concern to everyone, including the fishermen, the trapper, or the farmer in the relatively peaceful and beautiful State of Maine. This is the problem.
>
> I am for this bill. I agreed to floor manage it, not because there is any pressure in my State and not because the problems exist in my State, but because as an American I do not think we can afford, as a country, to avoid taking this small step forward to make this country

one, toward making it whole, and toward making it healthy. The amendment would cut the demonstration cities program. If the amendment were adopted we would have to begin all over at some time in the future to prove the case again, and the problem will not wait for that time.

Until that point, Spector says, there was no certainty that the bill would make it. A few minutes later, however, the Senate voted lopsidedly, 53 to 27, against the Tower amendment. Shortly after that, by a 53 to 22 vote, the Senate approved the bill, with only a few technical changes. The House later passed a similar version, differences were ironed out, and a jubilant President Johnson signed the bill into law in October. Muskie's speeches and extemporaneous remarks on August 18 and 19, his handling of friendy and unfriendly questioning, his decisions on which changes to allow and which to oppose, were so effective that Majority Leader Mike Mansfield later observed that this was the only occasion he knew of in which a manager for a bill changed any significant number of votes. During the debate Senator Robert Kennedy of New York was quoted as calling the Muskie speech of August 18 the finest he had heard in the Senate. Senator Jacob K. Javits of New York paid Muskie this high compliment: "I am one of the very few men in this chamber who is really, thoroughly and right down to the ground a product of the big city from the poverty level up, where this problem festers. This is where I was born. This is what I know. I speak as a witness from personal experience. The cities are strangling. They are in the gravest danger. It is wonderful to me that a barefoot boy from Maine could say it as eloquently as he has."

Although he was from a small state that had no large cities, Muskie, by 1966, was a long way from being a barefoot boy, even metaphorically. He had become an authentic expert on urban affairs. There were several reasons for his growing authority in these matters. One was his assignment to the

Housing subcommittee of the Banking and Currency Committee. Another was his assignment, upon its creation in 1962, to the Intergovernmental Relations subcommittee of the Government Operations Committee. He was the first (and so far the only) chairman of this panel. Such committee assignments increase a senator's constituency, so to speak. Citizens in other states saw Muskie as their spokesman. In December, 1962, just a few months after the Intergovernmental Relations subcommittee was formed, it began hearings on big-city problems. At this point, Muskie started to develop a close working relationship with the mayors of big cities, and with the specialists and lobbyists active in the field. A third reason for his interest in urban affairs antedated even his committee assignments. After his election as governor of Maine in 1954 he was a sought-after speaker at Democratic rallies in the big cities of the North and the Midwest with large Middle-European populations. Candidates for state and local office showered him with invitations. "As he traveled around the country, principally to working-class neighborhoods in big cities, Ed Muskie saw what was happening," says a local officeholder who benefited from one of those appearances, and served with Muskie in the Senate later. "By the time he came to Washington he was already aware of and concerned about the cities." Another reason for Muskie's development as an urban specialist was that he had been the governor of a non urban state whose population was declining because its people were fleeing to the big cities to escape the poverty, tedium, and hopelessness of the farm country. One cause of the problems of large cities is the fact that rural newcomers like these have had no preparation for the urban experience. Finally, of course, Muskie lived from 1959 on in a large metropolitan area with every imaginable urban problem—Washington, D. C. Every senator is a potential urban expert, if he tries to be one, and Muskie tried.

Unlike many of the former governors in the Senate, particularly those from small states, Muskie usually sided with the big-city mayors in their protracted conflict with the governors over control of federal aid. In 1967, when his Intergovernmental Relations subcommittee was again looking into city problems, a spokesman for the governors took the view that only the states could properly serve as conduits from the federal treasury to the poverty-stricken cities. Mayor John Collins of Boston attacked that view, and Muskie publicly agreed with him. Earlier, in 1964, he had voted against giving state governments power to veto antipoverty projects worked out between federal and local officials—but he agreed that governors should have the right to veto programs devised by federal officials and private agencies. Also in 1964 he voted against Senator Everett Dirksen's plan to prevent the federal courts from carrying out the one-man, one-vote reapportionment mandate directed at state legislatures.

When it was first promulgated, the one-man, one-vote court order was expected to free the cities from their old thralldom to rural interests. It didn't quite turn out that way. Muskie was one of the first government officials to display alarm at what was resulting as representation in the state legislatures began to be reapportioned. At a Norfolk meeting of the AFL-CIO in August, 1967, he warned of "a new and discriminatory alliance between rural and suburban interests, leaving the central cities to fend for themselves. Nothing could be more dangerous. The needs of the central cities are the single most pressing problem in the domestic affairs of our country." This expression of awareness of the new power of suburbia was an echo of many earlier speeches. In January, 1966, long before he became the manager of the model-cities bill, he had told a meeting of the Downtown Progress Club of Washington that, "a beautiful, vigorous city center is a mockery of the American dream if it is a jewel in a setting of overcrowded and decayed slums." What was needed, he had said, was an alliance between city and suburb.

Muskie gave one of the best summaries of his philosophy in this regard in an interview with Gail Miller of *City* magazine

Senator Muskie, in his role as Mr. Clean, shown at a Senate subcommittee hearing as he argues for giving federal preference to "pollution-free" vehicles.

RUNNING MATES

A Bill Mauldin cartoon printed in the Chicago *Sun-Times* during the 1968 election campaign. Muskie is seen as "carrying" Humphrey.

Left to right are Jane Muskie, daughter Melinda, summer guest Gregory Singleton, son Steve, daughter Martha, the senator's mother, the senator, and son Edmund junior. Muskie's oldest daughter, Ellen, is not present at this 1968 gathering.

Vice-presidental candidate Muskie debates with student Rick Broady in Washington, Pennsylvania.

Surprise guests at a reception for Muskie in 1964 are President and Mrs. Johnson.

A glum-looking Hubert Humphrey and a not-so-glum-looking Muskie in a three-way handshake with Richard Nixon in Florida just after the 1968 election. All three are vacation bound.

Muskie in his resort-hotel bellhop's uniform poses with sister Lucy in 1935.

He sports a Navy ensign's uniform during World War II.

After the war a rumpled Muskie, standing with his father holds newborn son Steven in his arms.

Governor-elect Muskie (left), with his trademark bow tie, in Indiana with a group of Democratic leaders: Indiana Committeeman Paul Butler, Adlai E. Stevenson, Michigan Governor G. Mennen Williams, wearing *his* trademark bow tie, and National Committee Chairman Steven Mitchell.

Senator Muskie and President Kennedy at the Harvard-Columbia football game in 1963.

Governor Muskie holds up two ring-necked pheasants, each bagged with a single shot.

(United Press International Photo)

An avid huntsman and fisherman, Muskie has lately spent more of his outdoor time on the golf course.

Here he selects a club, tees off.

(United Press International Photo)

(Wide World Photos)

Senator Muskie tours Jackson State College after a campus shooting. He is
with student-body president-elect Warner Buxton (left), student Adrian
Peterson, W. Averell Harriman, and Senators Charles H. Percy of Illinois
and Ralph W. Yarborough of Texas.

Ellen Muskie becomes Mrs. Allen. Senator and Mrs. Muskie with their
daughter and Ernest Allen after their January, 1970, wedding at American
University Chapel, Washington, D.C.

(United Press International Photo)

in 1969. She asked him to comment on President Nixon's "New Federalism," which was supposed to return power from Washington to lower levels of government. Muskie had been interested in this concept before (it was then called "creative federalism") and was author of one approach to it, the 1968 Intergovernmental Cooperation Act. He said:

> This country is so big, its problems so huge, and the programs so complex that if states and metropolitan areas can develop workable and progressive governmental institutions, you can get a better job done. As far as I know, local conditions, priorities, and needs are best understood at the state and local level. Of course there are some risks involved in giving discretion for the administration of federal programs to local governments, not the least of which is the possibility of federal funds being used in ways contrary to national policy.
>
> Further, the establishment is always reluctant to give up prerogatives, and the establishment exists at the local as well as the federal level. So we need a policy which will create mechanisms designed to bring into play local administration and institutions with the assurance that they will seek sound leadership outside their own ranks, and the federal government has to keep a voice in the program that can be raised when necessary.
>
> There is a more positive face to state government than ever before; still, some states observe ancient concepts and they're going to have to be prodded into change. More and more states are responding to federal pressures and pressures from their growing urban areas. Still more will respond, but not all will become noble overnight. So the state should be empowered to shape, but not to obstruct, and therefore all programs—revenue sharing, welfare, civil rights—must have a strong federal presence.

Senator Muskie had come so far from being a barefoot boy that he resented other senators' moving in on urban problems. In 1966, just about the time the model-cities bill was coming to a vote in the Senate, Senator Abraham Ribicoff's Executive

Reorganization subcommittee, a Government Operations sibling of Muskie's Intergovernmental Relations subcommittee, began extensive and very well publicized hearings on urban problems. Muskie protested to Ribicoff, apparently in a most direct way. Ribicoff would not discuss the episode afterward, exhibiting a reticence that perhaps suggests a memory of unpleasantness. Some Senate employees who had at least close secondhand knowledge of the affair have said it was very unpleasant. Senator Muskie describes what happened this way:

"It really wasn't as bad as it may have been painted. The subcommittee on Intergovernmental Relations was given jurisdiction over all federal grant-in-aid programs. We'd worked in this field for a couple of years before Senator Ribicoff was elected to the Senate. The Advisory Commission on Intergovernmental Relations had been created as a result of my initiative on the Senate side. In due course Senator Ribicoff was made chairman of the subcommittee on Executive Reorganization. Well, he had an interest in the problems of the cities, which was perfectly proper. No reason why he shouldn't. But then he prepared these hearings on the problems of the cities, and in his first speeches his approach was through the whole grant-in-aid program. This understandably aroused my concern. I did not immediately challenge him on this because my inclination on this was, well, let's see which way he's going, and whether he's actually going to go into our area—unwittingly I'm sure. Finally it seemed to me he was moving into this area to the point where I ought to bring to his attention at least our jurisdiction in this field. So I wrote him a letter. We were involved in several exchanges of letters and at one point, until we reached a meeting of the minds, feelings, I guess, got a little high on both sides. But we eventually worked it out." Muskie said the affair was the understandable result of "sensitivity on the part of each of us to our jurisdictional prerogatives."

Some of Senator Muskie's friends believe this sensitivity to his prerogatives suggests that his famous reticence, his oft publicized reluctance to fight for Senate leadership positions are not the dominant characteristics of his personality. They say it demonstrates he can be aggressive when it is important to him to be. The Ribicoff-Muskie clash was only one of several such disputes with other senators involving fields in which jurisdictions clashed or overlapped.

Few, if any, senators compile perfect "pro-cities" voting records, and Muskie cast some dubious votes, particularly in his first term. In 1960, for example, he voted against authorizing 37,000 units of public housing, although then, in a compromise, he did vote in favor of 25,000 units. In 1961 he voted against the imaginative $100,000,000 open-spaces program, which helped crowded cities buy parks and greenery in a period when cities were both broke and expanding, and real-estate values in metropolitan areas were soaring. In 1963 he voted against a three-year, $500,000,000 program of grants-in-aid for urban mass-transit systems. In 1965 he led the fight in the Senate to cut rent supplements from $500,000,000 to $150,000,000. And there have been other votes like these. In some cases, Muskie regarded the reduction of the scale of a program, or the excision of part of it, as a tactical act designed to save the whole measure from defeat—as the half a loaf that is better than none to New England pragmatists. Sometimes it later turned out that this compromise was not necessary. But his opposition to the mass-transit grants was not just a matter of tactics. "A reasonable scale of priorities does not justify enactment of a $500,000,000 bill at this time," he declared, in a statement which hardly exhibited the priority setting expected of an urban champion. Such lapses did not hurt his reputation with his friends the mayors of big cities. In 1969 he spoke at a testimonial to Cleveland Mayor Carl B. Stokes. Milwaukee Mayor Henry W. Maier used the occasion to praise Muskie as "one of the few senators who really understand the problems of the cities."

"Urban problems" is often a euphemism for "Negro problems"—the nation's number-one domestic issue. In his views on this matter, Senator Muskie is an unmistakeable liberal. His record in this field has been a good one and after 1968, when as a vice-presidential candidate he first came face to face with many ghetto residents, and—what was even more important—with many white working men and women in "ethnic" neighborhoods who were agitated by the turbulence of the times, he became more outspoken on the subject than before. He had always said the right things. In 1960, still a very freshman senator, he spoke in Miami, to the Florida Civil Liberties Union, at a time when pressure for more effective civil-rights laws was building up. He addressed himself to the argument that law was not the proper instrument for dealing with the racial problem. "We cannot legislate trust and understanding," he conceded. "We cannot legislate confidence. We cannot strike down fear by legislative decree. We cannot by a stroke of the legislative pen create love and kindness in a human heart. But we can by wise legislation create a climate in which men separated by divisive differences can learn to live together. It is possible to establish rules to prevent abuses, to restrain the impulsive, to contain and eliminate excesses, to encourage responsible attitudes, to give support to moderation. When men are equal before the law and are required to treat each other as such, they are more inclined to believe in such equality." By the end of the 1960's such rhetoric had taken on a bloodless quality, for all its high-mindedness. It was in that sense typical of much northern liberal thought before the full fury of the civil-rights revolution and the backlash reaction engulfed the decade. In 1968, late in the vice-presidential campaign, in an impromptu speech to a hushed, somber, all-white audience of Maine Democrats, Muskie delivered a speech that by its emotional intensity demonstrated how far he—like others—had come, or been carried, in eight tumultuous years:

It's a great challenge we face in this country—not just in this election year, but in the years ahead. We made freedom work during the easiest years of our national existence, notwithstanding all the difficulties through which we've come. Wars, including the great Civil War, absorption of forty million immigrants, the Industrial Revolution, two great World Wars. None of those pose the kind of problems that we face here today. To put it in its starkest, simplest terms, we have the question of whether or not Americans who already have a stake in our society, who already are enjoying our affluence, are willing to share with those who do not.

The easy answer is to protect what we have, and let the others look out for themselves. That won't work. It simply won't work.

You can talk about law and order and pass criminal laws or any other legislation that you can conceive of. That answer won't work, unless in addition to insisting upon law and order, you do something about the conditions which make the have-not Americans restless and dissatisfied with their lots.

And I'm not talking about charity. I'm not talking about handouts.

I'm talking about people who live in conditions that no one in this room would accept quietly and passively without resistance.

I'm talking about our self-interests—yours and mine. Do we want to live in an orderly, peaceful society? There's only one way to do it. We've proven it for 180 years. For the life of me, I can't understand why we should begin to doubt in the year 1968 what our own experience teaches us. For many of us here—all of us, I think—are descendants of immigrants. We ought to know from the experience of our own families that human beings are going to fight to improve themselves, to get out of ruts, to get out of ghettos and and out of slums. You would, and I would.

To pretend that you can somehow suppress that urge by phony definitions of law and order is to overlook the plain facts of history. This idea of shielding off the well-to-do has been tried over and over again in history, and it's never worked. It's always led to trouble—for the affluent as well as the poor.

Those great historians, the Durants, tell us that it is inevitable in history that the rich will get richer and the poor will get poorer, and that when the gap gets big enough, this society explodes. They tell us that in their monumental history on the life of man. They've just issued a small volume summarizing their findings, and this is one of them—that this inevitably happens. We must not let it happen here.

We've had the one answer in history which makes it possible to avoid that outcome here—if we'll just understand the lesson and practice it.

When I consider how much more the average American has today than we had when I was a boy—we weren't affluent, but we weren't poor. And we were happy. And what we've added to that since is more than enough to share with those who have nothing.

The question is whether the affluent are ready to share, at a time when the affluent have never had more and the poor—have never had less by comparison. . . .

He was even more insistent and direct during that campaign in a speech to a Polish-American convention in Cleveland:

In this election year of 1968 our society and our system of government is being tested as never before. For the seeds of a new oppression are all around us.

They are fear, hate, and intolerance. They are the ugly facets of disunity and lack of trust—in each other and in our basic institutions.

Thomas Jefferson once said that the ultimate objective of government in our society is the happiness of its people.

When we say "the happiness of its people," we mean the happiness of all of them—without exception, without distinction.

That is the lesson I think we must learn in this campaign all over again.

It isn't an easy idea to pursue, because Americans are many different kinds of people, of different races, colors, cultures, national origins, and economic groups. We have different educational backgrounds and different tastes.

But the lesson of our country is that people, no matter how different, can live together and advance each other's interests.

This is what my father believed about America. This is what I believe.

Others do not share that belief.

Where there is poverty, they sow hate.

Where there is love, they sow distrust.

Where there is comfort, they sow fear.

Where there is common interest, they sow division.

You and I know that hate, distrust, fear, and division can only lead to anarchy and tyranny, the twin offspring of the enemies of freedom.

You and I know that no one can be free unless all are free.

You and I, having gained so much in this great land, should be in the forefront of those who want to help Americans who still suffer from discrimination—those who have not enjoyed the fruits of equal opportunity and equal participation in our society.

The great freedom fighter, Kosciusko, left all his money in America for the emancipation of the slaves.

Those of us who are his spiritual descendants should be the first to work for an equal chance for their descendants.

You and I should be the first to reject those who parade under the banner of suppression—disguised as law and order.

For we know that suppression breeds discontent.

Discontent breeds rebellion.

And rebellion breeds violence and oppression.

Public safety we must have.

Crime we must combat.

But we can carry out these objectives only within the guarantees of our constitution, and in a society where there is mutual trust, where poverty is no more, where youth has hope and age has dignity, and where men and women—of whatever color or social status—control their own destiny.

Two months before he died, Paderewski said: "I am grateful to the Supreme Deity that he permitted me to come here, to this free soil of the United States, that he granted me the strength still to serve Poland. . . ."

In each speech the effect on the members of the audience was stunning. One could feel them reacting in the complete silence. Reading the speeches is not the same as hearing Muskie deliver them. As a *New York Times* reporter once observed after another speech (on civil rights, in fact), "his speeches sometimes seem to acquire in the delivery a passion and an eloquence that partially evaporates when his words are reduced to transcript."

Between 1960 and 1968 Muskie neither earned particular distinction nor demonstrated any lack of understanding regarding civil rights, with a few exceptions. He voted to uphold the poll tax in 1962. In 1963 he voted against liberals twice on outlawing funds to segregated hospitals and medical schools. In 1965 he approved the nomination of a former Mississippi governor, J. P. Coleman, to the Fifth Circuit Court of Appeals. In the somewhat related field of civil liberties and crime control, Senator Muskie cast several votes in early 1968 that dismayed some of his friends who were active in the broad fight against those authoritarians who saw the civil-rights movements and urban crime in general and rioting in particular as sinister aspects of the same problem. Muskie voted to disqualify from federal employment anyone convicted of a felony in a riot. He voted for Senator Strom Thurmond's bill to make it a crime to use the facilities of interstate commerce to incite a riot. He voted against an effort to take away from police the authority to wiretap when they believe a crime is about to be committed. He voted against Senator Edward Kennedy's amendment to prohibit the interstate shipment of rifles and shotguns. And he voted against Senator Edward W. Brooke's amendment to prohibit the sale of bombs, hand grenades, and the like to unauthorized persons.

In 1964, during the epochal filibuster in the Senate over the omnibus civil-rights bill, Muskie was not given a floor assignment. Humphrey was the Democratic leader in that long fight. Senators Hart, Magnuson, Morse, Douglas, Long, Pastore, Clark, and Dodd were his Democratic lieutenants. Muskie was a foot soldier. No one was more attentive to routine duty in that campaign. Between May 6 and June 19 there were 118 roll-call votes, all important. Muskie voted on all of them, and always in support of the pro-civil-rights position. Only Senators Paul H. Douglas of Illinois, Kenneth B. Keating of New York, and Clifford P. Case of New Jersey matched that record.

In 1969 and 1970, Muskie, like the majority of the Senate, opposed the nominations of Clement Haynsworth and G. Harrold Carswell to the Supreme Court. In the Haynsworth debate, many objecting senators said Haynsworth's loose sense of judicial propriety was what led them to oppose him. There had been instances of his sitting in cases in which he seemed to have a personal interest. Muskie emphasized the South Carolina judge's civil-rights record. "It's taken us over a hundred years to shape public policy—Federal government policy —so that it moves in the direction of justice and equity and right. The President has indicated that he wants to change that thrust in some way. Since he won the election last November 5 he has the right, I suppose, to have any impact he can implement in that connection. This raises the question for each of us. I don't happen to agree that that thrust ought to be changed. By my vote on Justice Haynsworth I will be indicating whether I approve or disapprove the new thrust that the President has undertaken to give to the Court's decisions in this field."

In 1970, the pressure for civil rights, as it concerned school desegregation, had begun to shift from the South to the North. Senator John Stennis of Mississippi proposed legislation that would have required as much integration in northern schools (for the most part all white or all black because of residential housing patterns rather than the old separate-but-equal laws) as in southern ones. Achievement of this integration in the

North would have meant the extensive bussing of students. Stennis and other southerners rightly scored the hypocrisy of the nonsouthern states in this matter. Senator Abraham Ribicoff agreed, publicly, and scolded his fellow liberals. However, the goal of the southern senators was not more bussing and integration in the North, but less in the South. They felt that racial school integration would be so unpopular in the North, if the Federal Government started enforcing it, that the public reaction would cause Congress to relent and pressure to integrate would be relaxed everywhere, including the South. Nevertheless, most northern liberals, including Muskie, still opposed the idea and its was defeated. "The issue before us is not really bussing," he said. "Several years ago it was estimated that fifteen million public school children—about 40 per cent of the nation's total—traveled to school on buses. Parents do not ordinarily mind sending their children to school on buses so long as the schools provide a good education. It is what is at the end of the bus ride that counts." What would have been at the end often was an inferior and even unsafe school predominantly used by poor Negroes. Muskie proposed special federal aid "to state agencies and local school districts which on their own initiative or court orders, are attempting to end racial isolation and ensure equal opportunity and quality education."

Sometimes the enemies a man makes and the friendships he seeks tell a lot about him. Vice-President Humphrey says that when he was asking the opinion of Democratic governors and senators about his several possible running mates in 1968, "no one objected to Ed, though southerners weren't particularly warm." Senator Herman E. Talmadge of Georgia says, "I like Ed all right, but he is far from the moderate he's always described as. He has about the most liberal voting record of any senator I know. Especially on civil rights, so called." For this senator, and probably for most southern senators, whatever dislike is felt toward Muskie focuses on his ideas, not on him as a person. Some southerners do regard him with personal distaste, however. He made enemies in Mississippi when he clashed with Governor John Bell Williams during hearings on disaster relief after Hurricane Camille. In one televised exchange the venom was evident. "If I may say so respectfully, Senator," Governor Williams began, with a trace of sarcasm. Muskie cut him off with a barbed, "You don't need to be respectful as far as I'm concerned." Several months later Muskie flew to a funeral in Jackson, Mississippi, and a local columnist greeted him with memories of the disaster-relief hearings. He said the senator had displayed himself then as "puerile and distasteful."

The trip to the Jackson funeral was an uncharacteristic episode in many ways. In the field of civil rights, as in other fields, he had been criticized because while he almost always did the right thing, he seldom did it out front. The trip was designed to overcome that sort of criticism. It was also designed to earn him some publicity with both whites and blacks. And it did so immediately. His appearance at the funeral was featured on network news shows that day, and the next day his picture was on the front page of *The New York Times*. There was no immediate indication that his stock as a leader went up. His reputation as a nonpushy, take-it-slow political figure was solid, and more than one such event would be required to overcome it. The Jackson episode was important, nonetheless, for him and for the civil-rights cause, especially for those who sought an end to white-black polarization.

The funeral was for seventeen-year-old James Earl Green, a black high-school student who had been shot to death at a dormitory of Jackson State College, in Mississippi. He was one of two victims, felled in a hail of bullets from state police who were responding to nothing more threatening than shouts and such nonlethal missiles as bottles. This confrontation occurred in May, 1970, following by only a few days the shootings of four white students at Kent State University, in Ohio. Senators Birch Bayh and Walter Mondale went to the Mississippi campus immediately, to investigate the slaying. Muskie aides relayed a request from Charles Evers, a black Mississippi mayor, that someone, somehow, demonstrate that white Americans in important positions were determined to halt such brutality. Muskie liked the idea. He chartered a plane and invited a number of white and black political, educational, labor, legal, and sports figures to accompany him. Several students from Kent State were also invited. Among the better-known individuals on the trip were former Governor Averell Harriman; Senators Hart, Eagleton, Percy, Inouye, Yarborough, and Hughes; Representatives Adam Clayton Powell and Charles C. Diggs, Jr.; Whitney M. Young, Jr., executive director of the National Urban League; and writer Budd Shulberg.

The group, numbering eighty-two with press and staff included, left Washington on a chartered Southern Airways DC-9 on the morning of the funeral, May 22. On arriving, Muskie and his party first toured the Jackson State campus. State officials had tried to remove the bullet-ridden windows and panels before Muskie and the other investigators, official and unofficial, could get there, but students had stopped them. Students and other eyewitnesses led Muskie around the grounds, and told him their version of the incident. Then he and the rest walked down Lynch Street to the funeral. The ceremony, in which were combined the near-fundamental Missionary Baptist tradition and political rhetoric by Fayette Mayor Charles Evers, was a new experience for most in the Muskie party, and a moving one.

Flying back to Washington that afternoon, Muskie shucked the coat of his black suit, loosened his stylish wide tie, and made a brief speech on the plane's loudspeaker system. He referred to the shooting scene and said, "What we saw ought not to happen in America and ought not to be allowed to happen in America." He hoped those on the plane would give him ideas on what to do. His own idea was to insist on a "major federal investigation." If the people of the nation knew what had happened in Jackson, he said, they would not stand for it. He had faith in the people. But pressure had to be maintained. "It's all too easy in America to put such things behind us." He also urged that funds be raised for the eleven students wounded and hospitalized in the shooting, as well as for the assistance of the dead students' families. When he reached Washington he wired President Nixon to request an investigation.

When the trip was over, it was questionable if Muskie had demonstrated a newfound knack for the kind of leadership that is measured by being out front *first*. Bayh and Mondale were already back in Washington calling for a full-scale investigation by the time he left for Jackson. But he was indeed out front—and visible. (To most Negroes, Muskie had been an invisible man. Opinion polls consistently showed him, up to this time, far behind Senator Edward Kennedy and Hubert Humphrey in their support and affection. He simply was not known.) More than anything else, what Muskie's trip demonstrated were those qualities no one had ever charged him with lacking: compassion for individual victims of society's failings, deep concern about the polarization of the races, a desire to keep the disaffected from giving up on the system and the people who work within it, an urgent belief in cooperation. The Jackson trip allowed him to exhibit those qualities in a time of great stress.

A Negro attorney active in the civil-rights movement said after the Jackson trip, "I don't know any white political leader on the scene today who has worked out the problems of the seventies, and is busy communicating the answers to them. But Senator Muskie is beginning to. The important thing he is doing is offering positive answers to the poor of both races in the cities, while other politicians are offering negative ones that divide people even more." One example of what this attorney had in mind was the debate over the open-enrollment policy adopted by some colleges to make possible the admission of more blacks. Vice-President Agnew denounced this in terms that could only inflame and divide. Muskie rebutted the Agnew speech, and he did it in Louisiana.

CHAPTER SEVEN

MR. CLEAN

I n 1970 columnist Richard Wilson referred to "Senator Edmund Muskie . . . the Mr. Clean of the environment crusade." The appellation alone, without the Senator's name attached, would have identified him in the eyes of many, for he was far and away the nation's best-known pollution fighter. Publicists had been referring to him as Mr. Clean for several years. In 1964, long before there was an "environment crusade," a housewife in Cicero, Illinois, outraged at the dirty air there, directed her appeal to Muskie; she mailed him an envelope of soot. In the 1960's there were few areas of federal activity in which Congress supplied more leadership than the White House. Antipollution legislation was one of those areas, and Muskie was the premier congressional expert. Even more than Illinois housewives, the members of the younger generation took the issue to heart, and Muskie was a hero to them. On Earth Day in 1970, ten thousand youths at the Washington Monument applauded him more vigorously than they did such youth-culture heroes as Rennie Davis, Phil Ochs, and I. F. Stone.

In a sense this just happened. Muskie had been assigned to the Public Works Committee in 1959. In 1963, when Chairman Pat McNamara of Michigan created the Special Air and Water Pollution subcommittee, Muskie had enough seniority to become its chairman. His work was hard—and unsung, at first. "His motives had to be as pure as the air he was trying to get because there was no political mileage in it," says one senator. "Pollution legislation was a forlorn and only vaguely understood goal. He wrestled it out almost single-handed and alone." But by the later years of the decade, there was political mileage in it. So much, that Mr. Clean found he was spending a lot of time on the defensive. He was defending his subcommittee's jurisdiction and his ideas for new governmental arrangements against other committees and other new ideas. He was defending himself against charges that while he had been saying all the right things, he had allowed a friend to despoil a wild Maine stream, and that in order to win for his state the economic advantages of a refinery he was willing to run the risk of massive oil spills along Maine's world-famous, picturesque rock-ribbed coast. Most newsworthy of all, he was defending himself against an attack from Ralph Nader, who said Muskie wrote legislation that was in polluters' interest, not the public's.

Nader was the intense young lawyer who led the Center for Responsive Law, a consumer-oriented organization which he had created after his own single-handed assault on the automobile industry had resulted in new safety laws. Young law students and others who came to work at his center were known as Nader's Raiders. They conducted lightning investigations of government regulatory agencies and then issued reports critical of inefficiency, industry favoritism, and other aspects of what they saw as failures of the institutions to do their job of protecting the citizenry. In 1970 the center issued a "Task Force Report on Air Pollution." It was focused on the National Air Pollution Control Administration, but also attacked a Muskie-authored bill—the Air Quality Act of 1967—and Muskie himself. The key provision of the 1967 act allowed the Federal Government to establish "air quality control regions" around the nation, and to set standards for the air in those regions. This was not what President Johnson had asked for. He had wanted a law establishing national emission standards for major stationary air polluters, such as power companies and steel mills. The industries had opposed the Johnson request, preferring the Muskie approach, which eschewed emission standards for air-quality standards. The Nader group's task-force report pointed out the shared views of Muskie and industry, and said, "Senator Muskie has never seemed inclined (either politically or temperamentally) toward taking a tough stand against private industry." The report also said, "It is hard to avoid the belief that Muskie, an extremely astute politician who by temperament avoids conflict and unfavorable odds, was influenced by a desire to get the bill through Congress with a minimum of acrimony. He therefore took the path of least resistance."

The report contained other, similar anti-Muskie statements. It characterized the chairman of the Public Works Committee, Jennings Randolph of West Virginia, as a crude protector of the coal industry's profits at the expense of clean air and said, "There is really not much difference between these two men [Randolph and Muskie] on the important issues in air pollution control legislation." It talked of "Muskie's failure," and at one point observed that "on balance" he "has failed the nation in the field of air pollution control legislation." Of an episode in which a Republican Justice Department placated automobile manufacturers, the report commented that "so reluctant is he to become involved in controversy which involves industry, that he passed up the politician's dream issue, a chance to denounce the opposition party." Granting that Muskie had been an early fighter for clean air and water, the report went on to assert that his "leadership has wavered significantly over the last several years" and that any renewed interest in exerting that leadership was only due to his fear "that the President might steal the Senator's thunder on a good political issue." It said he was spending too much time running for president, and concluded, "Perhaps the senator should consider resigning his chairmanship of the Subcommittee and leave the post to someone who can devote more time and energy to the task."

These words were harsh—and sometimes actually unfair. Drained of their acid personalizations, however, some of the principal general charges did have substance. Of course, drained of their acid they were not exactly the same changes.

To begin with, in the debate on national emission standards versus air-quality standards it was possible for honest men to believe ardently in either approach, or in both. Industry was not alone in favoring local air-quality standards. Dr. Barry Commoner, chairman of the Department of Botany at Washington University, St. Louis, one of the nation's leading pleaders for a clean environment, was asked during testimony on the 1967 act if he thought emission standards would be effective. He replied, "I think national emission standards are useful as a backstop, but they will have to be translated into local situations by local analyses and, more important, by local follow-up of the impact of those standards on the air pollution problem as a whole. It seems to me that simply blindly saying . . . that the application of these [national] standards everywhere will result in the same kind of reduction in the problem . . . is oversimplifying the situation." Muskie felt the same way, and also held the view that in some areas one had to accept more pollution than in others as a realistic price for the benefits of an industrial society. Since these "worse" emissions had to be permitted in certain places, national standards were not practical. In that sense he *was* against taking what Nader's Raiders would have considered a "tough" stand against industry.

However, viewed in another light, Muskie's position could be characterized in terms that were not insulting, like those of the task-force report, but flattering. Ron M. Linton, an environmental consultant and former staff director of the Public Works Committee, puts it this way: "Muskie believed in the reasonableness of an adjusted society. In other words, we have to create goods and services for people . . . [and] we have to protect the physical environment from being degraded to where it causes health and economic harm. We have to find a mechanism to balance this thing, and this has been Muskie's approach." Linton believes Muskie was successful in finding a balance, and that if Muskie were not the congressional expert and chief law writer in this field, leadership "would have passed to the really fanatic conservationists, who I think would have . . . [tried to pass] laws that would have been a terrible economic penalty. They just dismiss that area. If you tell them a plant will shut down [because of too strict standards], they say, 'All right, let 'em shut down.' That's easy to say, but legislation had to offset the counter political forces you would get [from seeking standards that would lead to plant closings and the disappearance of jobs]." The end result of seeking that kind of legislation could have been no legislation.

President Johnson, among others, certainly was aware of the political realities in 1968. Even the Nader task-force report conceded that at that time there was no realistic expectation that Congress would approve of national emission standards. Probably what the White House wanted was to recapture the initiative in antipollution legislation—to propose bold action. Although theoretically Congress is expected to write the nation's laws, and the executive branch to carry them out, that situation has existed only in grade-school textbooks in most of the period since the activism of the New Deal era began.

In actuality, the President proposes legislation and Congress enacts it. In the 1960's, one of the very few areas where Congress took the initiative was pollution control. There was speculation in Washington in 1967 that Johnson proposed an unpassable law specifically because he was smarting from a Muskie-Congress success in 1966. In that year the President made only modest proposals for water-pollution legislation. The administration draft bill asked for 50 million dollars added to the grants for community sewage-treatment facilities that had been authorized in earlier laws. This proposal anticipated that the program of federal aid for such facilities would go no further than 1967. But Muskie proposed, and the Senate passed, a bill authorizing 6 billion dollars—120 times more than the Administration requested!—to be spent through 1972. The Administration rushed, when it saw what was happening, to get on board. It endorsed the Senate bill, but asked for only 3.5 billion dollars for treatment-plant grants. The House approved a bill for 2.5 billion dollars in grants through 1971. The compromise that emerged from conference authorized the expenditure of 3.6 billion dollars through 1971, a clear victory for the Senate and Muskie.

This history, as much as a desire to fight pollution at the source with emission standards, was probably what prompted the Johnson proposal in 1967. The fight against pollution is, like most, an evolutionary process. Things were possible in 1967 that were not possible in 1965, and so forth. In 1970, three years after the 1967 Air Quality Act, the Department of Health, Education, and Welfare issued a report on national emission standards, as required by the 1967 act. It went beyond existing law in recommending national (as opposed to regional) air-quality standards, and emission standards for "major new [that is, newly constructed] stationary sources." This was a compromise between the Muskie view of 1967 and the Nader view of 1970.

The task-force report's criticism of Muskie as a man who by nature avoided conflict and unfavorable odds was also generally true. He had worked out compromises in committee that allowed most pollution legislation to be passed by lop-sided margins. The 1963 Clean Air Act was passed by a voice vote; nobody objected to it enough to force a roll call. The Senate passed the 1965 Water Quality Act by a vote of 68 to 8. It passed the 1966 Clean Water Restoration Act 90 to 0. And it passed the 1967 Air Quality Act 88 to 0 (after a unanimous committee vote for it, and this accolade for the committee from Senator John Sherman Cooper of Kentucky: "I have never seen in my service in the Senate a better demonstration of the committee legislative process than in its consideration and development of this measure"). One would not expect such unanimity if the legislation were uncompromising to the industrial interests. Muskie himself once remarked, only partly in jest, after a bill zipped through the Senate, "Maybe that wasn't as good a bill as I thought." Even in this field, how-ever, he could be obstinate when he decided that industry should be required to do something it didn't want to do, and he could insist on going against the grain of congressional thought, rather than seeking the line of least resistance. It was his style to compromise, but he didn't always do so. In 1968, he went against the grain of industry and significant congres-sional thought in behalf of a point he thought important. He held out for a whole loaf instead of half. He lost a bill because of it, but in the long run won a better bill.

In 1968 the Senate and the House passed different versions of a water-pollution bill. Muskie and the Senate wanted stricter provisions for oil-spill cleanups. But oilmen's views prevailed with enough House conferees to cause their rejection of the Senate version. The year ran out with neither side giving in, and Congress adjourned. The next month, with a new Congress just convened, an offshore well in the Santa Barbara Channel began leaking oil, which fouled long stretches of beautiful California beaches. Newspapers and tele-vision screens carried pictures of birds unable to fly or to swim because the oil clotted their feathers. It was one of those events that capture the public's imagination. As a result of that event, and of other oil accidents, Congress passed the Water Quality Improvement Act of 1970, which included provisions for dealing with such problems that were tougher than those of the 1968 Senate version. "As strong a piece of pollution legislation as ever written," noted *Congressional Quarterly*. Muskie believed during this period that his reputation for willingness to work out compromises was controverted by the incidents, such as the 1968 episode, of his stubborn insistence on his point of view in conflicts in Congress. He even indicated once that he thought this stubbornness was typical of his behavior. There were certainly limits to his willingness to work things out without ruffling anyone's feathers. Those limits became narrower after 1968, when he began to see himself as a national leader. He believed a man in his role should not compromise as readily as a legislator. In 1970 he forsook the idea that legislation had to involve compromise with polluters, and as a result, his subcommittee wrote and the Senate passed the toughest clean-air bill ever. The House had earlier passed a tame (for the times) bill. Muskie's bill called for national air-quality standards, emission standards for new construction, citizen suits against sources of pollution, and other similar approaches to cleaning up the air. Even more noteworthy, the Muskie bill required Detroit to produce a nearly pollution-free automobile by 1975 (or 1976, the Secretary of Health, Education, and Welfare having the power to grant a one-year extension if he found manufacturers needed it). Automobile men howled. They said they couldn't even meet a Nixon goal of 1980. If ever there was an opportunity for easy compromise, this was it. Detroit's top executives insisted that the technology for meeting such a deadline didn't exist. The economic consequences of any shutdowns were unthinkable. It would have been a simple matter to change the "deadline" to a "target date." But Muskie held firm. He said the industry had not shown a sense of urgency, so the Congress would have to. Senator Robert P.

Griffin of Michigan complained, but neither he nor any other senator voted No and the bill passed 73 to 0, a testimony to Muskie and the temper of the times rather than to the existence of any compromises in the bill. Then it was sent back to a late conference with the House members, who had traditionally been more amenable to industry's point of view.

During this period he also on occasion placed himself in direct confrontation with industry in a way that made the Nader charge less than fair. He consistently feuded with New England private power interests in the controversy over building a public power project in Maine—the Dickey-Lincoln School project—which he favored. And he was in conflict with the power industry everywhere on the question of allowing nuclear power plants to employ a certain cooling process, which would raise the temperature of large bodies of water. Finally, he angered many industry officials when he endorsed "Campaign GM," which involved pressure from owners of General Motors stocks to force that corporation's board to fight pollution. He was the first of only a few senators to endorse this effort—which was initiated by Ralph Nader.

The Santa Barbara incident demonstrated that public opinion was a strong force for a clean environment and conservation, and that the issue had finally arrived. The oil and gas lobbyists who had defeated Muskie's bill in 1968 were powerful men who didn't lose many fights, but growing public interest in environmental affairs was creating competition in Congress for what one Senate aide was quoted as calling "a piece of the action." President Nixon stressed environmental problems in his 1970 state-of-the-union speech and issued a special presidential message on the environment. The Library of Congress's Legislative Reference Service had to set up a new division in late 1969 to handle requests from Congressmen who wanted to make speeches on, and introduce bills related to, the general pollution-environment-conservation question. Muskie and others who had been in the thick of the fight long before it was so politically productive had mixed reactions to all this. On the one hand they were glad to see the old battles being won, the new pressures on behalf of their old causes. On the other hand, they were human enough to be jealous.

Two incidents of this sort involved Muskie centrally. In 1967 he directed his staff to work out a plan for a new select Senate committee on "technology and the human environment." The Intergovernmental Relations subcommittee held hearings. Establishing a new committee is a ticklish business, because many old jurisdictions are involved. Muskie thought everything had been worked out to everybody's satisfaction, but when the Government Operations Committee met to vote on the final version of the plan, Senator Fred Harris of Oklahoma objected that his Research subcommittee was being unfairly treated, and the Muskie proposal was defeated. Muskie thought Harris was being unfairly possessive. And vice versa. They clashed sharply. Muskie later described the conflict as "pretty vigorous." Harris said he had never participated in nor heard of a worse senatorial argument. One witness not involved called it a shouting match. Another said it was not so much loud as venomously bitter. Subsequently, Harris and Muskie agreed on a different plan to set up an even more powerful joint House-Senate committee on the environment, and forgot whatever personal animosities their argument had created. Harris described their later relationship as "very warm and friendly."

In 1969 Muskie, Senator Henry Jackson of Washington, and Representative John D. Dingell of Michigan scrapped over the distribution of authority in environmental matters. Essentially, the dispute concerned determination of which committees of the House and Senate would have jurisdiction over the environment-related activities of existing federal agencies, over new agencies, over future legislative proposals, and over some appointments to high-level environmental agencies. Jackson, Muskie, and Dingell had competing and conflicting interests. Jackson was chairman of the Senate

Interior and Insular Affairs Committee. Dingell was chairman of the House Fisheries and Conservation subcommittee. Dingell believed that the dispute was personal on Muskie's part, that Muskie was resentful of others competing with him for leadership in the antipollution field. There was more to it than that. The orientation of Muskie and others on the Air and Water Pollution subcommittee was largely toward the East; that of the Interior and Insular Affairs Committee was traditionally more toward the West, with the result that this committee, like the Department of the Interior, had been associated far more with resource management than with true conservation or the fight against pollution. In any event, Muskie and Jackson worked out their dispute relatively smoothly—but not Muskie and Dingell. Where Muskie and Dingell were concerned, the argument was incandescent. "He laced me up and down," said Dingell of one meeting. A witness said Muskie used "gutter language." Dingell said it wasn't the first time: "He's the most miserable man in the whole Congress to deal with." Dingell never forgave Muskie. An aide to Senator Jackson has noted, "These guys [Muskie and the subcommittee staff] were in the trenches a long time before the war became popular. . . . It's natural for them to resent it and to be suspicious of the newcomers' contributions."

In May, 1970, on the day after the Nader task-force report came out, Muskie called a press conference. It was held in a small chandeliered hearing room across the hall from his Senate Office Building suite. The halls were aswarm with high-school students and tourists, and some of them joined about a hundred reporters and cameramen crowding into the brightly lit room. Muskie looked grim. He dueled with questioners, defending the Air Quality Act of 1967 and the argument that setting air-quality standards was better public policy and environmental science than setting emission standards. Often the questions and answers were too complicated or technical for many in the audience. The technicalities could have been argued endlessly, as they already had been and would in fact continue to be. The real issue concerned *Muskie's* standards and the differences between his style and Nader's. Finally, he addressed himself to that:

> I'd like to make this clear. Our way of being tough in our part of the country is to do it without name calling or recrimination. But to develop clear ideas of what we stand for and to press for them as hard and as effectively as we can. We don't think it is necessary to be noisy to do this. We don't think it is necessary to be nasty to do this. We think there are effective ways to be tough that are sometimes silent and are sometimes restrained. I can't be something that I'm not. I come from my region. I reflect its attitudes about the way to get things done and always will. That doesn't mean we don't get things done. We do. And I think sometimes more effectively than different and noisier approaches. We happen to live in a time of confrontation. I understand, of course, the deep-seated unrest and discontents that are responsible for that confrontation. So confrontation serves a useful purpose as an outlet, as an escape valve. But in order to really make this society work, at some point we're going to have to move across the lines of confrontation, reach agreements, get results that will improve our country. To do it needs toughness. It needs courage. But it also requires effectiveness. And these are the qualities that I understand and my people understand in my part of the country.

How damaging the Nader attack had been could not be determined immediately. Both *The New York Times* and the San Francisco *Examiner* supported Muskie. The *Times* observed that "the movement for a cleaner America needs both these men," and that Muskie "is in no danger of losing his credentials now as a foremost protector of the environment." The *Examiner* said, "Nader and his group would accomplish more by backing Muskie in his struggle against public apathy, industrial resistance and reluctance on the part of Congress to appropriate antipollution funds than by making a senseless attack on one of the nation's environmental pioneers." The next month Nader went to Maine to announce that he was directing a study of pollution by the pulp and paper industry there, including one plant in Muskie's old home town.

Republicans, and Muskie critics and competitors in the Democratic party, had been expecting for some time that Muskie's Mr. Clean reputation in Maine would come under attack. But they had not expected the attacks to come in connection with the pulp and paper industry. Muskie had never really been involved as closely as the Maine Republicans with this source of pollution. His supposed vulnerability had to do with a man who raised beets and potatoes and with an oil refinery.

"Freddie" Vahlsing (few call him anything else) is a businessman and an acquaintance of Muskie's who has contributed to his past campaigns and has flown him around the state several times. He was also a resource rapist and an industrial polluter of remarkable dimensions. To growing numbers of Yankee conservationists who see Maine's natural beauty threatened, her resources ravaged, and her way of life altered by the growth of the eastern megalopolis which now stretches from southern New Hampshire to northern Virginia, Freddie Vahlsing is the symbol of the approaching danger. That he is a despoiler of natural resources is indisputable; what is important here is his relationship with Muskie and the question of whether the champion of clean water helped him to foul the Prestile Stream.

Freddie Vahlsing is perfectly typecast for the role of villain. A flamboyant (he carries a seven-million-dollar insurance policy on his life), effervescent millionaire with ill-fitting forty-five-dollar suits, dirty fingernails, and a rasping voice, Vahlsing first came to Maine with his father, Fred senior, who headed a wealthy firm, based in New Jersey, which processed fresh produce and frozen foods. Fred Senior grew, bought, and processed Aroostook potatoes, living happily and at peace with his northern Maine neighbors. "The old man was easy to get along with. He was liked, respected, and trusted," says one Aroostook potato grower. Freddie, who took over and enlarged the family's business activities when his father retired, cut a wider swath. An engineering graduate of both Princeton and Tufts, and the holder of a Phi Beta Kappa key from Princeton, Vahlsing has drive, zeal, and determination. In 1952 when he was twenty-six, he sailed his own boat across the Atlantic from Amsterdam to Newport with a few friends. Thirteen years earlier his father had taught him to fly; today he logs about 150,000 miles a year in his private twin-engine plane. He is ebullient and sensationally optimistic, and—until he turned his hand to sugar beets—he was a businessman with the reputation of never having been bested in a deal.

In any other part of the state Freddie Vahlsing would have been a genuine oddity, but Aroostook County, with an area greater than all of Connecticut, is not typically Maine, and the citizens of what in Maine is called "the County" do not conform to the Maine stereotype. In topography too the County differs from the rest of the state. There is no coastline and the Appalachian range, which ends to the south, is replaced by relatively flat, rocky fields and gently rolling hills. The people are different. There is no Down East accent in Aroostook, and there is little of the native caution and reserve that characterizes the typical Mainer. The County resident is warm and open, with an optimism that is far more western than eastern. In their own way Aroostook residents can be as flamboyant as Freddie. An Aroostook farmer once built what was said to be the largest barn in the world for no other apparent reason than to build the biggest barn in the world. It promptly burned. He rebuilt it and again it burned. He said the hell with it and went on to other things. The harness horse John R. Braden was the pride of Aroostook County when he raced throughout the state, and after one stirring victory was brought into the dining room of the Northeastland Hotel, in Presque Isle, to eat oats off a table at a banquet in his honor. Nobody in Aroostook thinks that odd. Aroostook residents are expansive when the economic backbone of the County—the potato—is firm; when it is not, and during the past twenty years poor potato prices have outnumbered the good, they suffer and potato-house fires are not uncommon. The cause of such fires is often unofficially blamed on "friction: a large mortgage rubbing against an insurance policy."

Freddie was accepted in Aroostook; he expanded his father's operations there and in 1961 opened a large potato-processing plant which produced frozen French fries in Easton, a small town of about 1,500 near the Canadian border. The potato wastes from the processing plant poured into the Prestile Stream, a small waterway which meanders through Easton to Mars Hill, a few miles to the south, and then crosses the border into Canada, where it joins the St. John River and moves south to the sea. By 1964 the plant had been enlarged several times, in part with loans from the Area Redevelopment Administration, and was seriously polluting the Prestile, which then had the water classification B, one of the highest classifications in the state, indicating that it was fit for swimming and after minimal treatment, for drinking. It was considered by fishermen to be a first-class trout stream. Until 1964 Vahlsing's relations with Muskie had been slight. "The first time I ever saw Fred Vahlsing was in 1962 when I was up in Aroostook," Muskie recalls. "He'd been in operation for about a year and I didn't know him from Adam. I just wanted to see this [potato-processing] operation of his and he showed me through it with a great deal of pride." During the next three years, when Vahlsing had sought ARA loans for expansion, Muskie and his staff assisted him. "We gave him the help we could as we have with all such projects all over the state," Muskie says, emphasizing that Vahlsing received the same treatment as any other Maine business applying for ARA assistance. That treatment, Muskie says, consisted of going "over the application and suggesting the strongest ways of

presenting the project. As I remember it, in the cases with
Freddie, it was all handled by correspondence."

The pollution of the Prestile continued. The state's Water
Improvement Commission had warned Vahlsing several times
between 1962 and 1964 that he was violating the law, and
threatened him with court action. In response, Vahlsing spent
$400,000 installing a waste-treatment plant, which has never
functioned properly. Fish were dying in heavy numbers;
children were warned not to swim there. In all, during the
three-year period between 1962 and 1965 the Water Improvement Commision found thirty-one violations of the standard
required by the stream's B classification. Strangely, the state's
attorney general's department took no significant action.
Vahlsing continued to pollute the Prestile and publicly maintained that his waste-treatment plant was performing properly.

A 1962 decision of Congress to amend the Sugar Act first
brought Muskie and Vahlsing together. The new Sugar Act
permitted the construction of six additional refineries and the
allocation of new sugar-beet allotments. Aroostook, which
grows a seventh of the nation's potatoes, decided to make a
pitch for a second cash crop. In late 1963 the Governor and
all four of Maine's members of the Congress testified before a
Department of Agriculture hearing in support of a Maine
sugar-beet allotment. Of the five, Muskie was the only Democrat. Maine was granted a 33,000-acre allotment, and Aroostook farmers and businessmen immediately began to search
for a company to build and operate a sugar-beet refinery. The
Great Western Sugar Company initially agreed to build the
refinery, but first-year test plantings of sugar beets produced
such poor yields that the company withdrew. At that point,
Vahlsing, who had had no experience with either sugar beets
or a sugar-beet refinery, stepped forward to construct and
operate the fifteen-million-dollar plant. "Vahlsing kept the
sugar-beet allotment alive," Muskie says. "He did a remarkable
job in terms of getting the plant built on time and in over-

coming a lot of other roadblocks." Finances were one. With Muskie's aid, Vahlsing secured six million dollars in federal ARA loans for plant financing, and the state agreed to put its credit behind another eight million dollars in private loans. In addition, Vahlsing invested his own capital, through the family holding company, a corporation called Vahlsing Christina, and made loans to Aroostook farmers for sugar beet farming equipment.

A more serious roadblock was the state's high water standard for the Prestile, a standard Vahlsing was already severely violating with his potato wastes. When the ARA had originally promised loans to Great Western, the plans had called for construction of the refinery in Caribou, on the Aroostook River, which was larger than the Prestile but equally polluted. When Great Western backed out and Freddie stepped in, his intention of building the proposed plant on the Prestile became cause for concern. The ARA was aware that Vahlsing had been served with a cease and desist order from the state Water Improvement Commission because of the Prestile pollution and was concerned that its loans might be jeopardized if state action forced closing of both the potato plant and the refinery. And no one knew, least of all Vahlsing, how much a sugar-beet refinery might additionally pollute the Prestile. The solution was brutally simple: to downgrade the classification of the Prestile to a D—the state's lowest level—to ensure that the Prestile could not be illegally polluted. The Maine Legislature, then controlled by Democrats for the first time in a half century, responded reluctantly. Muskie came forward to marshal the Democratic votes, publicly supporting the downgrading, making it clear that he stood with the sugar-beet industry. Republican Governor John H. Reed, himself an Aroostook potato farmer, made a rare appearance before a joint convention of the Legislature to support the downgrading. The combination of Muskie and Reed was enough to get the measure passed. Now it was official at last: The Prestile was designated an open sewer in early 1965. Ignored were the arguments of conservationist legislators who vainly protested that the reduced classification was aimed at benefiting only one industry. Nobody listened when they noted that the town of Mars Hill had constructed a large municipal sewage-treatment plant to end its own pollution of the Prestile. Muskie, through his aide Don Nicoll, put the best face on the situation. Muskie, Nicoll said, "does not favor a permanent reduction in the quality of the . . . stream." The "temporary" downgrading, Nicoll said, was necessary because of the likelihood that "with a new plant there will be some problems in the initial stages of plant operations." Muskie reemphasized that position in a newsletter to Maine newspapers two weeks later.

The sugar-beet refinery was completely pollution-free when it went into operation in January, 1967, but the potato-processing plant continued to befoul the Prestile, killing fish and producing a water odor that literally drove nearby residents out of their homes. In winter, when the stream froze, the ice was black. And there was worse to come. In the summer of 1968 Freddie decided to process two hundred carloads of potatoes during a period when the water level of the Prestile was low. The pollution load reached a new high. Robert Caines, a sturdy, crew-cut resident of nearby Centreville, New Brunswick, and a former mayor of the little town of seven hundred, watched in disbelief and rage as the stream's life died. "We threw some trout into it [the Prestile] and they lived less than a minute," he says. "Eels live longer in contaminated or polluted water than trout, but even the eels in the stream had their eyes turn white and dissolve. When we threw fresh eels into the stream they tried to swim along with their heads out of the water before being killed. Other fish would jump right out of the water and die." Caines and several other Canadian neighbors decided to take action. They publicly announced that they were going to build a dam across the Prestile at the Maine border. On July 9, as Royal Canadian Mounted Policemen casually directed traffic, and a crowd of spectators cheered encouragement, five bulldozers constructed a hundred-foot-long, ten-foot-high dam across the Prestile at the international boundary line. The action, which violated a number of international and provincial laws, was a desperate and symbolic gesture by the Canadians against the Vahlsing empire across the line. The dam was voluntarily removed a few days later. Today, a large stone marker commemorates the site of the futile effort to stem pollution. A plaque states: *This International Monument symbolizes the beginning of the citizens' war on pollution in western New Brunswick and eastern Maine, and marks the site where aroused citizens built an earthen dam to stem the flow of pollution from the Vahlsing Inc. complex in Easton, Maine, July 9, 1968. This date marked the beginning of our war on pollution. The war continues.*

Vahlsing, meanwhile, had been otherwise occupied. His broad, white-toothed grin, his backslapping greeting, and his bellowing voice had become familiar at Democratic state conventions and at party fund-raising dinners. He had contributed to Muskie's reelection campaign in 1964 (exactly how much is unknown, since state law requires that the statements of contributions and expenses filed by candidates be kept only two years) and made a modest contribution to Muskie's 1968 campaign. He had also donated to the successful campaigns of two other Democrats: William D. Hathaway, running for Congress from the Second District, and Kenneth M. Curtis, running for governor. His Maine attorney was George J. Mitchell, formerly a Muskie aide in Washington, a Democratic state chairman, and now the state's Democratic national comiteeman. Vahlsing's plane seemed always available to fly politicians and reporters to Easton to inspect his facilities. His largesse appeared boundless. When a Portland newsman ripped his suit slightly getting out of Freddie's plane, Vahlsing promptly bought him a new one. Governor Curtis was flown in Vahlsing's plane to a Washington, D. C., fund-raising dinner for the Democratic National Committee, and Freddie played host to state party leaders there at a cocktail party in his hotel suite. From time to time Muskie and other Maine Democrats found themselves traveling in Freddie's plane to Easton for the ceremonies which marked the establishment of new facilities. When ground for the refinery was broken, 1,300 people were invited for a banquet of roast beef, turkey, king crab, and sugar-beet greens. Freddie picked up the tab. "I've flown with Freddie on two or three occasions," Muskie acknowledges. "I would be in the state and he would ask to fly me up to Easton to attend some celebration or ceremony in connection with his plants. But he didn't serve me as a substitute for Northeast Airlines." Vahlsing, then forty-two years old, was also much in evidence at the 1968 Democratic convention in Chicago, which nominated Muskie for vice-president. He kept two chauffeur-driven limousines available to shuttle Maine delegates between the hotel and the convention hall in the cab-struck city. His hand was always grabbing for dinner and drink checks. When Muskie attended a late-night cocktail party for the Maine delegates after his nomination he made his way through the crowd at the Chicago Holiday Inn to a dais to thank the delegation. There, suddenly at his side was a beaming, grinning Vahlsing. "Hello, Freddie," said Muskie, "what are you doing here?"

That was the question a lot of Mainers started asking when, in late 1969, the once sweet smell of sugar beets turned sour. Aroostook farmers had never grown enough beets to make the refinery profitable; indeed, at one point Vahlsing had imported sugar cane in an effort to keep the plant open. By the end of 1969 Vahlsing's loan payments were in default, and in early 1970 the state, which had backed eight million dollars in refinery loans with the credit of its citizens, began making monthly payments of about fifty thousand dollars to Freddie's creditors. The state agency which had backed these loans, as well as others for Freddie's potato-processing plant, was the Industrial Building Authority which had been established under Muskie's auspices during his second term as governor.

Vahlsing stockholders began grumbling as well. A group of stockholders in Texas Plastics, a Vahlsing-controlled company, filed suit charging that Texas Plastics had illegally loaned money to Vahlsing Incorporated and Vahlsing Christina. Vahlsing was unable to pay Maine farmers for their sugar beets; his taxes to the town of Easton were in arrears and in dispute. A second Vahlsing sugar-beet refinery, Maine Sugar Industries, of Montezuma, New York, was also in danger of collapse.

Now there were ugly questions. Why had Mr. Clean favored a downgrading of the Prestile? Why was Vahlsing seen in Muskie's company so often? And the ugliest of all: Since the sugar-beet refinery wasn't a polluter, why had the Prestile been downgraded? Could it have been to legalize Vahlsing's pollution of the Prestile with his potato wastes? The Maine Legislature, meeting in special session in early 1970, authorized a $75,000 study of the entire Vahlsing sugar-beet operation, not entirely out of the best of motives. One Republican leader, when asked if the investigation was politically inspired, smiled and replied, "You bet your ass it is." Vahlsing, no longer ebullient and now scarcely visible (he was nowhere to be seen at the 1970 Democratic state convention), went to the state Supreme Court in a vain effort to block the investigation: "No one needs a $75,000 investigation to find out what the problem is. There simply have not been enough sugar beets grown in Maine." Instead, he proposed a merger of Maine Sugar Industries and Texas Plastics with the financially sound Vahlsing Incorporated, a maneuver which, coupled with a stock sale, could bail him out. The merger proposal failed and Vahlsing subsequently entered into agreements with creditors holding about $8,800,000 in debts. To some creditors Vahlsing turned over stock in Maine Sugar Industries; to others he signed long-term notes providing for repayment. Vahlsing announced that "MSI is deeply gratified at the confidence placed in it by creditors" and said the agreements were a "major milestone" in making MSI a profitable enterprise.

Meanwhile, Muskie became increasingly defensive on the subject: "If I felt for one moment that the sugar-beet refinery meant that the Prestile is condemned to the status of an open sewer, I would not have supported the proposal to reclassify the stream. The reclassification was intended to be temporary. It was designed to meet an immediate problem in connection with the financing of the plant." Muskie maintained that he had only "reluctantly" supported the downgrading and then only after assurances that a waste-treatment plant would be built into the refinery. Whatever Muskie's failings in the Prestile turmoil, investigation indicates no basis for a charge that the Prestile was downgraded simply as a ruse to permit Vahlsing to discharge potato wastes legally. In lowering the classification from B to D, the Legislature had added a proviso that the reduced classification would not become effective until the sugar-beet refinery was operational. Three months after the refinery opened, when it was apparent that pollution was not a problem, the Legislature upgraded the stream to a compromise C. If Vahlsing's aim had been to legalize his pollution of the Prestile the plan had succeeded for only a few short months. One of Muskie's aides pointed out glumly, "If it weren't for that damned potato plant, this whole affair would have been a classic case of permitting flexibility to allow a new industry to get off the ground. But the potato plant spoiled everything." Including, most obviously, the Prestile.

Muskie's personal relationship with Vahlsing has been substantially exaggerated. "There's never been a personal or social relationship between us," Muskie maintains. In mid-1970 he said, "I haven't seen Freddie or talked to him in a year and a half." The two are public acquaintances, not private friends. Vahlsing agrees. "I like everybody," he once said. That may be Freddie's basic problem. An egotistic extrovert, he purposely made himself so visible that in the public mind he became much more closely associated with Muskie and the Maine Democratic party than in fact he was. "People talk about Freddie's parties," Muskie grumbled. "There's no way I can stop people from having parties at a convention." Another Maine Democrat has said, "Freddie goes to a Democratic dinner and he sticks out like a sore thumb. He's loud and he's brash and he's up in front." The pulp and paper manufacturers whose plants have polluted Maine rivers on a scale to dwarf Vahlsing's performance on the Prestile may have a cozy relationship with the Republican party, but at least they have the caution to keep out of the limelight.

The Vahlsing affair, while heavy with overtones of partisan politics (Clark Mollenhoff, President Nixon's resident muckraker, was keeping a close eye on Vahlsing when he resigned in May, 1970, to return to reporting), nonetheless was disturbing to those who had lauded Muskie as the champion of clean water on the national level, only to learn that he had supported a plan to permit the befouling, however temporarily, of one of his own state's waterways. Yet Muskie's explanation was pure Muskie: He had explored the options, he was flexible, and he was willing to compromise. Aroostook County, an economically depressed area, had desperately wanted a second cash crop. It had been possible that the sugar-beet refinery might be a polluter during the break-in period. Well, let it, he had reasoned, but only temporarily; the risk of some—nobody knew how much—pollution was justified for the sake of developing the new crop. And the compromise had been successful. The refinery had been clean. But anyone who has viewed the Prestile Stream, or smelled it in the summer, may raise the question of whether it was physically possible to pollute an open sewer.

To appreciate why Maine would accept the Vahlsings of the industrial world one must understand the economic climate of the state. The people are poor and isolated. Maine is the only state which borders on just one other, and Maine people see themselves as at the end of the line. One of every five Maine families earns less than three thousand dollars a year. Industries that have been willing to come to Maine, primarily those concerned with wood, food, and leather products, tend to offer jobs requiring little skill and paying low wages. The result is that although Maine has a higher percentage of manufacturing employment than the national average, the average industrial wage lags one fifth behind the rest of the country. Since the bulk of the employment opportunities are for either unskilled or semiskilled workers, the demand for skilled labor simply has not kept up with the supply as education levels have increased. The result has been a constant emigration of Maine youth during the past two decades and a population growth of zero, which until only recently was viewed as a distinct liability. Almost one of every six Maine citizens is over sixty-five years old. The political response to this situation has been predictable. The attraction of industry—almost any type of industry—has become a state goal. If environmental pollution is the price that must be paid for gaining industry, Maine has been all too willing to pay it. Only recently, pushed by such conservation-oriented groups as the Maine Natural Resources Council, the League of Women Voters, the strident Maine Biologists Association, which instituted a national boycott of Vahlsing products, and a weekly state newspaper, the Maine *Times,* has Maine begun to recognize that the price is monstrous when weighed against the meager returns.

This increased awareness of the need for environmental control as an explicit state goal is a major factor in a second issue over which Muskie agonizes as he struggles to reconcile his campaign for a pollution-free environment on the national level with a parochial desire for economic improvement in Maine. The issue—the coming of big oil to Maine—divides the state, and as in the case of Freddie Vahlsing, places the reputation of Mr. Clean on the line. The question is whether an oil refinery, to be certainly followed by a satellite petrochemical industry, should be permitted on the Maine coast. Muskie and Maine must decide whether the risk of pollution

—of the air, of the water, and of the state's natural beauty—
is overbalanced by the need for jobs in industry-starved Maine
and by the desirability of lowering some of the highest fuel
rates in the country.

The oil industry is not attracted to Maine by the state's
need for industry, by its natural beauty, or by the urge to
satisfy a consumer demand for lower fuel prices in the New
England region. To the oilmen Maine has only one basic
attraction—deepwater ports, which can accommodate the
giant oil tankers which have become so mammoth that they
have outgrown practically every established port on the east
coast of the United States. Only on the Maine coast, in places
like Machiasport and Eastport in Washington County and in
Casco Bay in Portland, are there harbors deep enough to
handle the supertankers. The oil industry hopes to bring these
supertankers to Maine loaded with crude oil, process the oil
at a refinery, and then transship it in conventional tankers to
markets along the east coast. The crude oil would come from
overseas, or perhaps, by way of the Northwest Passage from the
new rich Alaskan oil fields. The oil companies investigating
Maine sites have been particularly impressed with Machiasport, near the Canadian border, which has depths immediately
offshore ranging from 80 to 170 feet at low tide. By 1969
three companies—the Occidental Petroleum Corporation,
which had struck oil on holdings in the deserts of Libya;
Atlantic World Port Incorporated, a New England firm owned
by a large northeastern oil distributor; and Atlantic Richfield
—had made formal presentations for a refinery. But there were
problems for all three. Occidental and Atlantic World Port
had not been allocated oil-import quotas by the Federal Government. If they were to process foreign crude oil they would
need quota "tickets" and permission from the Federal Government to establish a foreign-trade zone in the area. Atlantic
Richfield, which would process domestic oil and hence would
need no import allotment, had to prove that use of the
Northwest Passage was economically feasible. In 1969 the

giant tanker *Manhattan*, financed by Richfield and Humble Oil, was sent into the Artic to test the passage. The result was indecisive. Whether it was economically feasible to bring oil from Alaska to Maine, refine it, and sell it at a profit, was still in doubt.

When the possibility of an oil refinery was raised, state officials promptly sought federal permission to establish a foreign-trade zone, a move which was opposed by the major oil companies and the political representatives of the oil-producing states, who saw it as a first step toward an increase in the amount of foreign oil which could be imported into the United States. President Nixon, under pressure on the one hand from New England to admit more inexpensive oil to the United States from abroad and on the other from United States oil interests concerned with maintaining present oil price levels, responded by appointing a special presidential oil-study committee. After ten months of study the Cabinet-level task force recommended in early 1970 that the present import-quota system be replaced by a tariff policy which would permit any company able to pay the duty to import foreign oil, on a sort of first-come, first-served basis. The effect would be to push up the cost of foreign oil somewhat while— it was hoped—pushing down domestic oil prices, until they met somewhere in the middle. The domestic oil industry responded with horror, and President Nixon promptly adopted a characteristically political stance by ordering a new study. Said Muskie of the new study, "It's an insult to all New England." Muskie's attitude had been that, at the very least, there should be greater allotments of foreign crude oil to high-use, oil-deficient areas such as the northeast. The presidential study mentioned neither a foreign-trade zone in Maine nor a Maine refinery, and permission for the zone was held in abeyance. During the delay, opposition to a refinery in Maine began to grow. Residents of southern Maine, who had seen the distant Machiasport project as no threat to their own coastline, became increasingly concerned when the Denver-based King Resources Company announced plans to construct near Portland (on Long Island, in Casco Bay) what would be one of the country's largest oil-storage depots and transshipment centers. King and other companies also began exploring the possibilities of an oil refinery in the Greater Portland area. Bumper stickers with such legends as "Oil Men Are Slick Operators" and "Save the Maine Coast" began to appear. Knowledge of the *Torrey Canyon* oil spill and the oil leak in Santa Barbara spurred opposition. Supporters of the oilmen's proposals argued that Portland harbor was already the second-largest oil-handling port on the east coast, with more than 26,000,000 tons passing through each year, and had long avoided a major oil disaster. Finally, in August, 1970, President Nixon announced that he was scrapping further consideration of the institution of a tariff system.

Muskie had cautiously favored the project at the outset because of his desire to see lower fuel bills in New England. His initial concern had focused primarily on the possibility of a refinery in the Portland area, a dangerous undertaking, he felt, because of the heavily traveled shipping lanes in the vicinity. After all, he noted, virtually all the fuel oil used in Maine came to the state by sea, so unless the public was willing to accept a substitute for oil, it would have to live with the risk of spills, while taking all possible steps to prevent them. But by mid-1969 he was obviously harboring doubts. "The pressures on our coastal resources are growing by leaps and bounds," he said, "and we do not have much time in which to plan for their protection. . . . Proposals are coming almost too fast for us to react. The Long Island development . . . and the oil refinery proposals for Machiasport are harbingers of what is to come. And they are the most dramatic signs of change for our state. Are we prepared to deal with them in the context of a wise public policy?" In 1969 the answer to his question was clearly No. However, in early 1970, in response to an outcry of alarmed public opinion, and with Muskie's applause, the Maine Legislature passed almost

unanimously some of the strongest oil-handling and environ-
mental-protection bills ever enacted by a state. One of these
established a coastal-protection fund to be used in cleaning up
spills, which would be financed in part by a tax on every
barrel of oil moving into or through the state. The Legislature
decreed that liability for anyone causing an oil spill was both
absolute and unlimited. No longer was it necessary to prove
negligence. Finally, in the most far-reaching action of all, it
approved a site-location bill which put final authority to
approve any major industrial project—including an oil refinery—in the hands of the state's Environmental Improvement Commission. Oil companies promptly responded by going to court to attack the constitutionality of the bills. Muskie
followed by having his Senate Air and Water Pollution subcommittee hold hearings in Machias, to see, said an aide, "if
it is possible at all to build a clean refinery." Muskie came
away from the Machias hearings still highly skeptical of the
ability of the oil industry to construct a pollution-free refinery
but at the same time unable to foresee a reasonable alternative
for Washington County which could match the economic
returns of an oil facility. Reluctantly, in the fall of 1970, he
concluded that he was opposed to an oil refinery until proper
environmental safeguards could be developed.

Maine attitudes, as reflected in the passage of the strong
environmental legislation, were clearly changing. Only a few
years before, Maine would have welcomed almost any industry that promised to employ Maine workers. The change was
expressed perhaps most vividly by the president of the state
Senate, Kenneth P. MacLeod, who said privately of the pressure for oil development, "Sometimes I'd almost like to see the
Legislature approve the money to build a wall fifty feet high
around the state and keep *everybody* out for the next five
years." Another legislative leader said in reference to Freddie
Vahlsing that if industries weren't willing to foot the bill for
ending pollution they should be driven from the state to the
accompaniment of a brass band at the Kittery bridge, on the

New Hampshire border. Even in Machiasport, where poverty is a constant neighbor, reaction to the prospect of an oil refinery was markedly cool. Author Frank Graham, who had fled New York for Washington County, felt that what he was trying to escape was catching up with him: "We have problems here all right but I don't think we want to solve them by making this into another Bayonne." In an eleven-town referendum in Washington County to sample public sentiment, an oil refinery was approved by only a narrow two-hundred-vote margin. The president of Atlantic World Port, which had sponsored the plebiscite, said candidly of the results, "We didn't win anything." Much of Maine's public opinion seemed to have gone far beyond Muskie's "flexible" approach in dealing with environmental problems.

The stridency of Maine opinion may be remolding Muskie's views. When he became governor, he muses, the big issue was industrial development, how to provide more jobs and more industry. "Today," he says, "it's different. People say, 'We'll take your new jobs, provided they don't do anything to the environment.' Now if Machiasport get a green light, all of us in Maine are going to have some tough questions to answer with respect to the environment. There's no question that Machiasport would mean lower fuel costs. But we have to ask ourselves, Is that benefit worth it, in the face of the risks that go with oil?" Muskie poses the question characteristically, outlining the alternatives, but there is little doubt that he is backing away from the support of big oil for Maine. National political aspirations may be a factor as well. He must protect his reputation as Mr. Clean, a reputation that is daily being placed under more scrutiny in view of the turmoil created by Machiasport and Freddie Vahlsing. And there is no longer a consensus in Maine, as there was in 1954, for the encouragement of all types of industrial development, regardless of the environmental consequences. Both Maine and Muskie are having serious second thoughts.

CHAPTER EIGHT

HAWK

INTO

DOVE

Senator," said Stewart Alsop on the television program "Meet the Press" in August, 1969, "I find it a little difficult to understand precisely where you stand on the overriding issue of Vietnam." He wasn't the only one. The strange thing about this confusion was that Muskie had been involved with the Vietnam question in various official capacities since the earliest escalation of the war. By the time of Alsop's question, he had probably made more of a record on Vietnam than on any other foreign-policy issue. He had probably made more of a record on Vietnam than a majority of his colleagues in the Senate. He had been to South Vietnam on a presidential fact-finding mission in 1965. He had been an official observer at the Vietnamese elections in 1967. In 1968 he had testified before the Democratic party's Platform Committee on the subject, and he had been the lead-off speaker in support of the majority plank on Vietnam in the debate before the full convention. Of course, he had spoken about the issue during various arguments in the Senate, and had voted on bills, amendments, and resolutions related to the war. In his vice-presidential campaign he had occasionally discussed the matter. He had been on several national network programs where his views had been explored. Yet, as the question showed, the Muskie position on the overriding issue was not clearly evident.

One reason for this was that during the Johnson Administration, the spotlight of publicity in the Vietnam debate had been shining only on the most outspoken critics of the war, and Muskie was not one of these. Another was that on this issue, as on others of great importance outside his areas of special competence—pollution, urban affairs—Muskie tended to explain both sides at such length, before indicating his own position, that people lost interest, feeling as if they were listening to a lecturer, not an advocate. ("A criticism I have read from time to time is that Muskie sees more than two sides to a question. He sometimes sees seven," Muskie said to a reporter once. "Well, sometimes there are seven. There are certainly more than two sides to this war thing.") Another reason for a public vagueness about the Muskie war stance was that he often waited until after the debate on a particular point had left the center ring before making up his mind. Muskie "appears determined to be the last man to commit himself to any point of view," Washington *Post* columnist David Broder wrote in June, 1969.

The record was there, however, and while Muskie's views on Vietnam were not out in front—until 1970—or as definite and dramatic as those of some of his colleagues, they could be determined. If they were graphed, it became evident that like many other Americans in and out of public life, he was ex-

periencing a declining belief in the wisdom of the adventure
in Southeast Asia. His fever chart showed a line sloping
gradually downward from 1965 to 1969, then plunging.

In November, 1965, President Johnson asked Senate Ma-
jority Leader Mansfield to lead a study mission through
Europe to Southeast Asia. Three years before, when Mansfield
had led a similar presidential study mission, he had asked
Senator Muskie to go along, but Muskie had been unable to
do so. In 1965, when Mansfield repeated the invitation,
Muskie accepted. There were five senators in all—Daniel
Inouye, George D. Aiken, Caleb Boggs, Mansfield, and
Muskie. They returned in December and reported gloomily
that "a rapid solution to the conflict in Vietnam is not in immediate prospect. This would appear to be the case whether
military victory is pursued or negotiations do, in fact, ma-
terialize. . . . If present trends continue there is no assurance
as to what ultimate increase in American military commitment
will be required before the conflict is terminated. . . . The
situation as it now appears offers only the very slim prospect
of a just settlement by negotiations or the alternative prospect
of a continuance of the conflict in the direction of a general
war on the Asian mainland." This statement would come to
seem so clearly a warning, that is was impossible by the end
of the decade, five years later, to reconcile its existence with
the fact that only a handful of American public officials were
speaking out against the war in 1965 and 1966. Two months
after the Mansfield mission submitted its report to the Senate,
Senator Wayne Morse of Oregon proposed the repeal of the
Gulf of Tonkin resolution, which allowed the United States to
intervene massively in Vietnam. If the Senate had backed
Morse, this gesture might have led to actions that recognized
the full truth of the Mansfield report—that is, deescalation
and disengagement. But only four senators joined Morse. The
same year, only two senators voted against appropriations for
fighting the war.

Muskie was not one of the senators supporting Morse or opposing the appropriations. His own views were not quite so pessimistic as those expressed in the Mansfield report's conclusion. He wrote his constituents that March, "I don't believe that we really doubt our capacity to manage the war in South Vietnam and to convince Hanoi that the conference table is the best course for North Vietnam." He said there were five ways to approach the war: unilateral withdrawal, unlimited escalation, sharply increased military effort short of unlimited escalation, a policy of make do and hold, and unremitting pressure in a carefully measured response to the aggression of the enemy. He favored the last. He also favored, in that dim, dark past, a little less national debate on the subject: "Let us not forget . . . that the enemy is closely watching this exercise in national policy making. Undoubtedly he is encouraged by every concession to his ultimate objective which may emerge from our debate. Each of these sources of encouragement undoubtedly delays the day when he might otherwise be prompted to move toward the conference table. . . . This is a price we must pay, and which we pay willingly for the right to challenge and discuss national policy. And so let us debate, let us discuss, let us consider. But then, let us decide—unite— and press forward in a way that will convince the enemy that we mean and support what we say!"

A year later he told a college audience the same thing, and stated that he still favored the "unremitting pressure" of the Administration's position. That fall he went back to Vietnam, when President Johnson named him as one of twenty-two observers of South Vietnam's elections. He was a diligent observer. Reported Stanley Karnow in the Washington *Post:* "One of the most earnest and energetic of the observers so far has been Senator Edmund S. Muskie (D-Maine), who reportedly surprised U.S. Officials this morning by handing them a list of South Vietnamese editors, lawyers, and other intellectuals he wished to interview. Muskie also took an independent pitch this afternoon by detaching himself from his party, scheduled to fly to Trang, and attending a marathon press conference held by 11 presidential candidates." Muskie reported on his return, "I feel better about our prospects following my visit to Vietnam." He illogically defended the Thieu-Ky regime against charges that it was proved unrepresentative by winning only 35 percent of the vote, with the assertion that such a showing had been predicted in advance. But it was getting harder to defend logically some of the goings-on in Vietnam. Things were not working out as Americans had expected. In December, 1967, Muskie restated his views on Vietnam. Basically his stance was unchanged, but he prefaced the restatement with, and repeated at the end, a quotation from Benjamin Franklin, to the effect that Americans should "doubt a little of (our) own infallibility." He was doubting.

A central issue in the debate on the war at that time was the American bombing of North Vietnam. Advocates of the bombing, led by the President, said that it was necessary to protect American troops in northern South Vietnam, and that it created pressure on North Vietnam to come to terms. Opponents took the opposite view, claiming that our troops would be as safe without the bombing, and that a *halt* in the bombing was likely to lead North Vietnam to the conference table. Muskie declared publicly in an interview with Japanese journalists in January, 1968, that the United States should take "reasonable risks" in order to get negotiations started. He did not say so, but the implication was that a bombing halt would be such a risk. About the same time, he wrote the first of two letters to President Johnson urging just such an initiative. The letters remained a secret until the following fall.

Twice in August of that year Muskie showed publicly that he was seeking a position that would appeal to both the hawks and the doves in his party. In each instance he approached the question as a hawk, while trying to bend the least amount possible to attract the doves toward his side. At the party's Platform Committee hearings in Washington he said he thought a bombing halt "may be justified." It was up to the President to decide first if such a step was not too risky for "troops in the field." He also opposed South Vietnamese Communist participation in the first stage of negotiations. Later that month, in Chicago, he was the first speaker in the three-hour debate on the two planks on the war that had been sent to the full convention for a vote. He began with a conciliatory approach. "We overemphasize our differences and ignore our wide areas of agreement," he said. But the differences were important, and he knew it. The minority plank called for "an unconditional end to all bombing of North Vietnam." The majority plank said: "Stop all bombing of North Vietnam when this action would not endanger the lives of troops in the field." The minority plank also clearly implied that the United States was going to get out of South Vietnam and therefore the present government of that state had better make the best political deal it could with its adversaries: "We will encourage our South Vietnamese allies to negotiate a political reconciliation with the National Liberation Front. . . . The specific shape of the reconciliation will be a matter for decision by the South Vietnamese, spurred to action by the certain knowledge that the prop of American military support will soon be gone." The majority plank said only: "Encourage all parties and interests to agree that the choice of a post war government should be determinated by fair and safe-guarded elections open to all major political factions and parties prepared to accept peaceful political processes."

The majority plank, which the convention approved, was written by Johnson-Humphrey backers. The minority report was a compromise worked out by the competing members of the party's left—the McCarthy and the Kennedy men. Muskie's defense of the majority view, after his opening conciliatory statement, was spirited and not calculated to soothe: "The choice is this: a negotiated settlement with, or a negotiated settlement without, safeguards to protect free elections; a negotiated settlement which forces a coalition government on the South Vietnamese, or one that supports their right to decide that question; a bombing halt with, or a bombing halt without, consideration of the air protection of our troops against the military risks arising north of the Demilitarized Zone—the kind of protection I remind you, that brought relief to our boys at Khe Sahn."

During the ensuing vice-presidential campaign, Muskie, of course, continued to follow the Administration line until Humphrey himself deviated from it. It was never clear just how much leeway Muskie believed he should have in his role as candidate for the second spot (or as a Humphrey backer at the convention). Probably he felt that on this or any issue, the vice-presidential candidate had the obligation to follow the lead of the presidential candidate. When in August, 1969, Muskie appeared on the David Frost television show, Frost asked him if he would have run a different campaign if he had been the presidential candidate. He said, "In retrospect, with the wisdom of hindsight, I think it might have made a great difference if . . . [Humphrey] had at an earlier point made a sharper break [from President Johnson on Vietnam]. For example, if he had chosen to support the so-called peace plank on Vietnam. . . ."

Muskie's public criticism of the war began in connection with the Vietnam Moratorium Day observances of October 15, 1969—national demonstrations against the continuation of the war. Peace advocates had concluded by that time that Nixon's policies were not really different from Johnson's even though the new president had announced the beginning of withdrawals of United States troops and a shift of the fighting burden to South Vietnamese troops—"Vietamization." Muskie endorsed the Moratorium as a "constructive way to intelligently discuss Vietnam." He participated by making a speech at Bates College, in Lewiston, Maine. It was clear that he now favored the views embodied in the old peace plank. The bombing of North Vietnam had long since been stopped; at Bates, Muskie endorsed the other controversial proposal of this plank: "We should make it clear to the government in South Vietnam that our withdrawal is geared to a specific time frame to which they must adjust."

In November, President Nixon went on national television to defend his policies. The divisions in America had never been greater. Pressures were building up that would eventually lead to such tragedies as the shooting to death of college students by members of the National Guard and state police. The President was harsh to his critics, charging them with prolonging the war by encouraging North Vietnam. He said his policy to bring peace was working. Muskie answered him in a Senate speech four days later, criticizing as "verbal re-escalation" the President's statement that winning in Vietnam was essential to peace "not just in Vietnam but in the Pacific and in the world." The Muskie speech was ignored by the press. Other anti-Nixon speeches appeared to have no more effect. The President's popularity rose, and the issue of the war seemed to have been effectively smothered. That strange state of affairs lasted into the new year. In March, Muskie requested and received from the National Press Club an invitation to speak to the prestigious and news-making forum. In his speech, he attacked the silence which he believed now enveloped the nation, and challenged the press to be as aggressive as it had been during the Johnson Administration. In his view, he said, the press was no longer so aggressive, in part because Vice-President Agnew had intimidated the networks. Discussing Nixon's policy itself, Muskie said that Vietnamization couldn't work, that we had not made it clear to the Saigon government that American troops would ever leave, and that the Thieu-Ky government did not deserve support as a democratic regime. He advocated stepped-up activity at the peace talks in Paris, and the announcement of a timed withdrawal of American troops. And he urged "a new national debate." He was resuming the bombing—of President Nixon. Later in the month he began a series of speeches harshly critical of the Administration's Southeast Asian policies.

In April, President Nixon announced on television that his Vietnamization policies were working well. Muskie criticized the speech as "hollow rhetoric" and said that Vietnamization only meant "the continuation of Asians killing Asians. It does not end the war." Less than ten days later, President Nixon surprised the world by sending American and South Vietnamese troops into Cambodia. An unprecedented reaction followed. Hundreds of colleges were closed by rioting. Four students were shot to death by law officers at Kent State University in Ohio, and two at Jackson State College in Mississippi. Before this eruption, Muskie had described the Nixon action as "a cause for gravest concern." Afterward, he introduced a resolution he called "a declaration of peace for Indochina." Its key passage: *"Resolved* . . . the United States Government declare that all its forces and military personnel will be withdrawn from Indochina in a specified time, not to exceed eighteen months from the date of "adoption of this resolution."

Muskie had come to a position as extreme as that of the tiny band of war critics of the early years of the war. He was one of many. "The whole country's view has changed over the same period of time," he said in an interview in mid-1970. "I don't know of anyone's that hasn't." He was asked if his views had shifted because of the alteration in his own position. That is, where he had been a loyal Democrat during a Democratic administration, he was now a leading presidential aspirant during a Republican one. This was not an easy question, since the answer could be easily misinterpreted. Many public figures would probably have waffled or lied. But Muskie said, Yes, the changed role *was* a factor in his changed views. "Parties do have their institutional role with respect to each other. Nixon criticized President Johnson for some of the things he's doing himself. This role has to be fulfilled. The party out of power has more obligation to criticize policies than when it is in power. That's the basis of our party system." Furthermore, he said candidly, his personal situation compelled him to take a more active role in the debate on the war. As a potential presidential candidate, as a party leader, he was under pressure to lead on this issue as on all other important ones.

On the "Meet the Press" program Stewart Alsop had said to Muskie, "I have talked to a good many of your Democratic colleagues, and they all seem to have only one major criticism of you as a potential presidential candidate. That is that you haven't broken your lance in any really major cause, that you haven't been actually out front and center on the really controversial issues. What is your comment on that criticism?"

Muskie had replied, "It might be one I would make myself. In part it is a question of style, I think. I like the rational approach to issues, and sometimes to break your lance it is necessary to be a little irrational in order to stimulate controversy. I have not avoided tough political problems. I think my career over twenty years, running for governor, first, and then all through the years has indicated that. But it is a question of style, and this is something I have got to answer for myself. I do think that a man who is a candidate for president ought to be willing to assert that kind of leadership, 'the break the lance' kind of leadership. I don't know whether I am adapted to it. We'll take a look at it."

Along with the special pressures arising out of his position, Muskie experienced the same reactions as other Americans, in and out of public life, to the war that went on and on. All public-opinion polls showed growing dislike for the American role. There were revelations of such moral calamities as the American atrocities in the field. There were growing fears about the strife at home. In November, 1969, Muskie commented on the My Lai atrocities * in an interview at the Embassy during a trip to England: "In a sense this tragic incident puts all of us on trial. All Americans see in it the

---

* This most publicized of the American atrocity stories concerned the slaying of a large number of Vietnamese civilians by infantrymen in 1968. The incident came to public attention late 1969, when the army announced it would court-martial one officer on charges of premeditated murder of 109 civilians.

questions that bother us all about our involvement in South
Vietnam. It shows the impact we have on Vietnamese society
—and what the war may have done to our own people, in the
sense of brutalizing our young men. Something has happened
to our sense of values."

In mid-1970 Muskie was asked to indicate briefly what had
changed his views over the years. He said, "Our objective has
never been total military victory. Our objective was limited
to the creating of a climate in which the South Vietnamese
people could decide their own political future. There's always
been the problem of when have you arrived at that point. Do
you keep exerting an effort until there's a guarantee of some
kind of future for them or do you move along until you've
done what you think you can, then leave them to settle it for
themselves? In terms of that objective we've bought them five
years of time since 1965, at considerable cost. I don't think we
can afford to buy them much more. It's a question of what we
can afford to do for them. At some point they're going to
have to try their own wings. That point right now is dictated
in great part by our own realities here at home. That's the first
point. The second point I would make is that the war and our
disagreements about it have just had a traumatic effect upon
our relationship to each other which could destroy the in-
tangible things that hold a country together. It's just asking
too much of our country to destroy itself while it seeks to
build a future for this country in Southeast Asia. The third
point is that it has drained resources that ought to be applied
to our own problems."

His questioner persisted. "Were the three reasons co-equal?"

Muskie replied, "I think the three points go together.
Whether they are all co-equal, certainly I am more disturbed
emotionally by what this is doing [at home], destroying the
fabric of our mutual trust and confidence, than by either of
the other two arguments."

Senator Muskie never did get a seat on the Foreign Relations Committee. He first tried in 1959, and Lyndon Johnson

rebuffed him. He tried again in 1961, when a "New England seat" became vacant because John Kennedy had left the Senate for the White House. Naïvely, Muskie thought that since he had supported Kennedy for president, he would be favored to take over his seat. But New Englander Thomas J. Dodd of Connecticut had supported Lyndon Johnson, and the new vice-president had more influence in the Senate than the new president. Dodd got the seat. In 1965 Senator Eugene McCarthy was on the Steering Committee, which made assignments. He called Muskie and told him he could get him Foreign Relations, but he would have to give up either Banking and Currency or Public Works. Muskie said he wasn't willing to do that, and sacrifice his seniority. Muskie recalls, "Gene said, 'Well, then I'll take it myself.' So you see, he went on the committee as casually as he later came off." This was a reference to the fact that in 1969 McCarthy left the committee, enabling Senator Gale W. McGee of Wyoming, a forthright hawk, to become a member. McCarthy's move angered his supporters. Muskie again tried to get on the committee that year, for since the idea of running for president had occurred to him during the 1968 campaign, he now felt that sacrificing seniority on his other committees was worth the chance to become an expert, or at the very least a specialist, in foreign problems. Aspiring presidents are judged so much by their activity and ideas in this field. McGee had first claim, however, because he had been on the committee once before.

Despite the lack of the sought-after committee assignment, Muskie managed to get a good bit of action in this field in his first two Senate terms. In 1959 he was assigned to the Reorganization and International Organizations subcommittee of the Government Operations Committee, and in 1960 to the same committee's National Policy Machinery subcommittee. Later he was chairman of the Banking and Currency Committee's International Finance subcommittee. In all these positions he could work in areas on the periphery of the essential and more glamorous foreign-policy issues of the day. From the beginning of his Senate career, he showed ingenuity in getting overseas to meet international leaders and to be seen in troubled areas. In 1959, at the end of his first session in the Senate, he went on a month-long Public Works Committee junket to Russia. In 1961 he went to Berlin to participate in a panel discussion that would be televised as one of the "America Wants to Know" series, with Willy Brandt, Marguerite Higgins, and Eugene Lyons. And as we have seen, he went to Southeast Asia, the Near East, and Europe with Senator Mike Mansfield's fact-finding mission in 1965, and returned to South Vietnam in 1967 as one of the American observers of the elections. Between 1965 and 1970, he attended several conferences of the interparliamentary type, in Europe, Japan, and the western hemisphere.

On the Russian trip Muskie made a side visit to the birthplace of his father, Jasionowka, Poland. He wrote of the experience in a newsletter to his constituents: "As we approached the village . . . I became profoundly moved as I considered that in a matter of minutes my eyes would see the fields, streams and trees and possibly even faces that my father's eyes had seen last more than a half century before." He described the dilapidated manor house of the estate his grandfather had managed, now a state farm. His eyes lingered on "a small duck pond which may have been a favorite spot for children in my father's day." He was there for only an hour. He tracked down the widow of his father's brother, a tiny old woman of eighty who lived with her war-widowed daughter and granddaughter, and his cousin showed him a picture of his father and mother. His father's sister was dead. Her three sons were away at work. As the news of the American senator's presence spread through the village, people thronged the street. Two state policemen looked on. Muskie left the small house to go to the cemetery, but he found no trace of his grandparents. He summed up his impressions of the visit: "This is indeed the saddest part of Poland." Senators and other friends who have heard Muskie tell the story have described it as a moving experience. Some see in his sorrow for the poverty and lack of freedom of his relatives and country-men a clue to his anti-Russian, anti-Communist, cold-warrior stance. This was his posture all through the late 1950's and the early 1960's. However, it would be a mistake to interpret the senator's philosophy regarding foreign policy and national defense as one shaped by this perspective. Most liberal Demo-crats were resolute cold warriors during this period. Muskie, furthermore, was never actively involved with those conserva-tive nationality organizations that typified the right-wing anti-Communism of quasi-exiles. Senator Phil Hart says, "He has a sense of history about him. Whether that comes from tales his parents told him, the history of his own people, some per-sonal experience of which none of us are aware, or just the man's chemistry, I don't know. It is sometimes suggested that Polish-Americans are especially hard-nosed anti-Communists, and that Catholics generally are, but I've never found Senator Muskie's attitude to be based on that they-overrode-the-old-country-and-you-can't-trust-'em-now business."

Muskie was not now a hard-line cold warrior. He opposed the "conservative" stand on relations with Communist gov-ernments. In 1963, when Ohio's Senator Frank J. Lausche advocated denial of most-favored-nation trading status to Po-land and Yugoslavia, Muskie, like most senators, voted against him. In 1967 he voted against an amendment to the bill to extend the life of the Export-Import Bank which would have prohibited the financing of purchases by nations in conflict with the United States or by third parties that traded with such belligerents. The amendment passed easily. The year be-fore, Muskie had been in the liberal minority that opposed a sense-of-Congress resolution complaining about the Western nations' investments in and assistance to Communist China's steel industry. He voted for the test-ban and nonproliferation treaties. Muskie was never doctrinaire in his cold-war philoso-phy. In 1961, for example, after his trip to Germany, he pro-posed *de facto* recognition of Communist East Germany.

In 1969, when Muskie's International Finance subcommittee wrote a new law regarding United States trade with the Communist nations of eastern Europe, he was instrumental in arranging a compromise version that, while not as liberal as some senators wanted, was more liberal than the law then in effect. He had a small reputation in the field of international trade because of his subcommittee assignments. Generally he regarded himself as liberal but not too liberal in this matter. In a 1961 Senate speech he said, "I submit that neither extreme [of protectionism or free trade] will meet the interests of this nation or of the free world." In 1962 he supported the new trade-policy legislation which gave the President authority to cut tariffs drastically and to assist workers and industries harmed by any resulting increase in imports. He opposed all the amendments offered in the Senate that would have weakened the legislation. In 1967 he was Senate floor manager of the Export-Import Bank bill.

But he was a Mainer and a New Englander, with a need to assist the home folks. In 1965, 1967, and 1969 he introduced legislation that would have limited imports that had an adverse effect on domestic industries; shoe and textile manufacturers in particular were complaining of increasing imports. Muskie voted against the nomination of free-trade advocate Carl J. Gilbert as President Nixon's special representative for trade, and so did his Maine colleague, Margaret Chase Smith. The New England delegation in the Senate was split. Gilbert was confirmed 61 to 30. The other side of the quotas coin for Muskie and his fellow New Englanders was the matter of oil-import quotas. The region produced no oil and consumed a lot, and its senators objected to quotas that kept the domestic price artificially high. In 1970 Muskie was urging a policy of expanded trade, to be achieved by insisting on "realistic" exchange rates and on "equal treatment" in foreign markets (he was referring to tariff and nontariff barriers to trade employed by the Common Market countries and others), by encouraging "fair labor standards around the world," by providing assistance to exporting industries, and by increasing trade with Communist nations. He also advocated more generous aid to workers and industries harmed by increased imports. President Johnson and President Nixon had taken similar positions.

Muskie was consistently on the side of more foreign aid. During the 1960's American support of this approach to international affairs dropped precipitously, and so did the amount of money the Congress was willing to provide. Most of the opposition to foreign aid came from the right of center, but increasingly in the 1960's liberal disillusionment grew—first because of distaste for American support of military regimes such as the one in Brazil, and then because of the increasing belief in some quarters that foreign aid created the preconditions for such disasters as Vietnam. Muskie voted against cutting foreign-aid totals. He voted against cutting military aid, at least by as much as some senators advocated. In 1966, for example, he opposed cutting by $250,000,000 the funds appropriated in the Military Assistance and Sale Act, but supported a cut of $100,000,000. In 1963 Muskie voted against a restriction on the President's foreign-aid decisions affecting Communist-bloc nations, and against another affecting right-wing Latin juntas. In 1970, when United States annual spending for foreign aid had dwindled from the 3.6 billion dollars of 1960 to less than 2 billion dollars, Muskie urged that the United States greatly increase assistance to the developing nations. Speaking at an annual meeting of the International Development Conference, he declared that "the survival of the democratic process and of man himself" might depend on the willingness of the United States and other industrial nations to spend more on economic development in the poorer nations. He said that the minimum American contribution should be equal to the total of loans and grants of all other donors. That would have been 7.5 billion dollars.

Muskie's essentially conservative nature—as opposed to his essentially liberal views on issues of the day—often revealed

itself in institutional loyalties. In the field of foreign affairs
and defense policy, this was noticeable in his continuing support of foreign aid into the decade of the 1970's, and in his
support of the United Nations and the military draft. These,
like foreign aid, had been mainstays of the liberal position
in the era following World War II. In the late 1960's and
early 1970's, some liberals began to question their value.
Muskie still supported the draft, but urged that it be re-
formed. He first expressed this view in a situation that brought
his sentiments to a national audience during the vice-presidential campaign. He spoke to five thousand students outdoors
at the University of Colorado, calling for the changes a 1967
presidential commission had recommended. These included
lottery-type random selection. One of the principal complaints
about the draft during the period of the Vietnam War was that
it was unfair. The military needed only a minority of the
American boys reaching the age of nineteen each year. Those
nineteen year olds who could claim educational deferments
could in many cases escape service altogether by maintaining
their deferment for several years, until they were overage
(twenty-six) or married. The burden of service fell increasingly
on the lower and lower-middle economic groups. The commission recommended—and Muskie endorsed—a lottery which
would make all nineteen year olds equally vulnerable. In the
same speech he also applauded, but did not quite endorse, the
concept of "alternative service" to the military, which would
permit a young man to fulfill his service obligation by participation in the Peace Corps or VISTA. Some political leaders
in America preferred an all-volunteer army. This idea had
been around for years, but received little attention until the
Vietnam casualty rates began to soar, driving home the fact
that draftees formed a significant majority of the combat
troops. Even when the idea gained support, Muskie opposed
it, as he had in the past. As early as 1959, his first year in the
Senate, Muskie had voted against an amendment to the draft-
extension bill proposing a study of alternatives. In 1967 he
voted against a proposal to replace draftees in Vietnam with

volunteers as soon as feasible, and against a more drastic proposal to flatly forbid the use of draftees in Vietnam. In 1967
and 1968 he voted against allowing prospective draftees to
take their lawyers with them when called before their draft
boards. This procedure was regarded by many as a threat to
the selective-service system itself.

In 1969, speaking to a student audience at Miami University, Oxford, Ohio, Muskie went into detail about his objections to a volunteer army, and his proposals for reform of the
draft system. In this speech, he came out for the first time
in favor of an alternative form of service. He said in part:

> The entire system needs to be changed.
>
> First, four thousand local Boards with almost that
> many different procedures and classifications are unne-
> cessary. We should create regional selective service
> boards whose members have a better understanding of
> the problems of their constituents, and who more accu-
> rately reflect the Region's population.
>
> The Boards should be strengthened by the adoption
> of uniform national standards, more adequate appeals
> procedures, and a greater effort to inform the draft
> registrant of his status and the timing of his induction.
>
> Second, all men eligible for the draft should be se-
> lected by lottery at age nineteen, by the fair and im-
> partial random selection recommended by the Marshall
> Commission.
>
> Finally, when he is selected, the draftee should be
> allowed to choose among several options for National
> Service—military and otherwise—which have been de-
> termined to be relevant to the needs of the nation.
>
> Pre-selection deferments should be limited to strict
> criteria of health and occupation, but post-selection
> choices should be as broad as the needs of the country
> require and the imagination of our young people
> permits.
>
> There is an enormous force for good among American
> youth today, and there is no reason why this force should
> be discouraged by lack of opportunity.
>
> When we broaden the choice of service, we must

broaden it for all Americans. We cannot permit an edu-
cated elite to escape military service, dooming the poor
—black and white—to its limited opportunities.

Developing service alternatives open to all young
Americans will require imagination and initiative. Much
of that responsibility will be yours.

Alternative National Service should be as open as
military service. And its tasks should be no less taxing.

Its aims must not be subject to question or doubt. We
should not create a haven for draft-dodgers, a program
providing for two or three years of fun, or a series of
make-work projects.

We have seen the successes of the Peace Corps, the
Teachers Corps, VISTA, and some of the programs of
the War on Poverty. The young people who made those
programs successful have not found the going easy. But
they have found that a vigorous commitment to real
change in the lives of individual people can—bit by bit
—bring about a real change for the better in the world.

In October, 1969, Muskie went to New York to have lunch
with United Nations Secretary-General U Thant. Sol M. Linowitz, the former chairman of Xerox and ambassador to the
Organization of American States, arranged the meeting. He
and Muskie had been classmates at Cornell Law School back
in the 1930's. Muskie's hope was that he could interest
U Thant in a scheme of his to end the war in Vietnam. He
wanted the Secretary-General to act as "honest broker" in the
negotiations. It was not surprising that he would seek out
U Thant, for he had long held the United Nations and the
ideal it represented in high regard. In 1962 he spoke at length
on the subject, to students at Catholic University. He concluded with these words:

Is the United Nations worth it? Its aims, as stated in
the Preamble of the Charter, certainly are.

There is no alternative means to seek those aims. If we
were to abandon the United Nations, we would have to
create other similar means. We cannot isolate ourselves
from the problems of the world. We cannot isolate our-

selves from the impact of those who might seek to destroy us. We cannot isolate ourselves from the millions over the globe whose aspirations motivate them to break out of the prison of their present circumstances. Being of the world, we must be a part of it.

It is not easy to recall instances of United Nations successes. But there have been such. Most of them have related to its activities outside its peace machinery. Even with respect to the objective of maintaining the peace, in all fairness, I think it can be said that the world would be in a far worse state than it is but for the existence and the efforts of the United Nations organizations since 1945.

Muskie supported the United Nations through the decade. He voted for purchase by the United States of UN bonds when the organization was faced with a fiscal crisis in 1962. In January, 1969, he told a United Jewish Appeal audience in New Jersey that in his view the UN resolution of 1967 concerning the Arab-Israeli conflict was the "most logical" basis for negotiating a settlement. And in the fall of the year he went to the lunch with U Thant that had been arranged by Sol Linowitz. The Secretary-General turned him down. When this was made public in late October, Muskie repeated his thinking on the point: "I am certain that the only viable political settlement in Vietnam will be one which the South Vietnamese work out themselves, but a respected third party could pave the way for discussions leading to such a settlement.

"I continue to believe that U Thant's credentials qualify him for such a role. I continue to believe that it would be useful for our government to encourage him to assume such a responsibility.

"In the event that he continues to hold the conviction that he ought not to assume such a role himself, his assistance might contribute to the development of the 'honest broker' approach in dealing with political problems in South Vietnam."

The next month he urged that President Nixon use the good offices of the international organization to work for peace in Vietnam.

During all the years that Muskie kept the faith with respect to the United Nations and foreign affairs, and aid and trade, he also advocated keeping our powder dry. For months after the visit to Russia, in the election year of 1960, Muskie was a persistent "viewing with alarm" participant in the missile-gap controversy. Throughout that year the Democrats, led by Senator Stuart Symington of Missouri, charged that Russia now had a three-to-one lead over the United States in inter-continental missiles, which made the United States highly vulnerable to a first-strike attack. President Eisenhower and his military aides argued that taken as a whole America's strategic forces were still superior to Russian's. America's deterrence and attack capability lay in large part in manned bombers. In January, 1960, Muskie told of his concern over what he had learned of industrial growth in Russia on his trip. He said new productive capacity was being used for weapons, not consumer goods. The United States was not taking this into account, he warned: "Our programs are not adequately supported with funds geared to the real urgency of the [rocket development] situation." Again and again that year he turned to that theme. In the 1961 trip to Berlin, too, he played his role as a liberal cold warrior well. Naturally, he visited the wall (it had been built only a month before he arrived) and was aghast. "The impact of August 13 has been a serious one," he reported solemnly. While he was there he met with General Lucius Clay, who, he later indicated, hinted that the United States was ready to use nuclear weapons in defense of Berlin. "This . . . [was a] most reassuring conversation," he said.

Throughout the early and middle 1960's most senators voted for military and defense spending with hardly a second thought. Muskie was no exception. To be sure, the objection that defense spending was excessive was raised every year. But for most of the decade the senators who sponsored specific cuts in the Pentagon's budget, or a general reordering of priorities, were a lonely and unpersuasive squad. In 1961 Senator William Proxmire of Wisconsin proposed deleting $525,000,000 from the budget earmarked for B-52 and B-58 bombers. He was defeated 87 to 4. A 1962 attempt to limit funds for the RS-70, the white-elephant bomber that was later given up on, was defeated 72 to 15. In 1963 Senator Leverett Saltonstall proposed a 1 per cent Defense Department budget cut. He was overruled in a rare close vote, 45 to 43. In 1964 Senator George McGovern's proposal of a general 4 per cent cut in the Defense Department budget was smothered 78 to 5. Senator Gaylord Nelson proposed a 2 per cent cut; he was defeated 62 to 11. In 1966 McGovern proposed a 2.2 per cent cut in defense spending and was beaten 69 to 18. In 1967 Senator Wayne Morse proposed a 10 per cent cut in military spending; he was turned down 85 to 5. Senator Joseph Clark proposed a 3.5-billion-dollar cut, and was turned down 83 to 6. In every case Muskie voted with the majority. As this recitation suggests, through 1967, and into the third year of the full-scale war in Vietnam, challenges to the Pentagon were simply unrealistic. Only the tiny cuts proposed by Senator Saltonstall, himself a proper Yankee Republican and a member of the Armed Services Committee, received any substantial support.

In 1968, with a cloud of controversy darkening the prospects of the proposal for an expensive anti-ballistic-missile system, significant opposition to military spending first became evident in the Senate. Even Defense Secretary Robert S. Mc-Namara had spoken eloquently against this system's contribution to the "mad momentum" of the arms race when he endorsed it late in 1967. In April, 1968, Muskie voted *for* a proposal by Senator Philip Hart to reduce the expenditures for defense research and development from 7.9 to 7.4 billion dollars. This was defeated by only two votes. But in the votes on funding anti-missile programs Muskie was still to be found on the majority side—though the majorities were now much smaller than they had been in past years. The same day he supported Hart's half-billion-dollar cut, he voted against a $340,000,000 cut proposed by Senator Nelson that would have stopped development of the anti-missile system, and against a proposal by Senator John Sherman Cooper that would have barred use of funds for deployment of the ABM system until the Secretary of Defense certified that it was "practical" and its costs were known "with reasonable accuracy." If Muskie and one other senator had voted Yes instead of No, Cooper's amendment would have passed. In June, Senators Cooper and Hart teamed up to offer a proposal delaying the ABM for a year. Muskie went along with that, but it lost 34 to 52. On August 1 he voted for a Nelson amendment to the defense construction appropriations bill that would have deleted the funds for deployment of the ABM system that year. This lost 27 to 46.

In 1969 Muskie was a consistent opponent of ABM authorizations and appropriations. The Nixon Administration had taken the program to its heart, changing the name from Sentinel to Safeguard. Muskie and some other Democrats were accused of partisanship because of their opposition to the program. Some, like him, had supported it in its early stages, during the Johnson Administration. But Muskie, and others, had begun to have second thoughts in 1968, as the voting record shows. Democratic rhetoric was a little more purple when aimed at Safeguard than it had been when aimed at Sentinel, but the basic questioning had started before the change in names and administration. On August 1, 1969, a year after the vote on the Nelson amendment, Muskie announced his opposition to Safeguard in any form. In a long speech on the Senate floor, he made three principal points: that he had doubts about whether Safeguard would work; that it could make war more likely, not less, and lead to an escalation of the arms race; and that it was diverting money from desperate domestic needs.

> . . . an impressive array of scientific skepticism about the Safeguard proposal, persuades me that it would be a mistake to go ahead with this program, at this time, and in this form. If there is well-founded doubt that the system can function effectively—while it distracts our efforts from other, more appropriate steps and provokes our adversaries to a defensive escalation of the arms race—deployment would be a serious mistake. . . .
>
> The linkage between Safeguard and the MIRV's leads to a stark fact: by deploying a vastly expanded, hard point strike capability along with an ABM area defense system, American retaliatory nuclear forces could be converted into a system suitable for launching a first-strike attack upon the Soviet Union, while minimizing retaliatory damage to the United States. . . . In this context, Mr. President, the Safeguard is a destabilizing weapon, raising the risk of nuclear war rather than diminishing it. As the American MIRV nears perfection and the Safeguard nears deployment, we are reaching for a point of no return in the arms race. If the Senate authorizes the deployment of Safeguard, we may well be stepping across that point of no return. . . .
>
> The grim chain of urban sprawl and rural decline, of individual poverty and social disorganization, of wasted resources and hostile environments will not be broken by a government which is inactive—or preoccupied with hunting the next arms contract.
>
> The chain can be broken only if we set priorities, if we make a commitment to meet them, and if we organize ourselves to fulfill our commitments. I have indicated the priorities I would establish, and they are not the priorities of a fortress America. The priorities I would set are the priorities of men and women and children who have a right to enjoy for themselves the fruits of this world and to help insure the same right for others. The priorities we must set recognize the interrelationship of jobs, income, education, health care, housing, transportation, public facilities, recreation, and en-

vironmental protection in the balanced development of urban and rural communities.

These priorities will never be set or achieved so long as the United States is being bled by the continuing hemorrhage of spending on strategic armaments.

The significance of the conversion of the cautious Muskie was not lost on Senator Proxmire, who had been fighting defense spending for years. He said, "Mr. President, I wish to commend the distinguished Senator from Maine for a superlative speech. I am especially impressed by his presentation because I think we in the Senate, and I think people around the country during the last year or so, have recognized that he is a very careful man, very measured, and responsible, and unusually so."

Five days later, Muskie was one of the only eleven senators who voted for Margaret Chase Smith's amendment to the military procurement authorization bill that would have prevented any funds from being spent on any aspect of Safeguard. This was soundly defeated, 89 to 11. Immediately thereafter, the Senate voted on Mrs. Smith's proposal to bar funds to Safeguard but not to other anti-missile programs. The vote on this was 50 to 51, and so it too lost.* Muskie supported Mrs. Smith.

Muskie was certainly no longer the unquestioning supporter of the give-the-Pentagon-anything-it-wants point of view that had characterized him and almost every other senator in previous years. In April, 1969, he had made a speech at Brown University in which he attacked the "military industrial complex" and said Americans were intimidated by the economic power of the defense establishment. In 1969 he cast a vote symbolic of his view of priorities when he opposed the appropriation of funds for the supersonic transport (SST). This was not really a defense issue, but many of the members of the

* Vice-President Spiro Agnew, the president of the Senate, voted No to make the vote 50 to 51, for headline purposes. But under the rules of the Senate an amendment to a bill needs a majority to carry. The amendment failed even without Agnew's vote.

aforementioned "complex" also advocated development of this plane at government expense. Muskie was one of only twenty-two senators against funds for the SST, while fifty-eight senators favored the proposal. By contrast, in 1967 Muskie had voted with a 54 to 19 majority against cutting SST funds. In 1966 he had voted against reallocating some NASA funds to more down-to-earth programs. In 1968 he had voted against similarly reallocating some military and space funds. He moved a long way from his former position in 1969, and in early 1970 he stepped even further forward. He told the Democratic Policy Council's Committee on National Priorities that establishing national priorities meant little if the national budget did not reflect those priorities. He called for changes in the budget:

> First, we must make more than token changes in the level of military spending. We cannot have guns and butter in the manner we have always thought possible. We must examine every request for military spending with a new skepticism, asking not whether there is a less expensive military substitute, but whether there is a more effective non-military substitute. We must replace the spiraling costs of new weapons and greater overkill with genuine, persistent efforts at arms control. We must take honest risks in pursuit of peace and disarmament.
>
> Second, we must set priorities which protect total human environment—our air, water, and land resources, our health, our homes, and our communities—not priorities which lead to faster planes, mightier weapons, and more ventures into space.
>
> Third, we must make it clear that the unemployment caused by recession is no cure for the rising prices of inflation. Wage and price guidelines are preferable to having men and women thrown out of work.
>
> Finally, the Democratic Party must insist that the Federal Budget reflect the priorities we proclaim. There is no room in our society for empty promises and false commitments. These are the issues of people and peace. They are good ideas, they are good priorities.

During this period Muskie was referred to as "*a* leading candidate for the Democratic presidential nomination in 1972" or as "*the* leading candidate." Nevertheless, his attacks on the Administration policies with respect to defense spending were not well publicized. In October, 1969, he delivered a speech on security and weapons that did make headlines in an unusual way. He took up where he had left off in the anti-ABM speech. This time his target was the MIRV system, in which each missile carried many warheads. "We are already involved in a new cycle of an ever more costly and perilous competition for nuclear superiority," he said. "At the same time we and the Soviet Union have within our grasp a way to restrain this competition and to reassert a saner ordering of our national priorities. . . . We rationalized development of a MIRV system as a response to a limited Soviet ABM system and its possible expansion. The Soviets in turn started development of a MIRV system to insure parity in intercontinental missile systems for themselves. We moved to develop an ABM system in response to the Soviet moves to develop and deploy MIRV's. And so the arms race continues, unrelated to the real security of either nation." He said that what was needed was a break in this cycle. He recalled that he had endorsed the proposal made that summer by Senator Edward Brooke for a United States-Soviet moratorium on the testing and deployment of MIRV's. As yet, nothing had come of it. There should be a bolder move. "Let the United States unilaterally postpone the testing of all our multiple reentry missiles for a period of six months, announcing that we will not begin testing thereafter unless the Soviet Union initiates such tests." Muskie saw only slight risk in this step, since if Russia ignored the gesture, the United States could immediately resume MIRV testing.

The United States and Russia were about to begin the Strategic Arms Limitation Talks. Muskie's proposal was a bold thrust. Vice-President Agnew immediately attacked him, charging him with being willing to "play Russian roulette" with the safety of the American people. The attack brought the Muskie proposal before a wide audience. New York *Post* columnist Max Learner said the speech "might have gone almost unnoticed" if Agnew had not jumped in with his characteristic fury and colorful rhetoric. Muskie was pleased with the attack because it broadcast the idea of a unilateral step, and because it suggested to him that the White House politicians saw him out front in the race to oppose their boss in 1972.

In the spring of 1970, Muskie followed up this proposal with another one. He urged the Senate to support a "mutual interim strategic standstill." This would be a renewable six-month ban on "further deployments . . . [of] land and sea based ballistic missiles, strategic bombers and ABM radar construction and upgrading along with associated missiles." In his view the reason that arms-limitations talks had not been productive in the past was that the United States had held such a sizable lead. Russia simply had not been interested. "Now in 1970 there is the first clear opening. There is both a situation of mutal deterrence and an acceptable parity of nuclear strength between the United States and the Soviet Union. This unique and fleeting opportunity must not be allowed to slip away through design or delay." The idea that a "balance of terror" was the most stable strategic situation in a nuclear world had been developed in the universities and military think tanks early in the decade just ended. It was not an idea that had much appeal to the Nixon Administration. Defense Secretary Melvin R. Laird used the figures documenting Russian success in reaching what Muskie called "acceptable parity" as evidence for the need for further American efforts in developing strategic weapons.

Muskie summarized the benefits he foresaw under his plan this way: "The immediate benefit to the United States of a MISS [mutual interim strategic standstill] is that it would halt Soviet ABM and SS-9 [a giant missile] buildups and multiple warhead tests. . . . Another benefit . . . is that it keeps the door open for permanent agreement either along the same over-all freeze lines or along more limited lines. In this sense, it is a negotiator's pause. . . . If at the end of the freeze period we decide the MIRV's and ABM's serve some useful purpose vis-à-vis other nuclear powers, we can make other kinds of agreements which do not ban these systems. Finally if the talks make unsatisfactory progress or if we become dissatisfied with the freeze, both sides can go forward on their own." He concluded the speech after a blast at President Nixon for not showing more interest in negotiating in this field.

There could no longer be any excuse for anyone's not knowing where Muskie stood on the major foreign-policy and defense issues of the day. On these and all others, especially the war in Southeast Asia, Muskie's views were clear, and they placed him in the vanguard of the liberal wing of his party.

CHAPTER NINE

YANKEE

INSTINCTS

A few days after the 1968 Democratic convention, a reporter drove to Muskie's Kennebunk Beach summer cottage for an interview with the new vice-presidential nominee. Arriving early, he parked his car near the deserted beachfront and had begun the walk up the lane to the Muskie home when he noticed a single swimmer far out in the surf. It was Muskie, alone save for a watchful Secret Service agent, taking a solitary early-morning swim in the frigid Atlantic. He swam steadily for several minutes and then rested, allowing the tide to pull him toward shore. Then, cold and shivering, Muskie stood knee-deep in the surf and with arms crossed over his chest, and hands tucked under his armpits for warmth, gazed intently out to sea. Finally he seemed to shake himself, turned, and with head down, walked up the beach to towel himself.

The image of Muskie standing alone and exposed on the empty Maine beach is etched upon the reporter's memory. For while Muskie is a complex man with many facets, he is basically a man apart. Despite all his success as a public figure, he remains a private person. He shares little of himself with others, and even those who know him best confess they do not know him well. It is frequently said of Muskie that he has few enemies; it appears equally true that he has few deep friends. He is compartmentalized, and not many outside his family see the total man. "Ed is the kind of man who has golfing friends, or fishing friends, or hunting friends, or Senate friends but they are rarely the same friends," says a close acquaintance. "I've known him for almost twenty years and I've come to understand that he cherishes his privacy. I think very few people share that privacy with him for very long periods of time." Muskie's personality was shaped in early childhood, by a shyness he has never completely overcome and by a lack of boyhood friends. Muskie stood alone as a boy and was mocked; as a man he stands apart, as sensitive to exposing his deeper feelings as he is deliberate in formulating his public views. In the Senate he protects himself with a heavy, often impenetrable, barrier of staff members, sometimes to the annoyance of colleagues. If a disagreement occurs "he won't face you and have it out," says another New England senator. "He's always screwing around at the staff level." The result of this caution is a potentially explosive man, and the emotions he struggles to contain erupt in a waspish temper. His anger is often triggered by the trivial. For instance, he has bellowed at Jane upon learning that she's accepted a party invitation which conflicts with his own private plans. And his brooding temperament—for Muskie is a brooder who retreats within himself to consider a problem—is capable of producing a great sense of anger and indignation, often not

over the most crucial issues in the world. The victims of the
Muskie temper are usually the members of his staff, and
while most of them loyally deny the existence of his tantrums,
his administrative assistant Don Nicoll will concede that the
boss has sometimes blown his stack. But, adds Nicoll, Muskie
is aware that he can be harsh to his staff: "He goes out of his
way to be nice or say something kind after he's cooled down."
Muskie's former aide George Mitchell, now a close associate,
describes him as having "a good temper but a largely im-
personal one." Mitchell recalls that when complaining of poor
scheduling in Pennsylvania during the 1968 campaign, "he
got really warmed up and started going up my back and down
the other side. I just sat there and after ten minutes of a tirade
he finally talked himself out and it's followed by a long embarrassing silence. And then he calmed down and turned to
me and said, 'I wonder why you'd give up a good law practice
in Maine to come down here and work your tail off—to have
to take that kind of talk from me.' "

Sometimes men feign loss of temper to make a point or
win an argument. Nobody doubts that Muskie's temper tantrums are genuine. In the vicious encounters he had with
Representative Dingell and Senator Harris, both his adversaries were certain there was nothing fake or calculated about
Muskie's behavior. He was raging with true anger.

Jurisdictional disputes are not the only thing to raise the
Muskie hackles. He has grown accustomed to the deferential
treatment a prominent United States senator receives. On a
recent trip to the South he was delayed getting to Washing-
on's National Airport by traffic on the Fourteenth Street
bridge. He had asked Eastern Airlines to hold the flight for
him, but it left before he arrived. At the terminal he was taken
to a VIP lounge and told by an apologetic female Eastern
official with a charming French accent that to let the plane de-
part on schedule made one man unhappy, but to hold it up
would have made fifty people unhappy. Did the Senator see? No,

Muskie didn't see. He fumed at the personal inconvenience; he refused to discuss it.

Reporters who have covered Muskie are accustomed to his testy nature. After the 1970 press conference in which he denied Nader's charges that the air-pollution bill had been watered down for the benefit of industry, he was approached in the hall outside his office by a magazine reporter who had been sharply questioning him just moments before. Now, the reporter wanted to know, what did Muskie think would be the effect of Nader's charges on Muskie's reputation with the youth of the nation? Muskie turned on the reporter, his eyes blazing with anger, his lips and hands literally trembling. Obviously attempting to hold his emotions in check, he replied in a strained voice that he hoped his record would stand up against such charges. Muskie staff secretaries who watched the encounter whispered to one another that they had never seen him so angry.

Somewhat earlier, during the controversy over Judge Haynsworth's nomination to the Supreme Court, Muskie held a weekend press conference in Maine and was asked by a reporter how he planned to vote. "I can see that some of you fellows don't read the papers much up here," Muskie shot back, adding that he had already announced that he intended to oppose Haynsworth's appointment, and then explaining why. The reporter, angered, went back to his office and checked the entire Muskie file. Not a word from Muskie as to how he planned to vote. It was later discovered that Muskie had indeed previously announced his vote, tossing off the information almost as a throwaway line during the middle of a press conference in Chicago. The news of his decision had simply not found its way back to Maine.

Muskie's periodic petulance at press conferences seems rooted in the fact that he is basically distrustful of them. By nature a precise, deeply intelligent man, Muskie frets that the results of a complex, involved discussion of a public issue will be reduced to a distorted headline or to thirty seconds of film on the evening news. As he campaigned for reelection in 1970 he ruminated over criticism from some of his former Maine supporters in the Republican party who were distressed at what they felt was his too persistent criticism of President Nixon. "There is the problem of making sure that Maine people understand that I haven't changed," he said. "This is partly the business of the [news] media. I make a speech in some other part of the country and I hold a press conference and some reporter asks me a question; I didn't plant the question, I didn't raise the issue. But he's obviously looking for news or headlines and he asks me for something about the President with which I disagree. And that's all anybody gets. I can't recall making a speech that's filled with nothing but criticism, I try to be positive. But more often than not it's the press conferences and the story that comes out of them never says that it was a press conference or that I said this in answer to a question. The impression is that the criticism was the subject of my speech and that I spent the evening belaboring the President. It's the nature of the communications business and it is not representative of the way that I say things or do things. But the nitpicking aspect of it is the product of the system and it's nothing that I complain about. I recognize it."

Muskie's temper can also lead to stubbornness, a characteristic often overlooked by those who tend to see him as overly "flexible" (a favorite Muskie word) or as too prone to compromise. For Muskie can be stubborn, particularly when he feels his integrity has been assaulted. During the 1964 reelection campaign his opponent, United States Representative Clifford G. McIntire, charged that Muskie's vote which helped defeat the "peril point" amendment to President Kennedy's Trade Expansion Act in 1962 was a "factor" in the closing of a woolen mill in Lisbon Falls, Maine, arguing that if the restrictive clause had been a part of the act, domestic industries would have been better protected against foreign imports.

The "peril point" amendment would have permitted cutting off the importation of foreign-made goods whenever it was determined that the imports were threatening competing domestic industry. The amendment had failed by a two-vote margin; it would not have passed even if Muskie had voted for it. McIntire's charge was the kind of general rhetorical allegation to which politicians routinely resort. Muskie's aide George Mitchell, along with others on his staff, saw "the statement as so absurd on the face of it that it was kind of laughable." But Muskie did not laugh. He is specific in what he says, and expects others to be the same. Raging, he called McIntire's charge "a conscious, calculating, and vicious political lie." Mitchell, then relatively new to Muskie's staff, found the "peril point" amendment episode "instructive to me. I think it illustrates something about the nature of the senator." Muskie had already agreed to debate McIntire twice on statewide television, and Don Nicoll was negotiating with McIntire's staff about debate subjects. Muskie and Mitchell were campaigning along the coast, driving from Boothbay Harbor north to Belfast. During a stop at Thomaston, while Muskie addressed a street-corner crowd from a flatbed truck, Mitchell telephoned Nicoll in Portland to check on the progress of the negotiations. Nicoll reported that they were close to agreement on a topic involving a variety of national affairs. "The senator had finished his speech," Mitchell recalls, "and we were driving toward Rockland and he said, 'What did Don have to say?' When I told him, he immediately said, 'Now listen, Cliff has made this peril point thing the issue and that's what the debate is going to be about. He picked the issue, I didn't.' So when we got to Rockland I called Don again and told him what the senator wanted and he said, 'Gee, I don't think we can ever get them to agree to that.' When we started driving again I told Muskie it would be difficult and he said, 'Damn it, who wants to debate, him or me? You just call Don up when we get to the next stop and tell him that's what it's going to be.' Finally, by the time we got to Belfast, they had agreed to it." The topic of the debate was "Did Senator Muskie's vote on the 'peril point' amendment cause the closing of the Worumbo Woolen Mill?" As a serious subject for debate it was fully as laughable as McIntire's original charge. To Michell the episode illustrated that "when you get down to it the senator is a tough nut. He really is. He's capable of imposing himself on a situation. In that instance he recognized that Cliff was anxious to debate and so he was going to put it on terms most favorable to him. And he did."

The staff which Muskie interposes between himself and others is by senatorial standards only passable; as that of a major United States public official seeking the presidency it has been described as inadequate. Ralph Nader, during his curious battle with Muskie, termed the staff "amateur," an evaluation he said was shared by Washington political observers. Although there has been much criticism of the staff in Washington, the characterization as amateurish is an overstatement. This judgment must be viewed in the light of the general disposition to impute efficiency and talent to an organization which wins and to deny it to a loser. As a result, the tendency has been to view Nixon's 1968 campaign staff as a marvel of precision and public relations although in fact it may have been responsible for blowing an almost insurmountable lead. In general, the Muskie Senate staff is composed of relatively competent and devoted men and women in their twenties, thirties, and early forties, a sort of New England version of middle-class America. They represent a wide range of religious and educational experiences: Jewish, Catholic, Protestant; Harvard, Bowdoin, Mount Holyoke, and George Washington. Donald E. Nicoll, his administrative assistant, like Muskie a product of the Depression, remembers as a boy church charity groups bringing food baskets to his home on holidays, but other staff members have had comfortable and secure childhoods. Of all Muskie's staff, only

Nicoll is generally singled out for praise. He's held the job since 1962 and is probably the one man who best knows the many Muskie minds and moods. And like Muskie, he is a loner. As an administrative assistant he has as much authority as anyone at his level on Capitol Hill, but his name is largely unknown. Another administrative assistant said of him recently, "If you wandered around the halls and asked people like me who Don Nicoll is, few would know. It's curious to me that he is the most powerful administrative assistant and also the least known. Don isn't part of our club. We never see him." Now in his mid-forties, Nicoll still looks as he did in the yearbook photos taken at Boston English High School, Colby College, and Penn State, where he received a masters degree in American history. Small and slight, with mouse-colored hair falling inevitably over his brow, he seems too pale and frail to lift, let alone carry, his bulging briefcase. He has the qualities Muskie needs—a brilliant, inquisitive mind combined with an unflappable temperament. His intellectual curiousity ranges from the fate of the Maine clam to waste-disposal methods on the Rhine; he is probably one of the best generalists in Washington. Frank Coffin, then the young chairman of the Maine Democratic party, first spotted Nicoll's potential in 1954 when he hired the news editor away from a Lewiston radio and television station to become the party's first executive secretary. In 1956, when Coffin went to Congress, Nicoll became his administrative assistant, and he held this job until 1960, when Coffin was defeated for governor. He moved to Muskie's staff in 1961 as a legislative assistant and news secretary and became administrative assistant in 1962, when his predecessor, John Donovan, now a college professor in Maine, left to Join the Labor Department. Nicoll's contribution with respect to research and advice has been large, and in those areas he has been indispensable to Muskie. In public relations he has been a liability in the eyes of many Maine Democrats. His manner is restrained, clipped, and abrupt, both to those he respects and those he does not. "Don lacks any sort of human touch," says one acquaintance, "as well as any political sense. In a campaign, keep him as far away from politics as possible." Some credit Nicoll with masterminding Coffin's defeat in 1960. "There's no question that Don had a lot to do with losing that campaign," says Benjamin J. Dorsky, the blunt, cigar-smoking chairman of the Maine State Federated Labor Council. "It was his campaign, operated by him; he wouldn't listen to anybody else, and the responsibility for losing was his. He tried to change Frank's image, from one of a serious individual, into some sort of a comic. I remember they had him telling jokes at a political meeting and to illustrate one of the stories Don actually had Frank crawling under a table." Dick McMahon, manager of the early Muskie campaigns, describes Nicoll as "not listening enough to the folks back home, to Ben and to state committee members. He's impatient with them and he doesn't want to waste his time. But that's Don's only shortcoming. He's absolutely necessary to Ed, and if he lacks any political sense, Ed has got the personality to overcome it." Perhaps more serious is the complaint that Nicoll has created a one-man Senate shop by refusing to delegate more responsibility. George Mitchell doubts that: "I've heard that, but I worked there for three years and I found myself making a lot of decisions. Perhaps it's more a reflection of the people in the office. If a fellow wants to take a certain amount of initiative, has a willingness to assume responsibility, he can do it in that office." The fact remains that aside from Charlie Micoleau, an able researcher and strategist Muskie picked up from the Maine Democratic headquarters in 1970, few in Muskie's Senate office have elected to develop their own meaningful relationships with Muskie or to exercise much authority.

Although no longer on Muskie's paid staff, Mitchell is considered one of the top tacticians in the senator's coterie of advisers and the man he turns to for political advice in Maine. Now the state's national committeeman, Mitchell's influence is rapidly enlarging in Democratic national politics. He was one of the twenty-seven named to the McGovern Commision, which studied the need for modernizing the convention process, and earned a reputation as one if its most thoughtful and diligent members. Some fellow national committeemen consider him a future national chairman. In Maine Democratic circles Mitchell is ranked far above Nicoll in ability. "I think all of us here in Maine would be happier if George— not Don—were running the Muskie show," confides one Maine Democrat. It was Mitchell, during the 1968 campaign, who drafted some of Muskie's more memorable speeches, and he continues to contribute about one a month. Mitchell came away from the 1968 campaign, a hurriedly jerry-built amateur affair, with something less than awe for some of the Democratic party's more prominent strategists: "We'd never been through a national campaign before, so we had a couple of meetings with people who had been active in previous campaigns—people like Bill Moyers and Fred Dutton—and they were going to get a network of people to submit ideas to us. But it wasn't nearly what I had anticipated. We found that the really good, fresh ideas came from unexpected sources." During the middle of the campaign, Mitchell met with a half dozen young New York lawyers who had written to him volunteering their services. "Look," said Mitchell at a breakfast with the group, "I haven't the least idea what you fellows can do, so just imagine that you're the candidate for vice-president. Then sit down and write what you'd like to say to the nation and send it to me." Surprisingly, the results provided Muskie with some of his better speeches.

The best of Muskie's speeches, however, come not from his staff but from the Senator himself. He is not only one of the best speakers in public life in America today but is a magnificent writer as well. "Writing for Muskie is difficult because he's such an able writer himself," says one contributor. "He measures everything against his own standards and often it doesn't come up to scratch." As a result Muskie will often abandon a prepared text in favor of an extemporaneous speech of his own. His language is invariably polished, carefully honed and hauntingly rhythmical, ebbing and flowing like a Maine tide. He evokes images, not sharp or tangible, but cool and illusive. Nor is a Muskie speech easily dissected; like the man himself it must be experienced as a totality; the shading of one paragraph must be weighed against the nuance of another. A typical Muskie speech is an extension of the man: thoughtful, controlled, ever reasonable. This national image of reasonableness has led to some carping among his colleagues in the Senate. "This attitude of sweet reasonableness is something new," says one senator. "Whenever I had to deal with him he stuck to his point like glue."

Whatever the quality of his staff, Muskie is extremely loyal to his employees. In replying to criticism of Nicoll he has called him the most intelligent person on the Hill, in Washington, on anybody's staff. He has never openly fired an employee, even when circumstances might have justified it. In 1963, when President Kennedy spoke at the University of Maine a month before his death, a Muskie aide, John P. Jabar, of Waterville, excluded Republican Representative McIntire from the presidential receiving line. When McIntire protested that he had a right to be there, Jabar threatened to have the Secret Service haul him away bodily. The incident, which offended the Maine citizen's strong sense of courtesy and fair play, forced Muskie to apologize to McIntire. He later blistered Jabar privately, but he kept him on the staff. A few years later Jabar, a ten-thousand-dollar-a-year field assistant, was the source of even more acute embarrassment to Muskie. Without Muskie's knowledge, Jabar became president of two corporations in Maine which secured loans for the financing of nursing homes in Waterville and Augusta. Both Senator John R. Williams of Delaware and Representative H. R. Gross of Iowa questioned the propriety of a federal employee seeking Federal Government loans for private business activities. On paper, the lash-up looked particularly sinister. Associated in the nursing-home enterprises with Jabar was Paul J. Mitchell, the brother of George Mitchell, then chairman of the Democratic state committee. Also an officer in one of the nursing-home corporations was Jerome H. Barnett, the Maine field coordinator for the federal Economic Development Administration. One corporation received $415,000 in loans from the Federal Housing Administration, which was headed in Maine by Muskie's close friend and former campaign manager Dick McMahon. From the federal Small Business Administration the second corporation received a loan of $345,000. The SBA in Maine was headed by Maurice Williams, who had been Muskie's administrative assistant when he was governor. Muskie knew nothing of these projects or of Jabar's connection with them. When he did learn of them, he had Jabar divest himself of his interests in the nursing homes. The affair, which was first disclosed in the spring of 1968, just when Muskie was scenting the strong possibility of the vice-presidential nomination, disturbed him, but he refused to turn on Jabar. Several months later Jabar quietly resigned from the staff.

Muskie has remained scrupulously honest throughout his private life. He has lived exclusively on his public paychecks and what he has been able to earn as a speaker. His older sister, Irene, is frankly of two minds when she considers the possibility that Ed might become president. "In one way I think he'd make a good president because he's conscientious and honest. He's really a terribly honest man. The idea of cheating just wouldn't occur to him. But in another way I don't know. I just don't know whether he'd be able to take all the criticism that a president gets. He's so sensitive to criticism." Muskie has been basically a man of simple personal wants and he remains frugal. Early in the 1960's, when the Muskies moved into a new Washington home and money was, as always, scarce, United States Senator Edmund S. Muskie, the son of a tailor, made the living-room drapes. It is said that he has sat around the house in the evening licking trading stamps. "He was always a very conservative fellow that way," remembers Maury Williams. "When he was governor we'd do a lot of traveling around and we stayed at some beautiful places. I remember him saying, after we'd been visiting at a particularly lovely house, 'Well, they can have it. I've got what I want at China Lake.' And that's the way he really felt about that little camp." Only since the 1968 campaign thrust him into the center of the political spotlight has Muskie donned some of the more visible trappings of success. He's become a more stylish dresser, his ties are wider, his suits have a more expensive cut. But he is not a wealthy man. In 1968 he announced a net worth of $106,469, but of this total the largest part consisted of a Maryland home valued at $65,000 and the nonwinterized Kennebunk Beach cottage valued at $30,000. The two homes had mortgages totaling $48,647, or half their combined market value. Muskie's only liquid assets were $2,535 in cash plus $14,940 in securities. His other major assets included $18,550 in contributions to his Civil Service retirement fund and $12,930 in life insurance. It was not until 1969 that Muskie's income began to soar. He received $80,183.25, in speaking and writing fees, during the year, the high for any Senate member, and in 1970 was to get a guarantee (thought to be about $90,000) for a series of books on major public issues. Despite the newfound wealth, Muskie remains extremely conscious of his clean public image and wants to keep it that way. He knows he is constantly being measured in Maine against Senator Smith, who refuses to accept any campaign contributions, save for support from the GOP state and senatorial campaign committees. And he knows that the case of Thomas Dodd, who was censured by the Senate after a disclosure in 1967 that he had diverted campaign funds to his private use, has raised questions as to the use of campaign funds. "You can't develop a staff without money," he says, "but the problem of how you go about raising money without it being suspect or subject to criticism is very real." Some contributions in 1970 from sources that were considered dubious were returned.

While Muskie never had a group of close friends, either in the Senate or outside it, the pressures of national politics tend to make socializing even more difficult. One vacancy in the ranks of Senate friends has been left by Gene McCarthy, an old sidekick and neighbor who used to drop into the house in the evening for conversation, and Muskie seems genuinely to regret the loss. It is ironic that Muskie's only brush with the law came in 1965, when Mr. Clean and McCarthy, who was to be tabbed "Clean Gene" in the 1968 campaign, were caught bird hunting over a baited field on Kent Island, off Maryland's eastern shore, and were fined $27.50 apiece. The fine pained Muskie, who is widely respected as a sportsman in Maine. Since moving to Washington he has had less time for hunting and fishing and has moved instead to golf, a game he picked up a few years ago. Spurred on by a fluke hole-in-one which he hit immediately after learning the game, he continues to approach it with a sort of benevolent gusto, playing in the mid-90's. But Muskie, who looks at home in the woods or behind a duck blind, is just not constructed for golf and occasionally simply discussing his game makes him angry. His golfing partners at the Webhannet Country Club, adjacent to his Kennebunk Beach home, are a diverse breed, including Charles E. Lander, Jr., a telephone-company supervisor and an old friend from his early days in Waterville; Maine Superior Court Judge Alton A. Lessard; Portland businessman Arthur Benoit, Jr.; Robert Marx, a retired chief of the Maine state police; and John Levenson, a Chicago attorney and friend of thirty years, who also summers in Kennebunk. When he fishes, his companions are apt to be his eldest son, Steve; Gene Letourneau, the outdoor writer for the Waterville *Sentinel;* or Arthur Thibodeau, a retired Waterville police chief. Bird hunting, once a Muskie favorite, is a rarity these days

because the fall bird season usually coincides with a congressional session or a campaign. He has not hunted in Maine
since 1966. Photography, another favorite hobby (he is proud-
est of a color photograph of President Kennedy taken while
they were sailing off Boothbay Harbor in 1962), has also been
abandoned. "I haven't had the camera out of the case since
last Christmas; I just don't have the time," he said in mid-
1970. The same is true of gardening (as a boy in Rumford he
was a 4-H Club member, and once cultivated a patch of prize
carrots): "I just don't have the time." Nor can he recall the name
of the last novel he read, or when. "These days most of my
reading is about issues, problems. The cities, pollution, Vietnam—there isn't time enough to read everything about Vietnam."

Muskie's personal relationship with his fellow Maine senator, Margaret Chase Smith, is reserved. They come from
opposite sides of the political fence, they stand tall in the
same state, and each is envious of the other. In 1964, when
Senator Smith became the first woman ever to seek the presidential nomination of a major political party, the move upset
the delicate balance of power between the two, and Muskie's
staff worked to restore it. After all, Muskie was seeking reelection that year and needed to maintain his own political
clout. Shortly after Mrs. Smith announced she would seek the
nomination, a friend of Muskie's was discussing the problem
with Don Nicoll. What are the options open? he asked. "How
about vice-president?" said Nicoll calmly. The boomlet for
Muskie—never serious—was begun, and friends and aides
worked to plant the seeds of the possibility with reporters.
One aide recalls a meeting with a reporter for the *Wall Street
Journal*. He worked the conversation around to possible Democratic vice-presidential choices and then suggested Ed Muskie
as having a chance. "Ed who?" the reporter asked.

In Washington, Muskie golfs frequently with Maine Democratic Representative William D. Hathaway, proof that he
doesn't carry a grudge onto the fairway. For in 1968 Hathaway

led a convention fight to deprive Muskie of designation as the Maine delegation's favorite son. Hathaway, a strong supporter of Bobby Kennedy, was aware that if Muskie were the favorite son, Maine's votes might go in a bloc to Humphrey. Muskie, seated on the platform at the state convention, was stunned as Hathaway spoke in opposition to the favorite-son designation. Muskie sat cross-legged and alone, in obvious anguish as the debate continued for more than an hour, until his supporters had won. Finally he stepped to the microphone, gaunt, rumpled, and bitter, to glare in silence for a full minute at the packed convention hall. This, he said, was the most embarrassing and painful day in his political life: "If I realized six or eight weeks ago that . . . I would be subjected to the ordeal I underwent today I would never have given my commitment" to permit the favorite-son designation. He told them in measured tones, his shaggy, craggy head shaking with emotion, of how tortured he had felt as the debate had continued, and how he had longed to stand up and call it off; of how he had kept silent only because he felt honor bound to abide by the sense of the convention. To hear his fellow Democrats claim that he might use the favorite-son role as a means of frustrating the will of the Maine delegates at Chicago was agonizing, he said. "To be the favorite son was an honor I did not seek and do not want. I pledge my word," he said, anguished that a pledge was even needed, "that the free democratic process will prevail in the Maine delegation and I will not frustrate the free democratic process." The speech was over. The audience, which had been nearly mesmerized by perhaps the finest performance of the tall Lincolnesque figure, rose and cheered as one. He turned slowly away from the microphone then, brushing a tear from his eye. "He couldn't have been madder at Hathaway for what he did, and I suspect he'll never forget it," Mitchell says. "I know I wouldn't. But Muskie isn't a vindictive guy. He's been remarkably restrained and decent with his relationship with Bill since then." Two weeks after the convention, Muskie and

Hathaway were playing golf together. "There were no hard feelings," Hathaway says, "but I made sure I played behind him all that afternoon."

The Hathaway episode is an indication of the amount of power Muskie does not wield within the Maine Democratic party. Considering that he is both the Moses and the patronage saint of the party, his direct influence is minimal, although his imprint is plain. He has steered clear of supporting primary candidates openly, and according to Mitchell, "he's extremely sensitive to the possibility that people think he's running the show." Muskie, who began the adventure in 1954 not with the idea of becoming a successful political figure, but rather in order to build a solid two-party system in Maine, recognized early that the party could not bear the imprimatur of a single man if it was to be more than spasmodically successful. Muskie has been inordinately successful, but then so has the Maine Democratic party. To a degree that few politicians would believe, Muskie keeps out of the machinery of the state party. When, in early 1968, the amateurish forces of Gene McCarthy in Maine attempted to capture a bloc of seats on the Maine delegation, they were unable to comprehend the absence of Muskie's influence on the delegate-selection process. Some of the McCarthy people gave the impression that they actually thought that all Muskie had to do was push a button in Washington and the entire Democratic party in Maine would jump. At one point prior to the convention, Mitchell, who was to be its chairman, called Muskie to discuss the plans and referred to the pending battle among the Humphrey, McCarthy, and Kennedy slates. "Don't mention it to me," Muskie said. "I don't want to have anything to do with it." Not that there was any real need for Muskie to attempt to persuade delegates how to vote. Maine rank-and-file Democrats, who had only begun to taste victory under Muskie, were of the pragmatic school. They believed that only if Humphrey were nominated did Muskie stand a chance of being picked as a running mate, and they responded accordingly. With few exceptions they opted for Muskie; hence they supported Humphrey.

Muskie's low-key approach to power in Maine, like his wariness of stretching for leadership positions in the Senate, is both typical of the man and a reflection of the Yankee nature. For Muskie is, in character and temperament, an extension of the composite Maine citizen. Just as the average Maine man is reasonable and prudent, so Muskie and indeed Margaret Chase Smith, crystallize those qualities on the national scene. Both, to an uncommon degree, reflect the traits of the citizenry they represent. The flinty Maine voter is distrustful of the flamboyant and the impulsive; he admires silence and common sense. If the Maine lobster catch is declining, the Maine fisherman doesn't waste his time jawboning about that fact; he looks for the cause and then struggles for a solution. So with Muskie it is not enough to recite the nation's ills or the failures or omissions of the opposition; his character and Maine's demand the search for solutions. In that sense Muskie is more a carpenter than an architect, more a doer than a dreamer. And it is largely because of these qualities—because Muskie seriously studies a problem, genuinely strives to understand and to appreciate varying points of view and finally, to reach a sane, sensible, workable conclusion—that he has inspired the trust and confidence of the Maine voter. It was this sense of genuineness and reality which catapulted Muskie to national prominence in 1968. "Muskie was the only guy in 1968 that didn't sound like a worn-out political hack," says former presidential adviser Richard N. Goodwin. "He was the only one talking to the people who didn't sound like a holdover from the 1930's." Now, as he looks ahead to 1972 and the possibility of the presidency, Muskie is under some pressure to abandon those very qualities which first propelled him to success. In an age of instant coffee and instant news, Muskie is being urged to be quicker off the mark, to be more flamboyant, to fire more quickly, to be more critical. Yet those are not Maine characteristics, and they are not Muskie's. His solid reputation in the Senate has not been made by shooting from the hip. When Muskie came to the Senate he took a deep interest in those then unimportant committee assignments which were thrust upon him by Johnson. Instead of languishing, he showed genuine concern about such legislation as the Solid Wastes Disposal Act long before anyone, including himself, realized that human excrement would one day become a national political issue.

Kansas editorialist William Allen White once wrote of Calvin Coolidge, "Above all, he was honest. And he was also courageous but he never let his courage get the best of his judgment. When in doubt, he stopped." Much the same may be said of Muskie. He is thorough, precise, cautious—so cautious in fact that deliberateness sometimes crosses over the line into procrastination. But his Yankee instincts are basically sound. When a freshman senator arrived in Washington in the early 1960's, he was approached by Bobby Baker, then a powerful Democratic aide, with an offer to put him in contact with "some fellows who can help you with your campaign debts." The new senator, not liking the sound of it but hesitant to offend Baker, went to Muskie for advice. The reply was short and to the point: "Tell him you're not interested."

CHAPTER TEN

FRONT-
RUNNER

In the fall of 1969, after Senator Edward Kennedy announced he would under no circumstances seek the presidency in 1972, Senator Muskie resumed his quest for that office. As the front-runner he soon learned what he had begun to suspect before Chappaquiddick. The staff of a senator from a small state is not adequate for a serious presidential candidate. He told Associated Press reporter Joseph Mohbat of his troubles during a swing through the Middle West late in the year. "The problem is," he said, "we've spread ourselves so thin this year that we didn't do anything well. . . . I do get testy and irritable, and it's because I get so damned frustrated when I can't do something thoroughly.

"We're so busy in our office that only the unimportant things surface. Every damned day I leave the house with something specific I want to do when I get to work. And twenty-nine times out of thirty, I never get to do my own thing; I'm always doing somebody else's.

"The problem is how to control your own time so that you can do what you really ought to be doing—developing real, in-depth knowledge of the issues and speaking out on them.

"Well, next year we've got a campaign in Maine, there'll be some funds coming in, some extra staff. Then I'm going to start doing just that—in my own way I think is right."

Muskie brandished a sheaf of papers to illustrate his point.

"Look at this. It's an awful speech, just awful! I can't give this tonight. But we've nobody on our staff who has the time to research these issues and write a decent speech. We get volunteers to do some, but they're just not good enough. This is the whole problem this year. . . ."

For several weeks close friend and chief aide Don Nicoll had been working to set up an organization of very top-level volunteers who would help the senator mount his campaign. Muskie described it as consisting of two groups of advisers—those in Washington and those around the country. "Their purpose is to educate Ed Muskie," was the explanation. The Washington group grew to about three dozen men within a year, and was heavy with former Johnson-Kennedy policy makers. For instance, when it came to defense and foreign-policy matters, Muskie could count on former Secretary of Defense Clark M. Clifford; former Deputy Secretaries Paul C. Warnke and Cyrus R. Vance; former Ambassador W. Averell Harriman; Benjamin Read of the State Department; Harry McPherson, a White House counsel under Johnson; Leslie Gelb, a young and scholarly defense planner; and others. Arthur Okun, a former member of the Council of Economic Advisers occasionally offered assistance in his field. So did Ross Davis, former Small Business Administrator. On civil-rights matters, Muskie sought the opinions of William Taylor, formerly staff director of the Commission on Civil Rights. Another adviser on civil rights was Lester Hyman, formerly Democratic state chairman in Massachusetts. Joseph A. Califano, Jr., President Johnson's chief domestic adviser, also was available.

In addition to this group, there were numerous individuals around the country—lawyers, businessmen, professors, writers —who were available for all sorts of chores, from giving advice to making contacts, to arranging trips or invitations. For instance, Theodore Venetoulous, a Baltimore author and teacher, did some research and speech writing. Paul Brountas, a young lawyer from the prestigious firm of Hale and Dorr in Boston, volunteered his services as logistics and transportation expert, a skill he had learned during the vice-presidential campaign. According to Don Nicoll, there were about a hundred people in this second group.

Nicoll and Muskie both emphasized during 1969 and 1970 that this so-called Brain Trust was not nearly so formalized and structured as press reports indicated. "I've always picked people's brains," Muskie said. "After 1968 more people than before were available to me." Nicoll said there could be no formal structure because people were involved at several different levels of commitment. "We go to these people and say, 'Senator Muskie has broader needs than before. We are trying to get the best thinking available on all public issues. We need your help both in the form of ideas and judgment.'" He said some responded because they were loyal to Muskie, and wanted to see him get the presidential nomination in 1972. Some responded because they were good Democrats and wanted the leading party figure, whoever he was, to have the benefit of their advice. And some responded because they thought Muskie could most effectively present their ideas at the time—their loyalty was to the ideas.

An example of how the arrangement worked occurred before the Senate voted in February, 1970, on the Stennis amendment concerning desegregation of schools. That amendment was worded so as to seem to end the "hypocritical" legal situation which required desegregation in the South but not in the North. Berl Bernhard, a Washington lawyer, and Robert Nelson, a Muskie aide who had had previous involvement with the civil-rights movement, called William Taylor and asked him to have lunch with Muskie. Taylor had by then left the Commission on Civil Rights and was writing a book. Taylor discussed the Stennis amendment with staff people first. Then at lunch he presented Muskie with a statement explaining why he opposed the amendment. Muskie quizzed him about it at length, agreed with what Taylor recommended, and took that position in the Senate debate.

Another example of the 1970 version of the Muskie decision-making process was the National Press Club speech in which he called for a new national debate on Vietnam. Warnke, Vance, McPherson, Read, Gelb, Harriman, and "two young lawyers" (Nicoll's phrase; some advisers had personal or professional reasons for not being identified with Muskie or with partisan politics) participated as briefers. There were a number of meetings. Nicoll wrote the final version of the speech.

The members of the advisory group who talk about it publicly usually stress the receptiveness of Muskie to fresh ideas and information, and his ability to draw out facts and opinions that are obviously new to him. William Taylor says of their meeting, "He familiarized himself with the statement I prepared very rapidly and very well. He raised good questions, right to the point. He had clearly absorbed the facts of the problem." He says the meeting often took on the aspects of a cross-examination. (Ron M. Linton, who was staff director of the Public Works Committee in the early 1960's, once remarked that Muskie's "absorption" of new facts was unusual. "Halfway through the 1963 hearings I realized he had been reading just voraciously the material the staff had gathered. His cross-examination of the witnesses was really cutting right to the heart of the issues. I was absolutely amazed. It was the first time I realized how much he could absorb. By the time we finished the hearings, there was no question in my mind that he really knew more about air pollution than I knew, and I had started working on it months before he did.") Paul Warnke says Muskie was a "quick study" on complicated military policy matters. Several of the 1970 advisers have made the point over and over that "he *listens.*" That is the highest accolade a policy adviser can pay to a policy maker. Some of these men have told an interviewer that they were struck by the fact that it was never necessary to rebrief Muskie on a topic. What he learned on Monday he still knew on Tuesday. Sometimes he knew more than he had learned. He continued his education between briefings. He was always ready to break new ground at these sessions.

No one was pretending in 1970 that Muskie needed this assistance in his race for reelection to the Senate. The unwritten rules of politics prevented him from announcing his presidential candidacy so far in advance. So did political reality. But reality also required him to start preparing for 1972. As he put it, "When this year came along, and we had the Senate campaign to deal with, we tried to put together a campaign structure that could in part also help us do this other job of meeting the larger responsibilities that happened to be here. But if one were to seriously pursue 'seventy-two, you'd have to have much more than we've got." Did he plan to get much more than he had? "Not until November at least. After that we'll have to see what the situation looks like." In the spring of 1970 he opened a suite of offices in a new downtown office building on L Street, four blocks from the White House. Don Nicoll transferred down there, to run it, to write the first of the senator's by-lined books, to work with the Brain Trust (a phrase the press had adopted, and one that infuriated Muskie), and to handle a variety of chores, including those concerned with raising and spending money for the senatorial reelection campaign.* This was a ticklish problem. Since Muskie was a candidate for the Senate, a senator, a national political leader, and an author, what money could be used for what purposes was not easily determined. There was a lot of overlap. Muskie said, "I mean, I'm just one guy, in one piece."

Robert Nelson, also a New Englander, and a lawyer with experience in administration, was hired to manage the Muskie reelection campaign committee headquartered at the new office. He has described the new office's function: "This office was established with its priority purpose to provide backup, data, research material, and so forth and so on and some planning for the reelection campaign in Maine this fall. At the same time, we're trying to take some of the load off the really desperately overloaded Hill staff. We are taking off their shoulders what you might call political mail from people who are interested in the senator, what he is doing. We take care of people who want to help him financially and those who want to help him substantively."

The office on the Hill certainly needed help. Though its staff had been doubled in size, from fifteen to thirty, thanks to judicious use of an enlarged Senate allowance for clerical help, the increasing new demands on it kept the people there living a treadmill existence. And an uncomfortable one. There were still only five rooms in the suite for all the added personnel. There were dozens of volunteers coming in every Tuesday, Thursday, and Saturday to operate the signature machine, to file, to open mail, and to do other routine jobs. These volunteers included physicians, engineers, students, and housewives. The crowded confusion led office manager Jack Whitelaw to consider double-decking the suite. An engineer volunteer measured the noise level, and found it to be 76

---

* A national fund-raising committee was established in the summer of 1970, headed by Arnold Picker of New York, chairman of the executive committee of United Artists.

decibels in one room, 84 in another, about what it would be in "an average factory," Muskie told a housekeeping committee of the Congress.

The L Street suite was directly underneath the law offices of Verner, Lipfert, Bernhard and McPherson, one of whose partners had become, by 1970 and the start of the presidential drive, one of the three most influential men in the Muskie camp. (The other two were Don Nicoll and George Mitchell.) He was Berl Bernhard, then forty, staff director of the Commission on Civil Rights under John Kennedy, general counsel to the Democratic Senatorial Campaign Committee since 1967, and special counsel to the Democratic National Committee since 1969. The two had become fans of each other during Bernhard's service on the Campaign Committee, of which Muskie was the chairman when Bernhard was hired. In 1968 Bernhard worked in the Muskie campaign. After that he became both close friend and adviser. Like Nicoll and Mitchell, he had a loosely defined role. It was his judgment that Muskie valued, rather than his specialized knowledge. "He calls on me for a whole variety of things that go from speech writing to worrying about book contracts to what might be the best approach on an issue to what people should be involved on a certain project," Bernhard says. "He said that what he really needed was a generalist who would sit around and listen to all the specialists and try to translate it into publicly comprehensible terms, and who would question a lot of things the experts would say." In a sense Bernhard was Muskie's Washington lawyer.

Muskie really crossed the Rubicon in 1970 when he hired a television consultant. Again, technically this was for the purposes of the Maine campaign. (Muskie's Republican opponent was sixty-six-year-old farmer-turned-school-teacher Neil S. Bishop, of Augusta. In 1954 Bishop had been the leader of the "Republicans for Muskie." He subsequently ran for Congress, lost, and dropped below the political horizon, not to appear again until 1970. Muskie trounced him.) But obviously 1972 was involved. The consultant was Robert Squier, at thirty-five already a veteran in that new trade made famous, or notorious, by Joe McGinniss in *The Selling of the President 1968*, which told of the advertising and television techniques used by Nixon in his 1968 campaign. Squier got to know Muskie in 1968, when he was one of Humphrey's television consultants. Although he was originally hired for the 1970 race only, he saw his responsibility as going beyond that: "Our effort in that Maine race could be described as a kind of tune-up run, in which we get familiar with him, get him familiar with us."

Several months before the November election, Muskie went to Squier's office on the edge of downtown Washington. Squier "interviewed" him while a television camera ran. Then the tape was played back for Muskie. Occasionally Squier would stop the tape to discuss a certain point about Muskie's appearance or behavior. This sort of conversation is as secret as that between lawyer and client or doctor and patient. Squier talked about it afterward in general terms. He said he recommended to Muskie only that he shorten his answers and reverse the order in his answers: "After he's been asked a question he has a tendency to give you the landscape before he answers it. He gives the impression that he's waffling even though he's not." Squier has recommended changes in dress or hair style or speech mannerisms for some clients, but he felt this was not necessary in Muskie's case: "Muskie is perfectly tuned to the medium in my opinion. There are only two senators who are really natural television performers. One is Muskie and the other is Packwood. Television is more personal than personal communication. You're on a one-to-one basis with all your audience all the time. If a person comes on too strongly, if he is big in his gestures, if he is loud in his attacks, if his personal style is to lay it out hard, if he gives lengthy answers, then he's too much for the medium. He comes across too hot." Except for the excessively long answers, Squier found Muskie perfect. "Cool. Very cool."

Squier also said, "The real Muskie and the television image of Muskie are close together, and that's extremely unusual. That's going to be his secret weapon in 1972, in my opinion."

Squier believed Muskie's physical appearance was greatly in his favor. "Not too pretty . . . the Lincoln analogy comes most easily to mind." That was a familiar theme. "Thinking now of the presidency," Senator Philip Hart once said, "Muskie has a physical presence about him that is really impressive. It lends confidence. It's crazy to say it, but he looks solid, he looks strong." An unfriendly senator limited his praise of Muskie to the physical: "He looks good. He has a presence. He sounds steady. He has a commanding physical bearing." A New York writer, after quoting a woman as saying of Muskie, "Gee, ain't he handsome?" went on to this description: ". . . Muskie is not handsome at all. His 6-foot 4-inch frame, once slim and gangling, now swells pregnantly in lower mid-section. His face is as long and soulful as an under-nourished basset-hound. His teeth splay gently from a crooked mouth, over a chin of modest prominence. His nose is long and his ears are big too. But the effect, demonstrably, is altogether different. Women over 25 tend to regard Muskie as the greatest invention since the Mix-Master. . . ."

Republican strategists began in 1969 to see Muskie as President Nixon's probable opponent. "Some Capitol Hill Republicans feel Muskie has became something of an obsession downtown," Don Oberdorfer wrote in the Washington *Post.* Loye Miller, Jr., of the Knight newspapers, said after revealing a secret memo to state Republicans that called for planting tough questions at Muskie press conferences, "The GOP sees Muskie as the strongest threat to President Nixon in 1972." Columnist Max Lerner wrote that President Nixon's "elevated rhetoric" dealing with the environment "clearly means he expects Senator Muskie to be his 1972 rival." When Muskie called for an investigation of the Jackson shootings, the Justice Department initiated a federal grand jury probe. In 1969 Muskie proposed a superagency for fighting pollution; in 1970, Nixon asked Congress to establish one.

As time passed, columnists and other journalists were paying Muskie more attention too. In 1969, noting Muskie's complaint about coverage, Clayton Fritchey wrote that Senator Kennedy "makes page 1 news not only because he is a Kennedy but because he makes authentic page 1 news. . . . [Muskie] is not much for sticking his neck out." But in 1970, Fritchey wrote, "It is an interesting and significant fact that everything Muskie has said in the last week or two has been given prominent page 1 attention, a sure sign that the press instinctively realizes he is moving into a leadership role." Baltimore *Sun* columnist Thomas O'Neill said of Muskie, "No other hopeful for the presidential nomination has so far found it worthwhile to invest a lot of effort in getting it. They lack encouragement. Senator Muskie can see encouraging signs all around him. . . . The Democrats may well conclude in 1972 that his caution and methodic manner, his low key and unhysterical speeches that some find dull are precisely what the voters want after an emotional period in which few succeeded in lowering voices, even the originator of that notion who in the White House carried on a shrill vendetta against Congress." A nationwide Louis Harris presidential preference poll showed Muskie and Nixon neck and neck, 46 per cent to 48 per cent. Gallup Poll after Gallup Poll showed Muskie running better against Nixon than any other Democratic hopeful. A special poll in Delaware for the Democratic party showed Muskie ahead of Nixon.

In the summer of 1970, Senate Majority Leader Mike Mansfield made a curious statement about the chances of his party's front-runner. He was meeting with a group of reporters at one of the Washington breakfast interviews that are often so relaxed. "We haven't come forward with a candidate who can match Nixon," Mansfield said. "Of course what may happen in two years, I don't know. But as of now his chances are better than any Democrat's. The best man we have at present is Ed Muskie, but you have to get out around the country and develop charisma and charm and a following. He has all these things but not in enough degree at this time." This statement was duly reported in the next day's papers. It did not help and may have hurt Muskie's chances. Not every Democrat agreed with Mansfield, of course. Senator Stuart Symington was asked about it a few days later on a Sunday-afternoon network television interview. He called the remarks "unfortunate with respect to Senator Muskie. I think Senator Muskie is an outstanding American. Something was said about charisma—I don't think Abraham Lincoln would have gone over too well from the standpoint of charisma. . ." He said Muskie would make a good president. What made Mansfield's pessimistic statement so puzzling to some who heard it was a sentence he preceded it with. He told the breakfasting reporters, "I think if Muskie had headed the ticket in 1968, the Democrats very likely would have won."

Nothing more clearly underscored Muskie's position as the frontrunner for the presidential nomination in 1972 than his being selected as the voice to answer President Nixon and Vice President Agnew on nation-wide television on the eve of the 1970 election. Using time purchased by a hastily formed *ad hoc* group called the Committee for National Unity, Muskie accused Nixon of inspiring a political campaign built on lies, slander, name-calling, and "deception of almost unprecedented volume."

Referring to the Republican law-and-order campaign, Muskie said that "they imply that Democratic candidates for high office in Texas and California, in Illinois and Tennessee, in Utah and Maryland, and among my New England neighbors at Vermont and Connecticut—men who have courageously pursued their convictions . . . that these men actually favor violence and champion the wrongdoer." In quiet, measured tones Muskie added, "That is a lie. And the American people know it is a lie."

Backers of the Committee for National Unity included former New York governor and veteran diplomat W. Averell Harriman, who signed a $100,000 note to pay for television time with the understanding that he would be repaid from contributions received after the broadcast. Much of the speech was written by Richard N. Goodwin, a former speechwriter for Presidents Kennedy and Johnson, and by Jack Sando, a Muskie speechwriter out of the L Street office in Washington.

The idea of the nation-wide election-eve broadcast came from Geoffrey Cowan, a young Washington attorney who was active in Senator McCarthy's 1968 campaign. Cowan said later that Muskie was picked to represent the party because he was "the only guy with enough stature to oppose the president." The speech, which was generally well received throughout the country, spurred interest in Muskie as the likely Democratic nominee in 1972. Less than a week later, appearing on NBC's "Meet the Press," Muskie conceded that he had begun sounding out Democratic leaders about supporting him as the party's presidential candidate. When would he announce? "I don't intend to be coy about it," he said with a smile. "I plan to pick the time that will be best."

As 1970 ended with a Muskie victory in Maine, what were his chances for the 1972 Democratic presidential nomination and what were a Democratic candidate's chances of winning the election? Political prediction is treacherous, but on the basis of past election history, Muskie had to be accorded a very good chance of gaining the nomination, and the Democratic nominee had to be given a good chance of winning.

Americans seem to assume that a president will be reelected except in extraordinary circumstances. But in fact, reelection is unusual. Since World War II's end, only one man has been elected to the presidency twice—Dwight D. Eisenhower. In this century just three men have been elected twice—Eisenhower, Franklin D. Roosevelt, and Woodrow Wilson—while eight have been elected only once.* Not only was there no historical justification for supposing President Nixon's incumbency would ensure his reelection, but the public-opinion polls of 1970 showed Nixon continuing to be supported by less than half the electorate.

The postwar history of presidential nominees in both parties is marked by one significant fact. With only one exception all candidates have been men who first captured national attention and were first discussed as presidential timber at least three or four years in advance of their nomination. In an age in which the presidency carries with it such awesome power, the American people understandably prefer not to place their trust in strangers. Thus the 1968 candidates, Nixon and Humphrey, were men who had first sought the presidency eight years before. They had been at the very top level of political leadership ever since. (Even the third-party candidate, George Wallace, had first run for the presidency four years before, in the Democratic primaries.) In 1964 the candidates were the sitting president, Johnson, who had sought the post in 1960, and Barry Goldwater, who had been the emotional choice of many delegates at the Republican convention in 1960, and who was the undisputed leader of the party's right wing from then until 1964, with presidential talk constantly swirling about him.

The 1960 candidates were Nixon, who as the sitting vice-president had been a national figure for eight years, and John F. Kennedy, who had come to national attention in 1956 as a challenger for the vice-presidential nomination, and whose presidential ambitions thereafter had been widely circulated in a smooth public-relations effort. In 1956 the candidates were men who had run against each other four years before,

---

* Harding, Coolidge, Truman, Kennedy, and Johnson didn't seek elected second terms. Theodore Roosevelt, Taft, and Hoover did, and failed.

Eisenhower and Adlai Stevenson. In 1952 Eisenhower was a newcomer to politics, but he had been talked about nationally as a presidential possibility since D-Day, in 1944. The *Democrats* had wanted to nominate him in 1948. Stevenson was a relative surprise to America in 1952. He is the exception to the general rule. In 1948 the candidates were President Truman and Thomas E. Dewey, who had also run in 1944.

Should the pattern prevail in 1972, the potential Democratic nominees would be Muskie, former Vice-President Humphrey, Senator Edward Kennedy, Senator George McGovern, Eugene McCarthy, and former President Johnson. But Kennedy had announced that he was definitely out of the 1972 picture. McCarthy was presumed to be out as a Democrat; he quit the Senate and began to hint at his interest in a fourth party. Johnson could under no circumstances expect to be renominated. Muskie in 1970 consistently ran ahead of Humphrey and McGovern in public-opinion polls.

The possibility that an authentic dark horse could emerge was tiny, but still existed. There was occasional press speculation in 1970 about Senators Fred Harris of Oklahoma, Birch Bayh of Indiana, Harold E. Hughes of Iowa, Walter Mondale of Minnesota, former Attorney-General Ramsey Clark, even New York Mayor John V. Lindsay, a Republican.

Maine national committeeman George Mitchell, a member of the McGovern Commission that was reforming the rules for the selection of delegates to the 1972 convention, believed, as many others did, that the 1972 nomination would be won in the primaries. The primary was becoming more popular. New states—Maryland and Rhode Island, for instance—were requiring open primaries. "The only way the primaries won't be decisive," Mitchell said, "is if nobody wins. That is, somebody wins here and somebody else there and no clear leader emerges." Muskie could be expected to get off to a running start in the primaries. The first two were to be in neighboring New Hampshire and heavily Catholic Rhode Island. His supporters hoped he would generate so much momentum in these two primaries (to be held in March or April) that he would sweep through all the others he entered without serious challenge.

What kind of president would Muskie be? A good one, his Senate friends believed. "On balance, in terms of performing effectively in the office of the presidency, I think Muskie is ahead of all of us," said Senator Hart. "He has an ability to work with a group having different opinions and blend its thinking, which is constructive. I've seen this with legislative groups, and I suspect it would be true of community or international disagreements. There are occasions when he is very eloquent; he can be moving. This is useful for a national voice, as a president's must be." Senator Mansfield summed Muskie up as "steady, solid, a man for all seasons . . . his nature would be in his favor as a president." Senator McGee said, "If I know Ed Muskie, he would be a very firm and solid president. Not a president with a flair, but a president with a depth of conviction that would respond less than most we have seen to the political pressures of the time. I think one of his great strengths that comes through loud and clear is the integrity of his convictions."

In one important sense, a President Muskie would differ markedly from the presidents of the past decade. He did not display the early ambitions or the youthful political successes of the most recent occupants of the White House. Richard Nixon was a member of Congress at thirty-four, vice-president at forty, a leading presidential contender—and active seeker of that prize—in his party by forty-five. Lyndon Johnson was a member of Congress at twenty-nine, a senator at forty, floor leader at forty-four, an active presidential contender at fifty. John Kennedy was a member of Congress at twenty-nine, a senator at thirty-five, an active presidential contender at forty-one. All three were wealthy before they became president.

In contrast, Muskie at forty was still a small-town lawyer and a Democrat in a solidly Republican state. When he was fifty his most realistic political yearning was probably to become Senate floor leader for his party when Mike Mansfield retired, not likely for another ten or twelve years. Even this modest ambition was occasionally thrust aside, both in the belief that it was threatened by more aggressive colleagues and in the desire for more money and security for his large family than could be provided by a senator's salary. ("If there were the least trace of dishonesty in Ed Muskie, it would have shown long ago," said a Maine critic. "I know how hard up he was in 1964, and I know he could have taken advantage of his position. But he didn't.") Muskie was fifty-four years old before he began seriously to contemplate the ultimate political office, the presidency. Significantly, the thought that he would be a good president occurred to a lot of other people before it occurred to—or was —taken seriously by Muskie himself.

His pattern of life had been different from what most Americans today consider the normal national style. He was in his mid-thirties when he married. He lived in a small town until he was in his mid-forties. Until he was in his fifties his principal political responsibilty was to his state alone, a state whose population differed from that of the nation as a whole in most respects, being rural, poor, semi-isolated, not growing, nearly all white, elderly. Both his life and his political career constituted the sort of slow weathering process that reinforces, then highlights, a man's qualities of steadiness, solidity, moderation, and his understanding of personal politics and statecraft and social policy in human terms. The result was his devotion to the old traditions, institutions, and values— family, church, party, government, citizen army; trust, cooperation, compromise. The enduring cliffs and outcroppings of his state's coast, and the trim, clean New England town halls, where participatory democracy of simpler, more confident eras flourished, were both appropriate symbols for Edmund Muskie. For better or worse, he was the legatee of slow maturation in the town-meeting-and-bitter-winters environment of poor, little, sturdy Maine.

This book has attempted to provide some understanding of the character and history of Edmund Muskie. It has tried to show his views on the most important issues of his times. Most particulars of a Muskie presidential campaign in the primaries, and if he wins the nomination, in the national general election, can only be guessed at a year in advance. Issues change, and facts change, so an individual's stands may have to change as well. "One reason we are going slow on some issues now [1970] is that we don't want to get stuck with a position that may be right now but won't be two years from now," a Muskie confidant and adviser said. "If you don't change your stand, you could be behind the times. If you do, you look wishy-washy." A politician who wants to challenge the incumbent president, who has so much control over events, must be especially cautious. The nature of a Muskie campaign can be foreseen with great clarity, however, because of his repeated emphasis, throughout his life, on certain themes and because of the specific nature of American apprehensiveness in the 1970's, which has been referred to as a "crisis of confidence." More than most recent campaigns, a Muskie campaign would focus on the background common to all issues: American society and American government, themselves. In December, 1966, when the American malaise was just beginning to be perceived as one of perhaps truly critical intensity, long before Muskie had run for vice-president, before he had considered the even greater possibilities, before there was a Brain Trust, before there was a need to address himself daily to all the problems of the nation, to speak as a national voice, Muskie wrote to his Maine constituents about his concern for the developing public climate. Then he said, "This is a good time to remember what our national experience so well demonstrates—that a society built upon the potential for enlightenment, self-improvement and self-discipline of the individual citizen will work in the best interests of all. We can disagree with a problem and still deal with it effectively. We can criticize each other vigorously and still work together constructively. We know we can make our democratic system work, because we have done so. In this spirit, may all look forward to . . . [next year] as another opportunity to demonstrate the ability of a free and enlightened people to govern themselves."

A NOTE ON SOURCES

Most of the information in this book is based on what we learned in interviews with Senator Muskie, his friends, enemies, colleagues, family members, and staff members. The interviews were conducted in 1969 and 1970. We have been observers of the senator's Maine and Washington environments for the past ten years. We also made use of the research facilities of the Baltimore *Sun,* the Portland *Press Herald, Congressional Quarterly, The New York Times,* the Washington *Post,* and the Washington *Star.*

THEO LIPPMAN, JR.
DONALD C. HANSEN